6.00

# A *Handbook* OF CHRISTIAN TRUTH

# A *Handbook* OF CHRISTIAN TRUTH

Ex Libris

*Fred Falkinson*

## HAROLD LINDSELL
### *and*
## CHARLES J. WOODBRIDGE

Fleming H. Revell Company
Old Tappan, New Jersey

# Contents

**6    Contents**

To

OUR SONS JOHN

With the prayer that the faith of
their fathers may be their faith
too; and that as the Holy Spirit
called their fathers to preach the
gospel He may call them too.

# INTRODUCTION

This volume was written for two reasons.

First, because for many years the authors have felt the need for such a book. Admirable volumes have been written embracing, either singly or in small groups, many of the subjects contained herein. But this book is an effort to place in the hands of the Christian reading public a single, comprehensive volume covering the whole gamut of the Christian faith in its theological and practical expressions.

Second, the authors are motivated by a sense of mission. They believe that the Holy Spirit called them to undertake the project. To that end they have consistently sought the direction and guidance of the Spirit; they have undergirded the writing of the manuscript with prayer; and they have sought to be faithful to the Word of God.

The reader will soon notice that the book is expository. It is not a commentary, nor is it intended to be a seminary textbook in systematic theology. Rather it is a plain, simple statement of what the Bible teaches respecting the main doctrines of the Christian faith and the application of Biblical principles to all areas of Christian living.

Attention is called to the fact that the volume contains fifty-two chapters in essay, outline form. It is designed to aid pastors in their sermon preparation; Sunday School teachers in their classroom work; teachers in Bible Schools, summer conferences and institutes; and Christian laymen in general as they seek to grow in grace and in knowledge of the Lord Jesus Christ. Whether these fifty-two chapters are used as the basis of Bible studies at home, in church, or in school, their contents may be conveniently mastered during the course of a year.

Our prayer is that the book will prove to be a blessing to men individually and to the church universal, that it will be used in the winning of precious souls to the Lord Jesus and in building up the saints in the most holy faith.

# A
## *Handbook*
## OF
# CHRISTIAN
# TRUTH

# PART ONE

# The Bible

---

*God is.* The existence of God is the determinative fact of history. "But without faith it is impossible to please him: for he that cometh to God must believe that he is, and that he is a rewarder of them that diligently seek him" (Heb. 11:6). When this premise is granted all of life has its proper orientation. God is. This is the hub of truth. From it radiate the basic facts concerning the divine nature, attributes and purposes; concerning the origin, nature and destiny of man; and concerning the rationale of all life.

*God has spoken.* The divine self-disclosure, never a necessity, has its origin in God's sovereign grace. Jehovah has revealed Himself in nature (see Psalm 19:1); in the consciences of men (see Rom. 2:15); in inscripturated fashion in His Holy Word—the Bible (see 2 Peter 1:21); and supremely in the Incarnate Word—the Son of God, our Lord Jesus Christ (see Heb. 1:1-2). In His speech God has not stuttered. He has spoken simply, directly and definitively. His revelation is true and perfect. Our ceaseless refrain should be: God has spoken—"O earth, earth, earth, hear the word of the Lord" (Jer. 22:29).

The Word of the Lord is heard most clearly in the Bible. Our knowledge of all things pertaining to creation and redemption is derived from the Scriptures of the Old and New Testaments. If we would know the mind of God in any area of thought or life our primary source of reference must be the Word of God. The opening chapters of this Handbook are devoted to a consideration of the essential facts relating to the Bible.

# 1

# What Is the Bible?

The Bible is the source Book of our knowledge of God. It is the text-Book of divine truth, the guide-Book to everlasting life. The word "Bible" is derived from the Greek "biblos," "a book." The volume has several other titles, e.g. "the scriptures" (1 Cor. 15:3,4, i.e. "the writings"); or "the word of God" (as in Heb. 4:12).

## A. THE CONTENTS OF THE BIBLE.

The Bible is a library of sixty-six books, divided into two main sections, the Old Testament and the New Testament. The word "Testament" signifies a "covenant" or "agreement." (See Heb. 8:6-13.) The Old Testament was originally written in Hebrew (although parts of Daniel and Ezra are in Aramaic); the New Testament was written in Greek.

1. *The Old Testament* consists of thirty-nine books. In early days the Jews designated these "The Law, The Prophets, and The Holy Writings (or Psalms)." Observe this usage, for example, in Luke 24:25-27. Scholars sometimes subdivide the books thus:

(a). Five Books of the Law, known as the Pentateuch ("five volumes"): Genesis, Exodus, Leviticus, Numbers,

Deuteronomy. Moses wrote these and they contain the record of events from the beginning to the death of Moses.

(b). Twelve Books of History: Joshua, Judges, Ruth, 1 and 2 Samuel, 1 and 2 Kings, 1 and 2 Chronicles, Ezra, Nehemiah, Esther. These historical records refer entirely to Israel. Surrounding nations are mentioned only in connection with "the chosen people." The books describe the history of the Jews from Joshua's day to the return to Palestine from the Babylonian captivity.

(c). Five Books of Poetry: Job, Psalms, Proverbs, Ecclesiastes, Song of Solomon. These poetic works reflect the spiritual sensitivity of their Hebrew writers. Each has a message concerning God and human experience.

(d). Twelve Books of Prophecy (Minor, i.e. the shorter prophetic works): Hosea, Joel, Amos, Obadiah, Jonah, Micah, Nahum, Habakkuk, Zephaniah, Haggai, Zechariah, Malachi.

(e). Five Books of Prophecy (Major, i.e. the longer prophetic works): Isaiah, Jeremiah, Lamentations, Ezekiel, Daniel. The prophetic books of the Old Testament take us up to the fifth century B.C.

(Notice that the numbers 5 and 12 alternate. This will help you to remember the contents of the Old Testament.)

2. *The New Testament* consists of twenty-seven books. An easy way to remember this number: The Old Testament has thirty-nine books. Place a multiplication sign between the 3 and the 9. Three times nine equals twenty-seven.

(a). Four Gospels: Matthew, Mark, Luke, John. The word "gospel" is derived from the Anglo-Saxon "good news." The first three books are "the synoptic Gospels," for they approach the story from somewhat the same point of view. The Gospel according to John has a setting, style, and purpose all its own. (See John 20:31.) As a whole the books contain a *narration* of the life, teaching, ministry and passion of Christ.

(b). One Book of History: the Acts of the Apostles (sometimes called the "Acts of the Holy Spirit"). Luke is the author of this volume. He traces the history of the first century church from the time of Christ until the imprisonment of the apostle Paul, i.e. from about 29 A.D. to 64 A.D. Acts is the Book of *continuation.*

(c). Fourteen Pauline Epistles, letters written by Paul to churches and individual Christians: Romans, 1 and 2 Corinthians, Galatians, Ephesians, Philippians, Colossians, 1 and 2 Thessalonians, 1 and 2 Timothy, Titus, Philemon, and probably Hebrews.

(d). Seven General Epistles, not addressed to limited, specific groups: James, 1 and 2 Peter, 1, 2 and 3 John, Jude. These letters differ from the Pauline writings in this regard: their titles designate their authors, not their recipients.

The twenty-one epistles are the divine *explanation* of the Gospel.

(e). One Book of Prophecy: the Revelation. This is the Book of *consummation.*

## B. The Central Theme of the Bible.

The Bible unfolds God's redemptive purpose toward man. It is a vast panorama of truth about the nature and will of God, and the divine program for the ages. One central theme dominates the story, one melody rings throughout the cantata of redemption, one strand is woven inextricably into the fabric of revelation. The cardinal theme is Christ. He is the Key to an understanding both of the Old Testament and the New. Thus:

1. *Old Testament.* The law reveals the nature and will of God; but it is "our schoolmaster to bring us unto Christ" (Gal. 3:24). The historical books are a reservoir of facts about Israel; but they pave the way for the Saviour's coming. The poetic books inspire us with their sublime and heavenly music; but they sing primarily of the coming Redeemer. The prophetic books are windows opening upon mountains of God's transcendent majesty, ineffable holiness, awesome dignity, and

upon valleys of man's degradation and need; but they predict
the sufferings and glory of the One who would lift man out of
his fallen estate back to the bosom of the Father.

2. *New Testament.* The Gospels focus our attention upon
the advent of the Son of God. The Acts upholds Christ as the
One whose name must be proclaimed to the uttermost part of
the earth. The epistles abound in profound spiritual insights,
but they were written to explain Christ's salvation, its nature,
scope, and consequences. The Revelation, ominous in its de-
piction of judgment, devastating in its exposure of the consequences of sin, portrays Christ's ultimate triumph.

Thus the written word of God and the incarnate Word of
God, the Lord Jesus Christ, are inseparably linked.

## C. The Origin of the Bible.

The Scriptures originated in the mind of God, but the manner in which He arranged for their human authorship and
compilation is interesting.

1. The Old Testament, according to the traditional view,
was prepared somewhat as follows: Moses wrote the five books
of the Law and placed them in the Tabernacle beside the Ark
of the Covenant. Joshua added his record to the volume (see
Joshua 24:26), and Samuel continued the story (cf. 1 Sam.
10:25). This entire library was subsequently lost. When re-
discovered and publicly read, it produced a revival. (See 2
Kings 22:8.) The writings of the earlier prophets were then
added to the series. The later prophets were familiar with these
writings (e.g. Zech. 7:12). Thus the collection gradually expanded.

The assembling of the Old Testament books into an official
canon began shortly after the captivity (586 B.C.). The word
"canon" means a "rod," or "rule," i.e. a standard of that which
is to be believed. (See Gal. 6:16.) When Haggai and others
had completed their ministry, the need was felt for a formal
collection of the documents which the people already regarded

as of divine origin. According to the best tradition Ezra and Nehemiah, and after them a group of scribes, completed the canonization of the Old Testament.

2. The New Testament canon came into being as follows. When the books appeared, addressed usually to particular churches, copies were made and sent to other congregations. Exchanges of books took place. (See Col. 4:16.) Lists of these apostolic books were prepared. By the fourth century some fifteen such catalogues had been published. Gradually, not by the vote of any particular church council, but by the consent of the "universal church consciousness" that these books, and these alone were the inspired Word of God, the New Testament canon emerged as we have it today. We have here a magnificent example of the preserving and superintending power of the Holy Spirit.

## D. The English Versions of the Bible.

Perhaps it will be helpful to know the history of our major English versions.

The Latin version of the second century was the basis of Jerome's Vulgate (Latin "common"), prepared in Bethlehem in the fourth century. The Vulgate is the text from which the Roman Catholic Douay version of the Old Testament and the Rheims version of the New Testament are derived. For centuries it was the main Bible of the church. In the seventh century paraphrases of the Vulgate and a translation of fifty of its Psalms were made into Anglo-Saxon. The Venerable Bede translated the Gospel of John in the eighth century. But not until the time of John Wycliffe (1382) was the whole Bible known in English.

In 1526 William Tyndale's edition of the New Testament, based upon the original Greek, was published on the continent and smuggled into England. Soon after the "Great Bible" appeared (1539), the first authorized copy of the Scriptures in English. Then followed "the Geneva Bible" (1560), the first

English Bible to appear in Roman type, written by English scholars in exile; the "Bishop's Bible," a Church of England publication; and finally the King James Version, the "Authorized" edition, published in 1611 as the result of the labors of forty-seven scholars appointed by the King.

God has blessed the Authorized version. But in the nineteenth century the church felt the need for a revised version of the Scriptures, to be prepared on an international, interdenominational level. In 1880 the New Testament was completed, and in 1884 the Old Testament. Known as the Revised Version of the Scriptures, this is a masterpiece of scholarship. The American Standard Version was issued in 1901, embodying the finest scholarship of both Great Britain and America. In 1930 a committee was appointed to bring this version up to date. For sixteen years it labored. Finally on February 11, 1946, the Revised Standard Version of the New Testament came off the press; and the Old Testament version was issued in September 1952.

# 2

## The Inspiration of the Bible

---

The Author of the Bible is the Holy Spirit of God. Its pages
are an authoritative revelation, in written form, of the divine
nature and purposes.

### A. THE CRUCIAL NATURE OF INSPIRATION.

The most decisive, and unfortunately the most divisive, Biblical theme is the inspiration of the Scriptures. In the first
centuries after Christ the issue which absorbed the interest of
the church concerned the persons of the Trinity; in the six-
teenth century the vexing problem was whether ultimate authority rested in the Word of God or in the papacy; in the
twentieth century the inspiration of the Bible is the focal,
determinative point of conflict.

The view of inspiration which the church has always held
has been widely abandoned today. In its place men have substituted a pale, emasculated, sinewless view that the Bible
merely contains the Word of God. We believe that the Scriptures not only contain the Word of God, but that in their
entirety they *are* the Word of God.

Rising out of the contention that the Bible only contains the
Word of God, mighty doctrines of the Christian faith have
been denied: e.g. the virgin birth of Christ, His deity, miracles,

substitutionary atonement, and bodily resurrection. The camel of unbelief has nosed its way into the tent via a denial of inspiration. In many religious circles today it has the sole occupancy of the tent, to the detriment of Christendom and the imperiling of precious souls.

If the virility of Christianity is to be recaptured, the church must return to her faith in the inspiration of the Bible—that God has spoken clearly in His Word, and that apart from His revelation man is utterly devoid of hope.

### B. THE PURPOSE OF INSPIRATION.

The design of inspiration is to give to man an infallible rule of faith and practice. The Bible is God-given. Hence it is a dependable well-spring of information, a trustworthy light in human darkness, a reliable voice from heaven.

1. Our heavenly Father wanted His children to know beyond doubt who He is and what He did in the sending of His Son. Hence He spoke unequivocally in His Word.

2. He wanted to make the plan of salvation so clear that man would be without excuse if he rejected the Saviour. The Bible is perspicuous. Anyone may understand its divinely inspired teaching that man is a sinner, that Jesus Christ died for his sins, and that the way to Heaven is through saving faith in Him.

3. He wanted to give His children a set of principles to guide them in Christian living. In the realm of morals He spoke definitively.

4. He wanted all men everywhere to have authoritative information pertaining to every area of moral, rational, and spiritual life.

### C. THE MEANING OF INSPIRATION.

To "inspire" means to "breathe upon." The Bible is "theopneustos" ("God-breathed"). The sacred odor of heaven is upon it. Divinely directed men wrote as God breathed upon them.

1. "Inspiration" is not the equivalent of "revelation." Both are taught in the Scriptures, but they are not identical. Revelation is the direct impartation of previously unknown truth to the writer. For example, God gave Daniel details of the future by direct revelation. (See Dan. 7 and 9.) But the Holy Spirit did more than this. He inspired the Biblical writers. He gave them special revelation when necessary, but He also directed them in the choice of known historical material. He superintended the process of acquisition, selection and composition. The finished product is free from error and worthy to be designated the Word of God.

2. "Inspiration" is not mere "illumination." The Holy Spirit illumines one's soul before he can understand spiritual truth. (See 1 Cor. 2:10-12.) But when we speak of the inspiration of the Bible, we do not have in mind this sort of spiritual perception. We do not mean merely that the intuitive faculties of the writers were quickened, or their spiritual insights clarified. Their "inspiration" was different, not only in degree, but also in kind, from the heightened powers of ordinary men, even of men known for their spiritual genius. The inspiration of the Biblical authors was unique: it was special, direct, reliable, life-giving, inerrant.

3. "Inspiration" is not "dictation." Many passages of the Bible were actually dictated by God. On occasion God put His own words into the mouths of the writers, who recorded the words that He spoke. The ten commandments, for example, were "written with the finger of God" (Ex. 31:18). "The writing was the writing of God" (Ex. 32:16), reproduced for the readers of Exodus. When David gave to his son Solomon the divine pattern for the temple he said: "All this . . . the Lord made me understand in writing by his hand upon me, even all the works of this pattern" (1 Chron. 28:19). At times

the writers recorded truth without understanding it. (See 1 Peter 1:11.)

The normal procedure in inspiration, however, was different. The Holy Spirit controlled the authors' thoughts and judgments permitting them to express themselves in terms reflecting their own characteristics. The writers were not automata. They retained their own styles, personalities and self-command. Their personal powers were not suspended, but sharpened. The Holy Spirit commanded the operation; but Moses, John and Peter remained Moses, John and Peter while writing. Because of the close, sustained, continuous, effective supervision of the Holy Spirit, the Bible is the inspired Word of God.

4. The "inspiration" of the Bible does not suggest that God approves all of its statements. Surely this is obvious. How could the Almighty, for instance, approve all the remarks of the devil or of Job's friends? But the inspiration of the Bible guarantees that all remarks and events described in the Scriptures are accurately recorded.

5. The Bible is not "partially" inspired, or only "spiritually" inspired. It is inspired in all areas with which it deals, historical, geological, as well as moral and spiritual. It is "plenarily" and "verbally" inspired; that is, fully inspired, even in its words (see 1 Cor. 2:13), and therefore true from first to last and completely reliable.

## D. The Biblical Claim to Inspiration.

1. The apostles claim that the Bible is inspired. Paul writes: "All scripture is given by inspiration of God . . ." (2 Tim. 3:16). And Peter adds: "For the prophecy came not in old time by the will of man: but holy men of God spake as they were moved by the Holy Ghost" (2 Pet. 1:21).

a. *The Old Testament*. The writers of the Old Testament were confident that they were recording the Word of God. The phrase "Thus saith the Lord," or its equivalent, occurs over two thousand times in the Old Testament. The prophets believed that God spoke through their words. David, the "sweet psalmist of Israel," introduced a prophetic utterance: "The Spirit of the Lord spake by me, and his word was in my tongue. The God of Israel said, the Rock of Israel spake to me . . ." (2 Sam. 23:1-3). Isaiah wrote: "Moreover the Lord said unto me . . . For the Lord spake thus to me . . ." (Isa. 8:1, 11). Jeremiah claimed: "Then the Lord put forth his hand, and touched my mouth. And the Lord said unto me, Behold, I have put my words in thy mouth" (Jer. 1:9; see Jer. 5:14; 7:27; 13:12). Ezekiel was told by the Lord: "Go, get thee unto the house of Israel, and speak with my words unto them" (Ezek. 3:4; cf. Ezek. 3:7,10,11). Micah realized that his word was from God: "But truly I am full of power by the spirit of the Lord, and of judgment, and of might, to declare unto Jacob his transgression, and to Israel his sin" (Micah 3:8). Habakkuk heard God speaking: "Write the vision, and make it plain upon tables, that he may run that readeth it" (Hab. 2:2).

The writers of the New Testament frequently assert that the Old Testament authors were inspired. "God, who at sundry times and in divers manners spake in time past unto the fathers by the prophets" (Heb. 1:1). Old Testament prophecies concerning Christ, for example, were "spoken of the Lord by the prophet" (Matt. 1:22; 2:15). The Holy Ghost spoke "by the mouth of David" (Acts 1:16), and "by Esaias the prophet unto our fathers" (Acts 28:25).

b. *The New Testament.* Paul was confident that his words were the Word of God: "If any man think himself to be a prophet, or spiritual, let him acknowledge that the things that I write unto you are the commandments of the Lord" (1 Cor. 14:37). Or again: "For this cause also thank we God without ceasing, because, when ye received the word of God which ye heard of us, ye received it not as the word of men, but as it is in truth, the word of God . . ." (1 Thess. 2:13). The apostle knew that his gospel was a revelation from God and recorded it as such. To the Galatians he wrote (1:11,12): "But I certify you, brethren, that the gospel which was preached of me is not after man. For I neither received it of man, neither was I taught it, but by the revelation of Jesus Christ." (See 1 Cor. 11:23ff; 15:1-4.) Simon Peter declares that the writings of the apostles are on the same level as that of the Old Testament Scriptures. He exhorts his readers to "be mindful of the words which were spoken before by the holy prophets, and of the commandment of us the apostles of the Lord and Saviour" (2 Pet. 3:2). The apostles held so high a view of inspiration that the consensus of the first church council in Jerusalem was "it seemed good to the Holy Ghost, and to us, to lay upon you no greater burden than these necessary things" (Acts 15:28).

2. The Lord Jesus put His seal on the inspiration of the Bible.

a. *Negatively:* He did not reject the view entertained by His Jewish contemporaries. The Pharisees accepted the Old Testament Scriptures as the inspired Word of God. He rebuked them for their hypocrisy, but never for this attitude toward the Scriptures. His silence gave assent. Jesus was the great Teacher of the ages. He is God, the eternal Truth. Had He known that the Jewish concept was false He would have corrected it at once.

b. *Positively:* Far from criticizing the current viewpoint, Christ shared it and put His seal upon it. "The scripture," He declared, "cannot be broken" (John 10:35). He established the divine validity of the law: "Till heaven and earth pass, one jot or one title shall in no wise pass from the law, till all be fulfilled" (Matt. 5:18). He saw Himself as the fulfillment of Old Testament prophecies. (See Luke 24:25-27.) Moreover He pre-authenticated the New Testament by indicating to His disciples that the Holy Spirit would preserve them from error in its composition. (See John 16:13.)

3. What Christ and the apostles taught, we believe. This is

high and holy ground! Upon it the church has stood through the ages.

## E. THE CONSEQUENCE OF INSPIRATION.

1. To deny the doctrine is to deny the verdict of Christ and His apostles. Such a denial questions the integrity of the Son of God.

2. To affirm the doctrine is to take one's stand with saints, apostles and martyrs of all ages and thus to perpetuate the witness of the Holy Spirit to the hearts of men that the Bible is the Word of God.

3. God's people must handle this inerrant Book carefully and reverently; they must rejoice that God has spoken; and they must endeavor to walk in the light of His revelation.

# 3

# Why Believe the Bible?

The pivotal question of Christianity centers around the Bible itself. If this book is only a record of the religious quest of the Hebrew peoples, and if it deals only with their hopes, aspirations, and accomplishments in their upward search for God from polytheism to monotheism, then it cannot be the Word of God as we use that term here.

We believe that the Bible is God's word to man. We hold that from cover to cover, from Genesis to Revelation, the book is God's whole counsel to man and that it is without error in whole and in part.

To say that we believe the Bible is the Word of God is vastly different from stating the reasons why we believe that it is the Word of God. One may so believe on a pragmatic basis; another may believe after extensive research in the field of archeology; another may believe following an exhaustive internal examination of the Bible in the framework of lower and higher criticism; still others may come to this view through a combination of the foregoing and other reasons as well. Why then do Christians believe that the Bible is truly the Word of the living God?

## A. The Testimony of Christ and the Apostles.

We believe that Jesus is God. We confess our confidence in His omniscient authority. We also believe that the words of the apostles are authoritative. Both Jesus and the apostles consistently testify that the Scriptures are the Word of God.

## B. The Spiritual Test.

In the physical world things are physically revealed. Reactions in the material realm are, after all, responses to stimuli. Obviously such responses are not forthcoming unless the proper stimuli are present. A blind man does not react to the stimulus of a beautiful sunset; a deaf man does not react to the stimulus of a Wagner or a Bach. Dead men do not react to stimuli of any kind.

What is true in the physical world is also true in the spiritual world. People who are spiritually dead do not respond to spiritual stimuli. But when a man becomes a Christian the Holy Spirit takes up His residence in his heart. The believer is now alive spiritually as well as physically, and is able to respond to the witness of the Spirit of God to his spirit. The Holy Spirit convinces him that the Bible is the Word of God. This is known as "the testimony of the Holy Spirit" (*testimonium spiritus sancti*). So Paul proclaims: "Which things also we speak, not in the words which man's wisdom teacheth, but which the Holy Ghost teacheth; comparing spiritual things with spiritual. But the natural man receiveth not the things of the Spirit of God; for they are foolishness unto him: neither can he know them, because they are spiritually discerned. But he that is spiritual judgeth all things, yet he himself is judged of no man" (1 Cor. 2:13-15). "And it is the Spirit that beareth witness, because the Spirit is truth" (1 John 5:6).

Scholarly and scientific men with an objective bent of mind may strengthen one's faith in the inspiration of the Bible. But after all, it is the Holy Spirit, resident within the believer's heart, who bears witness to the truth and finality of the Scriptures. Let us remember, therefore, that the witness of the Spirit is of inestimable value in enabling one to know that the Bible is truly God's holy Word.

## C. The Pragmatic Test.

In recent years we have heard much about pragmatism. Almost constant reference is made to the idea that the acid test of a truth or an idea is: Does it work? An inventor produces a machine, but until he can demonstrate that it will really do the job he claims it can do, it is not accepted. Medicines are tested to demonstrate their efficacy; airplanes, tanks, guns, automobiles and a thousand other items are subjected to the acid test: Will they work, and will they do what the inventors claim for them?

In the field of comparative religions we ask of any religion in particular or of religion in general: Does it do what it says it will do? It is not an unfair test to apply to the Scriptures the standard we impose in other realms. Surely if the Bible is the Word of God, it can meet such a test. If it is true, then whatever it promises it will fulfill. Indeed, the Bible itself suggests the pragmatic approach as an evidence of its truth. "O taste and see that the Lord is good," says the Psalmist (Psalm 34:8).

Experimentally any man can make the test for himself. Meet the conditions of the Word and see whether or not its promises are fulfilled in your life. For twenty centuries men have witnessed to the fact that in their own experience they have found the Bible to be true. God promises pardon to the repentant and they have a sense of forgiveness; God has promised peace to the broken-hearted and they have His peace; God has promised to supply the material, physical, and spiritual needs of His children and these have been supplied. In no particular can it be shown that the Bible fails to do what it promises to do; whereas on the contrary, countless men testify fearlessly that the Bible has done exactly what it said it would do when certain conditions were met.

The Bible works! Any honest man who will put it to the test can discover this fact for himself. Jesus taught, "If any man will do his will, he shall know of the doctrine, whether it be of God, or whether I speak of myself" (John 7:17).

## D. THE TEST OF FULFILLED PROPHECY.

Reference is often made to "prophets" or "clairvoyants." Whenever men run into phenomena outside the ken of the average human mind, they think of the supernatural. To them this usually connotes some extra-sensory experience, or prophetic statements rising out of such an experience. Strangely enough, men cheerfully believe the weirdest tales involving the supernatural so long as these tales are not in the context of the Christian faith. But let a Christian mention the supernatural as related to prophetic utterances on the part of God's servants who were accurate in their predictions, and few will believe.

One of the grandest evidences that the Bible is the Word of God is fulfilled prophecy. By fulfilled prophecy we mean that men, before the events occurred and before anyone could have known what would happen, foretold historical events which transpired according to their words. The Bible is replete with prophecies which have been fulfilled literally. Among those which might be mentioned are the following:

1. Prophecies concerning the Jews.

a. *Their dispersion.* "And it shall come to pass, that as the Lord rejoiced over you to do you good, and to multiply you; so the Lord will rejoice over you to destroy you, and to bring you to nought; and ye shall be plucked from off the land whither thou goest to possess it. And the Lord shall scatter thee among all people, from the one end of the earth even unto the other; and there thou shalt serve other gods, which neither thou nor thy fathers have known, even wood and stone. And among these nations shalt thou find no ease, neither shall the sole of thy foot have rest: but the Lord shall give thee there a trembling heart and failing of eyes, and sorrow of mind" (Deut. 28:63-65). Behold Israel today scattered to the ends of the earth!

b. *Their reproach.* "And thou shalt become an astonishment, a proverb, and a byword, among all nations whither the Lord shall lead thee" (Deut. 28:37). This prediction too has been fulfilled.

c. *The loss of Jerusalem to the Gentiles.* "And they shall fall by the edge of the sword, and shall be led away captive into all nations: and Jerusalem shall be trodden down of the Gentiles, until the times of the Gentiles be fufilled" (Luke 21:24). For almost two thousand years this condition has prevailed.

2. Prophecies concerning Nineveh. The ancient city would become a desolation. "Woe to the bloody city! It is all full of lies and robbery; the prey departeth not . . . Because of the multitude of the whoredoms of the wellfavored harlot, the mistress of witchcrafts, that selleth nations through her whoredoms, and families through her witchcrafts. Behold, I am against thee, saith the Lord of hosts; and I will discover thy skirts upon thy face, and I will shew the nations thy nakedness, and the kingdoms thy shame. And I will cast abominable filth upon thee, and make thee vile, and will set thee as a gazingstock" (Nahum 3:1,4,5,6). "And he will stretch out his hand against the north, and destroy Assyria; and will make Nineveh a desolation, and dry like a wilderness. And flocks shall lie down in the midst of her, all the beasts of the nations: both the cormorant and the bittern shall lodge in the upper lintels of it; their voice shall sing in the windows; desolation shall be in the thresholds: for he shall uncover the cedar work" (Zeph. 2:13,14). And where is Nineveh today?

3. Prophecies concerning Babylon. When Babylon was

queen of the earth it was predicted that the city would become a perpetual desolation. "And Babylon, the glory of kingdoms, the beauty of the Chaldees' excellency, shall be as when God overthrew Sodom and Gomorrah. It shall never be inhabited, neither shall it be dwelt in from generation to generation: neither shall the Arabian pitch tent there; neither shall the shepherds make their fold there. But wild beasts of the desert shall lie there; and their houses shall be full of doleful creatures; and owls shall dwell there, and satyrs shall dance there. And the wild beasts of the islands shall cry in their desolate houses, and dragons in their pleasant palaces: and her time is near to come, and her days shall not be prolonged" (Isa. 13:19-22). "And Babylon shall become heaps, a dwelling-place for dragons, an astonishment, and an hissing, without an inhabitant" (Jer. 51:37). The glory of Babylon has long since crumbled into dust!

4. Prophecies concerning Egypt. The prophecy was made that Egypt would become the basest of kingdoms; that Memphis would be a desolation, and that No (Thebes) would be broken up. "It (Egypt) shall be the basest of the kingdoms; neither shall it exalt itself any more above the nations: for I will diminish them, that they shall no more rule over the nations" (Ezek. 29:15). "O thou daughter dwelling in Egypt, furnish thyself to go into captivity: for Noph shall be waste and desolate without an inhabitant. Egypt is like a very fair heifer, but destruction cometh; it cometh out of the north" (Jer. 46:19,20). "And I will set fire in Egypt: Sin shall have great pain, and No shall be rent asunder, and Noph shall have distresses daily" (Ezek. 30:16). Who can deny that history confirms the fulfillment of these stern proclamations of woe?

## E. The Test of Archaeology.

Men frequently ridicule certain stories in the Bible. For example, so-called experts at one time did not believe that

Abraham really lived or that the place from which he came, Ur of the Chaldees, actually existed. They claimed that the tower of Babel was a myth and that in Abraham's day men could not write. Archaeology has proved the skeptics to be wrong and has confirmed the Biblical accounts in a remarkable way.

Wherever archaeology has uncovered evidence the results have confirmed the Bible. In scores of cases the findings have demonstrated the validity of the Book. Archaeology refutes the critics' contentions that the Bible is inaccurate and fallible. It remains to be demonstrated that it is wrong in given particulars. Archaeological discoveries have done much to prove the truth of the Biblical records and to establish the believer in the conviction that the Bible is true.

Men whose hearts have not been opened and whose eyes are blinded by the prince of this world will never come to the truth of God even when the evidence is given to them. Essentially the problem remains a spiritual one. Only when men permit the light of the gospel to shine in their hearts through Jesus Christ will they believe that the Bible is the Word of God.

# 4

# The Study of the Bible

---

The Christian life is lived out by men of flesh and blood. Just as nourishment is required for the continuance of physical life, so it is needed for the development of spiritual life. Food, exercise, and rest are required for physical health. For spiritual health the exercise is service; the renewal of expended energies is through prayer; but the food supply is the Word of God. The question arises: "How can people who love God and want to be used of God make the Bible their own personal possession?" The answer is clear: By studying the Word.

## A. REASONS FOR STUDYING THE BIBLE.

1. We should study the Scriptures because the Bible is, in part, the source of faith. "So then faith cometh by hearing, and hearing by the word of God" (Rom. 10:17).

2. The Bible is the weapon by which the Holy Spirit brings conviction to the hearts of men and through which He accomplishes the work of sanctification. "And take the helmet of salvation, and the sword of the Spirit, which is the word of God" (Eph. 6:17).

3. The knowledge of God's Word makes possible a holy

life. "Thy word have I hid in mine heart, that I might not sin against thee" (Psalm 119:11).

4. The Bible provides light and guidance for the Christian. "Thy word is a lamp unto my feet, and a light unto my path" (Ps. 119:105).

5. The Word of God alone can keep one from error and provide an objective criterion by which to determine the truth or falsity of the ideas and claims of men. "All scripture is given by inspiration of God, and is profitable for doctrine, for reproof, for correction, for instruction in righteousness: that the man of God may be perfect, throughly furnished unto all good works" (2 Tim. 3:16,17).

## B. THE PROPER APPROACH TO BIBLE STUDY.

If one comes to the Word of God with a skeptical mind or an unbelieving heart it will not meet his needs. If he comes with hatred in his soul for the Lord Jesus, he will not receive from the Book food for his soul. One who denies the faith may indeed come under conviction when reading the Bible. Thank God for that. But when one has come under conviction and has been saved, his attitude will determine what benefit he will receive from Bible study. The correct approach may be summarized in the words:

1. ADMIT. One must allow the Word of God to enter his mind and heart. He may conceivably read the Bible without allowing its contents to filter through. But if he is really to profit by his Bible study, he must be willing to open his soul to the Word as a guest into the house of his heart.

2. SUBMIT. One does not necessarily accept what he admits. He may retain an open or a closed mind to information which has been conveyed to him. The second step is to submit, to accept what is written in the Scriptures for one's admonition. Acceptance is neither passive nor irrational. It arises as the result of the new birth. Yet even a man who has experienced the new birth may approach the Bible without the attitude of

submission. If one wants to be blessed, helped, and edified in his study of the Word, he must assent to its truth.

3. COMMIT. Just as one takes possession of truth in accepting it, so the truth must take possession of him in his committal to it. He must hide the Word in his heart until it becomes a part of his life and experience. This involves laying hold of it through faith and appropriation. When God tells one, for example, not to steal he must accept the truth and let it possess him, so that he actually does not steal. This is the acid test of the effectiveness of the Bible in one's life.

4. TRANSMIT. One must come to the Bible prepared to receive its truth and to pass it on. He is to know that he might be edified; but he is also to know in order that he might edify others. He must transmit to others what has become a reality in his own experience. To pass on the Word is a law of life and growth!

## C. THE SPIRIT OF BIBLE STUDY.

1. Believers should open the Bible with a spirit of awe and expectancy. They are handling the Word of God; not just an ordinary book, but one which reveals the mind of the Lord. If God is speaking, one can depend on the fact that He has something important to say. He who really believes the Bible will study it, therefore, with solemnity and eager anticipation.

2. Moreover, the Christian must be teachable. He knows that God has spiritual instruction for him, and he must be willing to be taught. This demands reverence, humility, and devotion. And it should issue in obedience to the injunctions learned.

3. Since the purpose of the Bible is to make Christ real, every earnest Bible student must study the Word with a desire to know the Lord Jesus better. This desire will not be in vain. The more one meditates upon the Scriptures, the more precious does the Saviour become to him.

## D. Reading as Distinguished from Studying.

Reading the Bible is profitable; but it is not studying the Bible. It differs from studying in that it does not necessarily involve method, whereas Bible study cannot be effective unless some method is followed. Christians are frequently burdened with a sense of fruitlessness in their Bible study. Their failure generally springs, not from lack of desire, nor from want of time, nor from a refusal to read the Bible, but from a lack of method.

Methodology in Bible study is important if best results are to be achieved. The choice of method depends upon individual preference. But one will probably use most, if not all, of the methods of Bible study suggested below.

## E. Methods of Bible Study.

1. *Book study*. The Bible is a library of books. Each is related to the others and together they form a unified whole. While each was written by a man and has for its background a particular historical situation, a divine unity runs through the entire volume. Some books are historical, some poetical, some didactic. Yet none is complete apart from the rest. To study a single book is profitable, especially when the book is considered in its relation to the rest of the Bible, to the total body of doctrine found in the Bible, and to the progressive development of Biblical truth. The historical background of a book, its authorship, purpose, and outline are well worth studying. Such study prevents fragmentation, and eliminates a casual one-sided approach to the Scriptures. It is systematic, it permits concentration and brings order to one's study.

2. *Topical study*. This type of study reveals divine truth as it unfolds, not in a single book, but in all the books. For example, the word "love" can be traced wherever it is used in the Bible, and from the study of the concept ideas will develop which will prove of profit to the student and to those with

whom he comes into contact. Important doctrines, such as grace, assurance, faith, and prayer provide good subjects for topical study. In the case of prayer, for example, such a study will reveal the principles of prayer, the privileges of prayer, the forms of prayer, the promises connected with prayer, and the practice of prayer. Every believer will find this sort of study edifying.

3. *Biographical study.* The lives of men and women are filled with instructive, and sometimes with exciting or thrilling material. The Bible recounts a great deal about individual characters, and the student can benefit from the study of their lives. Moses, Abraham, Sarah, Samson, Saul, Jesus, Paul, Peter and a thousand others come to view as one searches the Word. He sees men as they are. He observes their actions, both good and bad, as they pass before his eyes. He can study the operation of divine justice in payment for sin; he can behold salvation coming to sinful men; he can notice men's backsliding, repentance and restoration. No life is so sterile but that it will reward one for the time spent in studying it in its varied relationships to God and men.

4. *Other methods of Bible study.* One may study great passages such as 1 Corinthians 13, Romans 8, Hebrews 12, or John 1. He may study paragraphs, sentences, or even individual verses. This is narrowing the principle of book study into smaller segments. He may examine, outline, and digest single chapters without making a detailed study of an entire book. This type of Bible study, however, has its dangers. It may result in dilettantism and superficiality. One must ever remember that he is not just to taste, or to browse, or to wander,—but really to study the Word of God.

# 5

# The Drama of the Bible

---

The Biblical drama may be studied from two vantage points: first, as an unfolding of the varied relationships between God and man; second, as a titanic struggle between the Almighty and the devil, culminating in the permanent overthrow of Satan and his hosts.

## A. THE DRAMA: GOD AND MAN.

1. *The Perfect Fellowship*. God created man in order that He might have fellowship with him. He placed him in a lovely garden amid the most auspicious surroundings. At the outset the communion between God and man was beautiful and complete. And God demanded of man perfect obedience. Thus the boon of continuous, unbroken fellowship was grounded in obedience to the divine will.

2. *The Broken Fellowship*. But man, a creature endowed with the power of choice, was tempted and chose the wrong. Instead of God's will he chose his own desires. He disobeyed the clear word of God, and thus plunged the entire human race, although yet unborn, into misery and separation from God.

The entire human race? Yes. For Adam was the *federal* head of the race. He was not only an individual; he was also the *representative* man. When he fell all mankind fell "in him."

This is the clear teaching of the Scriptures. (See, for example, 1 Cor. 15:22.) The separation of man from God was the inevitable consequence of Adam's evil choice. So always the result of sin is separation from God. The Creator will not have fellowship with a sin-stained, uncleansed creature. Adam and Eve and all their posterity were placed under the curse of God.

The plot of the Bible centers in God's dealings with the fallen human race. Again and again He gave men opportunities to draw closer to Him. He dealt with them in judgment or in mercy; but men invariably rejected His offers of grace. The entire Old Testament reveals the utter inability of man to restore the broken fellowship. The drama centers around:

a. A series of judgments. The expulsion from the garden, the flood, and the confounding of speech at Babel. Here the rule is emphasized that sin always results in separation and judgment (Gen. 3-11).

b. The selection of a Nation (Gen. 12), Israel, to be the channel of God's gracious revelation, the repository of the divine promises and blessings and the vehicle for the transmission of the line of which Christ should be born. But the patriarchs, the early leaders of the nation, betrayed their trust, and the closing chapters of Genesis find the disobedient children of Israel in bondage in Egypt.

c. The statutes on Sinai (Ex. 20). After the exodus from Egypt under Moses' direction, Israel is put under the law, a "schoolmaster" to teach her the lessons of God's holiness, of her own spiritual weakness and of her need of divine redemption. But the nation's rebellious mood is indicated by her wanton idolatry even while Moses was receiving the law at the hands of God (cf. Ex. 32).

d. The setting up of a kingdom (1 Sam. 10). The wilderness was crossed and the land of promise re-entered. The period of the judges came to a discouraging close. Israel, weary of her theocracy (divine rule), demanded a king. In mercy God acceded to her request; Saul was anointed king. But the kingdom failed to draw the people back to God. Selfishness, intrigue and idolatry flourished. The kingdom was divided and ultimately fell prey to invading conquerors and the people of Israel were led away into captivity.

e. The supplications of the prophets. God pled with His people to return to Him, but in vain. (Consult especially 2 Kings 17:7-12.) The verses following read: "Yet the Lord testified against Israel, and against Judah, by all the prophets, and by all the seers, saying, Turn ye from your evil ways . . . Notwithstanding they would not hear, but hardened their necks, like to the neck of their fathers, that did not believe in the Lord their God." Israel's record is one of persistent stubbornness and failure. The last word of the Old Testament is "curse." The nation was still far from God in the days of Malachi, the last writer of Old Testament prophecy.

3. *The Restored Fellowship.* The New Testament discloses God's climactic intervention. Here the Almighty steps into history in human form to lift men back to His loving heart. His dearly beloved Son assumed flesh; was known to His contemporaries as a Prophet of God and Teacher of matchless skill; and bore the sins of men upon His sinless shoulders. (Study Rom. 8:3,4.) Through His perfect obedience, vicarious sacrifice and present intercession at God's right hand, He restores the sinner to God. By Him the broken fellowship between God and man is forever mended. Disobedience drove man from Paradise; through Christ and His perfect obedience Paradise is regained.

## B. The Drama: God and the Devil.

1. The theme is seen in the words: "And I will put enmity between thee (the devil) and the woman, and between thy seed and her seed; it shall bruise thy head, and thou shalt bruise his heel" (Gen. 3:15). This verse suggests:

a. That in the struggle precipitated by the fall of man there would be two opposing forces, the devil, who first tempted man; and the "seed of the woman." A continuing conflict would ensue between the forces of Satan and those of the Son of God.

b. That in the course of the warfare the devil would be permitted to "bruise the heel" of the forces of righteousness and of God.

c. That the ultimate issue would be victory for Christ, the Seed of the woman (see Gal. 3:16), when at length the serpent's head would be bruised.

2. Throughout the Scriptures from beginning to end the trail of the serpent is seen as he seeks to molest, or mar, or disfigure or obliterate the seed of the woman. The phases of his attack are four-fold:

a. He first tries to wipe out the race of men, for he understands that mankind is the vehicle for the transmission of the seed.

(1) Assured that Abel is the line of the seed, he prompts Cain to slay his brother. But God intervenes and raises up Seth, "the appointed one" (see Gen. 4:25).

(2) Foiled, the devil leads the race into such gross sin that the Creator feels compelled to visit the earth with the judgment of the flood. But in mercy, and to preserve the seed, there is a second intervention; and a remnant, Noah and his family, is spared (see Gen. 6-9).

(3) The devil instills pride into the heart of the race. Men are scattered and it appears that the seed might lose its identity. But God intervenes once more, and chooses a people, Israel, through whom the line of the seed might be carried on (see Gen. 11).

b. The devil now levels his attack against Israel. Here are some of the aspects of his attack. In each case God intervenes on behalf of the seed.

(1) Sarah, Abraham's wife, is barren and it appears that the line of the seed will end. But Isaac is miraculously born (see Gen. 21:1-8).

(2) Isaac's elder son Esau is a worldling. It seems that the seed will be corrupted. But God chooses Jacob to be the heir of promise.

(3) Jacob's character as "supplanter" is such as to threaten the seed-line with contamination. But he is converted, becomes Israel, "a prince with God," and the line continues (study Gen. 27-32).

(4) And so on through the bondage in Egypt, the wilderness journey, the days of the judges, the division of the kingdom, and the captivities. In each case it seems that the devil might triumph. The heel of the woman's seed is indeed bruised. But God always intervenes. And although the last words of the Old Testament are pessimisitic, even then God is about to initiate His supreme intervention in the coming of the Saviour.

3. Knowing that Jesus Christ is the Seed par excellence, Satan now spares no effort to destroy or corrupt Him.

a. The events of Jesus' infancy, the crowded inn, the slaughter of babes in Bethlehem, etc. reveal the devil's handiwork. But God the Father always protects His Son (see Matt. 1,2).

b. The temptations in the wilderness are devil-inspired but futile (see Matt. 4).

c. The devil cannot destroy the Son of God on the Sea of Galilee. He can prompt men to deny Christ or to betray Him. But no Satanic effort can lead Christ astray or bring Him to an untimely death.

d. At Calvary it seems that finally the Seed has perished. But God intervenes once more: Christ is raised from the dead and ascends to a position of power, beyond the reach of the devil.

4. Since that time the devil, aware that Christ the Head is at God's right hand, now attacks the body on earth, the church. The history of the church is a long and thrilling record of the devil's inventions and God's interventions. Some day the promises of God will be fulfilled. The Seed of the woman, the triumphant Son of God, will bruise the serpent's head and

the fearful drama will come to a victorious end. (See Rev. 20:7-10.)

## C. DRAMA AND DOCTRINE.

1. As the Bible drama is told the central doctrines of the Scriptures are brought to light. These teachings are either embedded in the events themselves, or illustrated by the characters and their deeds, or explicitly declared as a part of the counsel of God.

2. The importance of Bible doctrine is indicated: positively, in such injunctions as Paul's to Timothy: "Give attendance . . . to doctrine," "Take heed unto thyself, and unto the doctrine" (1 Tim. 4:13,16); negatively, in the clear insistence that believers are to have no fellowship with purveyors of false doctrine. (Study 2 John 7-11.)

3. The remaining chapters of this volume will deal with the major doctrines of the Bible, together with their implications in the varied areas of divine revelation.

# PART TWO

# The Unseen Powers

---

"Fear not: for they that be with us are more than they that be with them" (2 Kings 6:16).

Beyond the realm of the human senses of sight, feeling and touch a mighty conflict rages between the forces of God and the forces of the devil. The unseen powers of the world are guiding, governing and determining the destinies of men. He who would be wise in understanding the mysteries of life, and strong in power in the battle of life, must know who these invisible forces are and what they are doing.

The Bible is explicit in delineating the nature and operations of all beings having a part in this titanic struggle. The basic conflict is between God and the devil, good and evil, righteousness and sin, heaven and hell. Innumerable allies on both sides are arrayed against one another. No man can interpret history correctly, understand present events and trends, or solve the human predicament unless he is fully cognizant of the fact that the battle is real and that the issues of time and eternity hinge upon its outcome.

The shadow of this unseen strife falls across the temporal scene. The conflict between individuals, communities and nations is but an extension of the invisible warfare. For the Christian, however, the outcome is certain, the end is determined. God and righteousness will triumph. The doom of the devil and his hosts is sure. The believer may look up and face the future with high and holy courage, "for they that be with us are more than they that be with them." The following section of this book introduces the reader to these unseen persons and their work.

# 6

## God the Father

This chapter and the two which follow present the teaching of the Scriptures concerning the three persons of the Godhead: the Father, the Son and the Holy Ghost. Perhaps it may be wise to introduce this lofty theme by a brief statement on the Trinity as such and by an examination of some of the reasons men believe in God.

1. *The Trinity*. The word "trinity" does not occur in the Bible. The Scriptures teach that God subsists in three persons, Father, Son and Holy Spirit. "These three are one God, the same in substance, equal in power and glory." The three persons are mentioned together in at least three passages of the New Testament: the record of the baptism of Jesus, where the voice of the Father is heard, the Son is baptized and the Holy Spirit appears as a dove (cf. Matt. 3:16,17); the Great Commission, in which our Saviour instructs His disciples to baptize men "in the name of the Father, and of the Son, and of the Holy Ghost" (Matt. 28:19); and the trinitarian benediction: "The grace of our Lord Jesus Christ, and the love of God, and the communion of the Holy Ghost, be with you all" (2 Cor. 13:14). The mind of man cannot fully understand the mystery of the Trinity. He who would try to understand the Trinity

fully will lose his mind. But he who would deny the Trinity will lose his soul.

2. *Proofs of the Existence of God.* God has revealed His existence to men. His revelation is both natural and supernatural.

a. NATURAL.

(1) Through the religious nature in man, which demands an object of worship. This explains animism and fetish worship.

(2) Through the moral nature of man, the sense of "oughtness" which, although often neglected or dulled, is a persistent voice. Man's moral nature demands some Being to whom he is accountable and responsible.

(3) Through the law of cause and effect; logic teaches that every effect must have a cause. The universe is the effect; the original Cause is God.

(4) Through the law of design. Reason shows that the existence of design presupposes the existence of a designer. The interactions observable in nature and between man and nature indicate design. The Designer is God.

(5) Through the law of purpose. Whenever a purpose is evident, somewhere a purposive agent exists. The system of worlds is traveling towards a definite chronological objective. God holds the reins.

b. SUPERNATURAL.

The Christian accepts the findings of the natural which demonstrate the existence of God. But beyond this he has the supernatural revelation of God which comes to him objectively through the Bible, the Word of God; and the incarnation of God, or the living Word, Christ Jesus. The written Word witnesses to the existence of God. The incarnate Word is God manifest in the flesh.

●　　●　　●

## A. The Nature of God the Father.

1. *"God is a Spirit"* (John 4:24), an incorporeal, invisible, Reality. Only one God exists. He possesses a definite nature and unchanging attributes. ". . . the Lord he is God; there is none else beside him" (Deut. 4:35).

2. *God is a Person.* He has all the characteristics of personality: He knows, He feels, He wills.

"He that planted the ear, shall he not hear?

He that formed the eye, shall he not see?

He that chastiseth the heathen, shall not he correct?

He that teacheth man knowledge, shall not he know?"

(Psalm 94:9,10).

We should address God as a Person. He is interested in every aspect of His creation. We should gladly make all our wishes and needs known to Him.

## B. The Attributes of God the Father.

1. *God is eternal.* "In the beginning God . . ." (Gen. 1:1). There never was a time when He was not; there never will be a time when He will cease to be. He is "the everlasting God" (Isa. 40:28). "Before the mountains were brought forth, or ever thou hadst formed the earth and the world, even from everlasting to everlasting, thou art God" (Psalm 90:2). The contemplation of this truth is strangely comforting.

2. *God is omnipotent.* "And when Abram was ninety years old and nine, the Lord appeared to Abram, and said unto him, I am the Almighty God; walk before me, and be thou perfect." (Gen. 17:1; see Ex. 6:3.) All power belongs to God. No individual, or nation, or combination of forces terrestrial or celestial, can thwart His sovereign purposes.

(The use of *"omni"* adjectives [*"omnis"*—*"all"* in Latin] indicates a human effort to describe the totalitarian nature of the attributes of God. Man can see and understand only a minute segment of creation. His life span covers only a tiny portion of eternity. In seeking to describe God he must use immense words—words which describe facts far beyond his personal experience but within the scope of divine revelation.)

3. *God is infinite and omnipresent.* The Psalmist is eloquent: "Whither shall I go from thy spirit? or whither shall I flee from thy presence? If I ascend up into heaven thou art there: if I make my bed in hell, behold, thou art there. If I take the wings of the morning, and dwell in the uttermost parts of the sea, Even there shall thy hand lead me, and thy right hand shall hold me" (Psalm 139:7-10).

4. *God is immutable.* "For I am the Lord," He says, "I change not" (Mal. 3:6; see also Psalm 102:26,27; James 1:17). He is the cause of the changing seasons; but He Himself never changes.

> "Change and decay in all around I see;
> Oh, Thou who changest not, abide with me."

5. *God is omniscient.* "Great is our Lord, and of great power; his understanding is infinite" (Psalm 147:5). "Known unto God are all his works from the beginning of the world." (Acts 15:18; see also Psalm 139:1-6; Prov. 5:21.) He knows the mighty principles which He first called into being to govern His creation. He knows what keeps the planets in their orbits. He knows the sparrow that falls to the ground and the violet that lifts its dainty head in the forest. Above all, He knows you, intimately, personally, vitally. He knows your thoughts, words and deeds, and loves you still.

6. *God is holy.* "Holy, holy, holy, is the Lord of hosts: the whole earth is full of his glory." (Isa. 6:3; see also Psalm 99:9.) At the contemplation of God's holiness one is prone, not to analyze, but to fall in adoration at His feet.

7. *God is just.* He is impartial in all His dealings, equitable in all His works. "He is the Rock, his work is perfect: for all his ways are judgment: a God of truth and without iniquity, just

and right is he" (Deut. 32:4). God does not temporize nor compromise with iniquity. The balances in which the deeds of men are weighed are exact. "Great and marvelous are thy works, Lord God Almighty; just and true are thy ways, thou King of Saints" (Rev. 15:3).

8. *God is love.* (See 1 John 4:8,16.) His holiness and justice caused Him to mete out the penalty of death for our sins. But His love caused Him to send His Son to bear the penalty for sin on Calvary in the place of sinners. At the cross God's holiness and love were beautifully revealed. There "mercy and truth are met together; righteousness and peace have kissed each other" (Psalm 85:10).

### C. Our Attitude towards God the Father.

1. We must "worship Him in spirit and in truth." (John 4:24; see Matt. 4:10.) True worship is possible in one way only. The unbeliever may stand in awe at the contemplation of the wonders of creation. But only the believer, who has put his faith in Christ, can truly adore the Creator. (See Matt. 11:27.)

2. We must glorify Him in life and conduct. We belong to Him by creation and redemption. We must seek "first the kingdom of God and his righteousness" (Matt. 6:33), striving to do what is well-pleasing in His sight. We must maintain an unbroken fellowship with Him, remembering that we are ever in His sight, and that throughout eternity we shall be in His presence and share in His praise.

# 7

# God the Son

The second person of the Trinity is God the Son, our Lord Jesus Christ. He is consubstantial and co-eternal with the Father. One must understand who He is and what He did for man; for His person and work constitute the central theme of the Scriptures.

## A. The Eternity of Jesus Christ.

The One who crossed the stage of human history centuries ago did not commence His life in Bethlehem of Judea. From all eternity He existed in the bosom of the Father. "Very God of Very God," there never was a time when He was not. He is and always has been the only begotten Son of God, the eternal Word of God (John 1:1), the brightness of God's everlasting glory. "And he is before all things, and by him all things consist" (Col. 1:17). "Jesus Christ the same yesterday, and today, and forever." (Heb. 13:8; see also Heb. 1:3.)

## B. The Meaning of the Words "Jesus Christ."

1. "Jesus" is the Greek equivalent of the Hebrew "Jehoshua" (Joshua). It signifies "Jehovah is salvation." "Thou shalt call his name Jesus: for he shall save his people from their

56

sins" (Matt. 1:21). The One born of Mary is Jehovah Himself, the Saviour of men.

2. "Christ" is the Greek equivalent of the Hebrew "Messiah." (See John 1:41.) It means "the Anointed One," the promised Deliverer of men.

## C. THE INCARNATION OF JESUS CHRIST.

1. *Immanuel* ("God with us"). Only the one who is assured of the eternal existence of Christ can understand the stupendous nature of His birth. In Bethlehem the everlasting was confined within the dimensions of time; God the Son became man.

For the redemption of lost humanity, Christ "was made flesh, and dwelt among us" (John 1:14). This is known as the incarnation of the Son of God. The word "incarnation" is derived from the Latin "in" ("in," or "into"), and "caro" ("flesh"). "But when the fulness of the time was come, God sent forth His Son, made of a woman, made under the law, To redeem them that were under the law . . ." (Gal. 4:4,5). Christ Jesus, "who, being in the form of God thought it not robbery to be equal with God: But made himself of no reputation, and took upon him the form of a servant, and was made in the likeness of men . . ." (Phil. 2:6,7).

2. *The God-Man.* The second Person of the Godhead assumed a human body. Jesus is the God-Man (*theanthropos*), one Person with two natures, human and divine. He is God. He is Man. While He is both God and Man, He is one Person having two natures, each separate and distinct from the other without fusion or mixture.

This is a divine mystery. Our Lord fed the five thousand miraculously; yet He knew the pangs of hunger. He dispensed the water of life; yet He thirsted beside a Samaritan well. He stilled the troubled waves of the Sea of Galilee; yet He slept in a little boat. He spoke and Lazarus was loosed from the shackles of death; yet He wept when He heard that His friend had died. An earthquake occurred at His death; yet on the cross He experienced the piercing agony of human pain. Clearly He was both human and divine.

## D. THE WORK OF JESUS CHRIST.

More people have written about our Lord than about any other person who ever lived. His work as prophet, priest, and king causes the believer's heart to rejoice.

Some men regard Jesus as nothing more than a great man. They believe that He had a "spark of divinity" which, although it shone brightly, was similar to the spark which illumines every genius. To such people the ministry of Jesus is intriguing, but baffling. Yet they cannot let Him alone. They study Him. They try to imitate Him. They praise Him as man's greatest example. But they never find Him. Jesus' mission was divine. It originated in Heaven; it was manifested on earth; it continues in glory. He is Prophet, Priest, and King.

1. *Prophet.* Christ is the Prophet of the ages. (Compare Deut. 18:15 with Acts 7:37.) A prophet speaks on behalf of another. For example, Aaron was Moses' "prophet," or spokesman. (Cf. Ex. 7:1.) Jesus came to declare God's counsels and to reveal God's person. He came to point men to God.

His moral code is more precise and authoritative than any the world has ever known. His sermons are masterpieces of eloquent simplicity. His words are sublime. Beauty, dignity, warmth, and directness characterize His sayings. Some believe that Jesus' ethical precepts are the sum and substance of His ministry. This is a very dangerous position indeed.

As Prophet, Jesus made it clear that man is in spiritual need. He is a sinner. Beautiful as the Savior's teachings are, man is incapable of measuring up to His moral demands. Our Lord's precepts inspire but they also condemn. Man quickly discovers that in his present estate he is unable to keep them. The glory of the gospel is that Christ as Prophet furnishes man with a set of ideals, and as Priest redeems him from sin.

2. *Priest.* "Now of the things which we have spoken this is the sum: We have such an high priest, who is set on the right hand of the throne of the Majesty in the heavens" (Heb. 8:1). Redemption demands both priesthood and sacrifice. The Lord Jesus met both these requirements: He is both Priest and Lamb.

The sacrifice which Jesus offered was His own precious blood. He entered the Holy of Holies and sprinkled that blood upon the mercy-seat of God. He intercedes on the sinner's behalf. (Cf. Rom. 8:34.) The forgiveness of sins depends upon His priestly, mediatorial work.

(Study the phrase "greater than" in Matt. 12:5,6,41,42. Jesus is greater than Jonas: this is His prophetic work. He is greater than the temple priesthood: this is His priestly work. But He is also greater than Solomon: this is His kingly work.)

3. *King.* Jesus was born in David's royal city. Regal visitors from the East welcomed Him. A rival king, Herod, trembled at His birth. He was crowned King at His baptism. His royal manifesto was proclaimed in the Sermon on the Mount and in His parables of the kingdom. His royal credentials were the miracles He wrought. He was King of the Jews, of the royal line of David, the long expected Messiah of Israel.

The Jews rejected their King. For His diadem they gave Him a crown of thorns; for His scepter, a reed; for His throne, a cruel cross. But God raised Him from the dead and exalted Him to "the right hand of the throne of the Majesty in the heavens" (Heb. 8:1). From that position of honor He rules as Sovereign in the hearts of Jews and Gentiles alike who receive Him as Saviour and King.

The King's subjects have a duty and a hope:

a. Their duty is to render unto Him adoration, the loyalty of obedience, the fealty of unfeigned praise. They must acknowledge Him as King in every realm of life. They must seek first the kingdom of God. They must strive to extend His kingdom through testimony, service, and missionary effort, to the uttermost part of the earth. Christ is King! Then let Him indeed be Ruler over all.

b. Their hope is that the King will come again! Perilous times prevail. Wrong reigns supreme. Iniquity abounds. Callousness, carelessness, and confusion are rife. But this disorder will end. Christ will return in power and great glory to reign. The name written on His vesture and on His thigh will be "King of kings, and Lord of lords" (Rev. 19:16). The prophecy will be fulfilled: "The kingdoms of this world are become the kingdoms of our Lord, and of His Christ; and he shall reign for ever and ever" (Rev. 11:15).

### E. MAN'S RELATIONSHIP TO JESUS CHRIST.

One question determines the destiny of the human soul. The Roman procurator Pilate asked it centuries ago: "What shall I do then with Jesus which is called Christ?" (Matt. 27:22).

> "What will you do with Jesus?
> Neutral you cannot be;
> Some day your heart will be asking,
> 'What will He do with me?' "

## 8

# God the Holy Spirit

---

The third person of the Trinity is the Holy Spirit. He has existed eternally with the Father and the Son.

## A. His Titles.

He has many titles: for example, the Holy Ghost, the Spirit of Christ, the Spirit of holiness, the Spirit of truth, the Spirit of life, the Spirit of grace, the Comforter. The Greek word for the last of these titles is "paraclete," i.e. the "one called beside" the believer as a friend and ally. Note that the same Greek word is translated "advocate" in 1 John 2:1. At the right hand of God the exalted Christ is also our Ally, interceding for His own. (See Rom. 8:34.)

## B. His Nature.

The Holy Spirit is not a mere idea, or influence, or figment of the imagination. He is a person. Jesus said concerning Him: "But when the Comforter is come, whom I will send unto you from the Father, even the Spirit of truth, which proceedeth from the Father, he shall testify of me" (John 15:26). Notice the personal pronoun. (The Spirit is referred to as "it" in Rom. 8:26 because the translation there is of the neuter word *"pneuma,"* "spirit.")

Although the Spirit is invisible and incorporeal, He has the characteristics of personality: intellect, feeling, and will. This is important. He is no impersonal "force."

1. *He knows.* Paul writes that "the things of God knoweth no man, but the Spirit of God" (1 Cor. 2:11). If one would understand divine things, he must be indwelt by the Holy Spirit, who is the agent of spiritual understanding and enlightenment. The reverse side of this truth is that, apart from the Holy Spirit, all men, however cultured they may be, are blind to divine truth.

2. *He feels.* "Now I beseech you, brethren, for the Lord Jesus Christ's sake, and for the love of the Spirit . . ." (Rom. 15:30). He who sheds abroad in our hearts the love of Christ is Himself characterized by love.

3. *He wills.* "But all these worketh that one and the selfsame Spirit, dividing to every man severally as he will . . ." (1 Cor. 12:11). This selective activity is described at some length in 1 Cor. 12:7-10.

## C. His Work.

The Holy Spirit has always been active. As early as Genesis 1:2 it is written: "And the Spirit of God moved upon the face of the waters." (The Trinity participated in the work of creation. Cf. Psalm 33:6; John 1:3.) Throughout Old Testament days His influence is frequently noted. The Spirit of the Lord, for example, came upon certain of the judges (see Judges 3:10; 6:34; 11:29), upon King Saul (1 Sam. 10:10), upon David (1 Sam. 16:13), upon Azariah (2 Chron. 15:1), upon Zechariah (2 Chron. 24:20).

The Spirit was present in power in the days of Christ's incarnation. He was there when our Lord was baptized (Matt. 3:16). He led Him into the wilderness to be tempted (Luke 4:1). The Saviour's ministry was "in the power of the Spirit" (Luke 4:14,18).

The administration of the Spirit began after Jesus was glorified in death, resurrection and ascension. (Notice the time element in such passages as John 7:37-39; 14:16.) Pentecost witnessed its inauguration (see Acts 2:1-4). The Spirit's work today relates to every department of the believer's life, worship, testimony and service. We cannot enumerate all the Spirit's activities, for He is the very life of the church. Among His prerogatives are the following:

1. *The Holy Spirit exalts Christ.* This is one of His major functions. The work of the Spirit in one's heart makes Christ real, vital, and precious. Our Saviour said: "When he, the Spirit of truth, is come . . . He shall glorify me: for he shall receive of mine, and shall show it unto you" (John 16:13,14). Eloquence, oratory, illustration, pathos—no device of public speaking can bring the sinner to the Saviour apart from the exalting work of the Spirit.

2. *The Holy Spirit convicts men.* "And when he is come," Christ stated: "he will reprove the world of sin, and of righteousness, and of judgment" (John 16:8). "Of sin, because they believe not on me" (v. 9). From the context it is clear that the greatest of all sins, one which can be removed only by the Spirit's convicting power, is the flagrant sin of unbelief. May the Spirit Himself write this truth upon our hearts. All sins may be forgiven save a persistent, stubborn, changeless lack of faith in Christ. The one who rejects the Son resists the Spirit and repudiates the Father's provision of eternal life.

3. *The Holy Spirit regenerates men.* "Jesus answered, Verily, verily, I say unto thee, Except a man be born of water and of the Spirit, he cannot enter the kingdom of God" (John 3:5). Having exalted Christ and convicted the sinner, the Spirit persuades and enables him to accept the Son as his Saviour, and implants within his breast a new life.

4. *The Holy Spirit dwells within the people of God.* "Know ye not that ye are the temple of God, and that the Spirit of God dwelleth in you?" (1 Cor. 3:16). These words were addressed to the Corinthian church, which, although Paul

accuses it of carnality (cf. 1 Cor. 3:1-3), was yet the dwelling-place of the Spirit. The bodies of individual Christians are also temples of the Spirit. (See 1 Cor. 6:19; Rom. 8:9.) The Spirit of God purifies and strengthens the children of God. Supremely He produces "the fruit of the Spirit" within (Gal. 5:22,23). He is the builder of Christian character.

Few teachings of the Scripture need more emphasis than this. Multitudes today, for example, are afraid. The antidote to fear is the Spirit's work of shedding abroad in the believer's heart the love of Christ. For "perfect love casteth out fear" (1 John 4:18). The cure for worry, undue anxiety, is the peace which the Spirit produces. Indeed, growth in all the graces of Christian character is possible as the result of the presence and power of the indwelling Spirit.

5. *The Holy Spirit seals believers.* He sets His divine seal of ownership, authority, and security upon those who truly put their trust in Christ. "And grieve not the holy Spirit of God, whereby ye are sealed unto the day of redemption" (Eph. 4:30). The Spirit gives to the children of God the glad and confident assurance that they belong to the Father forever.

6. *The Holy Spirit guides the people of God.* He led Philip unerringly to the Ethiopian eunuch. "The Spirit said unto Philip, Go near and join thyself to this chariot" (Acts 8:29). At the Spirit's direction the early church separated Barnabas and Saul for their missionary task. (See Acts 13:2,4.) Today, utilizing the Word of God and the pressure of circumstances, the Spirit opens and closes doors for Christians, and puts within their souls a sense of spiritual compulsion. The mature believer can look backward across the years and trace with gratitude the strange but beautiful pathway along which the Spirit has directed his steps.

7. *The Holy Spirit prompts believers to worship.* We are to pray "in the Holy Ghost" (Jude 20; see Eph. 6:18), i.e. as the Spirit of God directs. Our praise and thanksgiving are inspired by the Spirit. As we are filled with Him we speak "in

psalms and hymns and spiritual songs, singing and making melody in your heart to the Lord; Giving thanks always for all things unto God . . ." (Eph. 5:19,20). True Christian worship, that which is acceptable to the Father, has its origin in the Spirit. Paul writes explicitly, "For we are the circumcision, who worship by the Spirit of God" (Phil. 3:3, R.V.). Ceremonial incantations, genuflexions, and ritualistic formulae are all in vain, an empty show, unless they are the result of the Spirit's working in the soul.

8. *The Holy Spirit empowers for testimony.* "But ye shall receive power, after that the Holy Ghost is come upon you; and ye shall be witnesses unto me both in Jerusalem, and in all Judea, and in Samaria, and unto the uttermost part of the earth" (Acts 1:8). When the Spirit of God came in power upon the church at Pentecost the message of the apostles became well-nigh irresistible. Thousands were converted. Paul's phenomenal success was due, not only to his dauntless courage, his eloquence and his loyalty to the gospel. All these were important. But to the Corinthian believers he wrote: "And my speech and my preaching was not with enticing words of man's wisdom, but in demonstration of the Spirit and of power: that your faith should not stand in the wisdom of men, but in the power of God" (1 Cor. 2:4,5); and to the Thessalonians: "For our gospel came not unto you in word only, but also in power, and in the Holy Ghost, and in much assurance . . ." (1 Thess. 1:5). If one would be a powerful witness for Christ, he must be "in the Spirit": dominated, controlled, motivated by the Spirit.

9. *The Holy Spirit enables men to appreciate, to understand and to discern what is taught in the Word of God.* "Now we have received, not the spirit of the world, but the spirit which is of God; that we might know the things that are freely given to us of God" (1 Cor. 2:12). The Spirit is the supreme Teacher. The study of languages, theology, hermeneutics and other disciplines is helpful. Ultimately, however, the Holy

Spirit opens eyes blinded by sin and allows the sunlight of truth to shine in. John writes: "But ye have an unction from the Holy One, and ye know all things" (1 John 2:20).

10. *The Holy Spirit will quicken the mortal bodies of believers.* "But if the Spirit of him that raised up Jesus from the dead dwell in you, he that raised up Christ from the dead shall also quicken your mortal bodies by his Spirit that dwelleth in you" (Rom. 8:11). Some day the bodies of believers will be raised from the dead, incorruptible, glorified. The Holy Spirit will be the one to execute the Father's decree: under His control the "redemption of our body" (Rom. 8:23) will be completed.

## D. OUR RELATIONSHIP TO HIM.

The child of God is utterly dependent upon the Spirit for his spiritual birth, life, victory and service. The Spirit lives within his heart. The more yielded he is to his indwelling guest the happier, healthier, holier, and more hopeful he becomes. This is the Christian's basic law of life. Would he experience daily the love and peace of the Saviour? Would he live on the highest spiritual plane? Would he have victory over temptation? Would he have a song in his soul? Would he be a blessing to others wherever he goes? Then he must keep yielded to the Spirit. Only thus will his life and witness truly count for God.

# 9

# *Angels*

---

Just as there is a personal devil so there are other created beings
who exist for the accomplishment of the divine program. We
speak of these beings as angels, although it is correct to say that
Satan himself was and is an Angel,—a fallen angel who lost his
first estate. In the section of this book which deals with Satan
this is brought out clearly; but now we must concern ourselves
with the angels who do the bidding of God.

## A. The Existence of Angels.

The Bible affirms that angels actually exist. Matthew states
that when the temptation of Jesus was ended, "behold, angels
came and ministered unto him" (Matt. 4:11). Jesus assumed
their existence when He said, "Take heed that ye despise not
one of these little ones; for I say unto you, That in heaven
their angels do always behold the face of my Father which is
in heaven" (Matt. 18:10). Speaking of His second advent He
declared, "But of that day and that hour knoweth no man, no,
not the angels which are in heaven, neither the Son, but the
Father" (Mark 13:32). Paul also teaches that angels exist: "Let
no man beguile you of your reward in a voluntary humility
and worshipping of angels, intruding into those things which
he hath not seen, vainly puffed up by his fleshly mind" (Col

2:18); "And to you who are troubled rest with us, when the Lord Jesus shall be revealed from heaven with his mighty angels" (2 Thess. 1:7).

## B. THE NATURE OF ANGELS.

1. *Angels* are spoken of in the Scriptures as "ministering spirits, sent forth to minister to the heirs of salvation" (Heb. 1:14). They are the servants of God accomplishing the purposes of God. God "maketh his angels spirits; his ministers a flaming fire" (Psalm 104:4).

2. *Angels are created beings.* There was a time when they were not. "Thou, even thou, art Lord alone; thou hast made heaven, the heaven of heavens, with all their host, the earth, and all things that are therein, the seas, and all that is therein, and thou preservest them all; and *the host of heaven* worshippeth thee" (Neh. 9:6); "For by him were all things created, that are in heaven, and that are in earth, visible and invisible, whether they be thrones, or dominions, or principalities, or powers: all things were created by him, and for him" (Col. 1:16).

3. *Angels are innumerable.* "And I beheld, and I heard the voice of many angels round about the throne and the beasts and the elders: and the number of them was ten thousand times ten thousand, and thousands of thousands" (Rev. 5:11); "But ye are come unto mount Sion, and unto the city of the living God, the heavenly Jerusalem, and to an innumerable company of angels" (Heb. 12:22).

4. *Angels are above the laws of matter.* Whereas men cannot go through doors or prison bars, angels are able to circumvent physical obstacles and to travel over distant spaces in a short time. When Peter was asleep in prison with guards about him the Bible relates, "And, behold, the angel of the Lord came upon him, and a light shined in the prison: and he smote Peter on the side, and raised him up saying, Arise up quickly. And his chains fell off from his hands" (Acts 12:7).

5. *Angels differ in rank and power.* The Bible speaks of archangels, angels, principalities, powers, dominions, thrones, might and authorities. (See Col. 1:16.) The angel God sent to aid Daniel engaged in a battle against the forces of darkness and was not able to prevail. Reinforcements came in the form of Michael, "one of the chief princes." His power enabled the first angel to succor Daniel. He ended his task with the words, "And now I will return to fight with the prince of Persia." (See Daniel 10:12-21.)

6. *Angels are greater in intelligence than men* despite the fact that men like to regard themselves as the highest in the order of God's creation. King David understood this when the woman of Tekoah said to him, "My lord is wise, according to the wisdom of an angel of God, to know all things that are in the earth" (2 Sam. 14:20).

7. *Angels excel in power.* "Bless the Lord, ye his angels that excel in strength, that do his commandments, hearkening unto the voice of his word" (Psalm 103:20). "Whereas angels, which are greater in power and might, bring not railing accusation against them before the Lord" (2 Peter 2:11). The power of angels is openly manifested in actual incidents relating to the world of men. So great is the power of a single angel that one's imagination is staggered at the thought of a being who wields such power. A few illustrations will suffice to indicate that angels can perform mighty deeds for God.

a. One angel slew 185,000 Assyrian soldiers in a single night: "And it came to pass that night, that the angel of the Lord went out, and smote in the camp of the Assyrians an hundred fourscore and five thousand: and when they arose early in the morning, behold they were all dead corpses" (2 Kings 19:35).

b. One angel slew 70,000 Israelites following David's sin in numbering the people. "And when the angel stretched out his hand upon Jerusalem to destroy it, the Lord repented him of the evil, and said to the angel that destroyed the people, It is enough." (See 2 Sam. 24:15,16.)

c. One angel thwarted the power of Rome and rolled away the stone that held our Lord captive: "And, behold, there was a great earthquake: for the angel of the Lord descended from heaven, and came and rolled back the stone from the door, and sat upon it . . . and for fear of him the keepers did shake, and became as dead men" (Matt. 28:2,4).

d. One angel will some day bind the devil and keep him imprisoned for a thousand years. The arch-enemy of our souls will be brought low, not by Christ Himself, nor by hosts of angelic creatures, but by a solitary angel: "And I saw an angel come down from heaven, having the key of the bottomless pit and a great chain in his hand. And he laid hold on the dragon, that old serpent, which is the Devil, and Satan, and bound him for a thousand years, and cast him into the bottomless pit, and shut him up, and set a seal upon him, that he should deceive the nations no more, till the thousand years should be fulfilled" (Rev. 20:1-3).

## C. The Mission of Angels.

In the affairs of men God uses angels to help His children and to carry out specific divine purposes. Among the works of angels are the following:

1. *Angels execute God's judgments and purposes.* An angel blocked Balaam's path: "And God's anger was kindled because he went: and the angel of the Lord stood in the way for an adversary against him" (Num. 22:22). We are told that at the end of the age "the Son of Man shall send forth his angels, and they shall gather out of his kingdom all things that offend, and them which do iniquity" (Matt. 13:41). Herod the king died as the result of a lethal stroke administered by an angel: "And immediately the angel of the Lord smote him, because he gave not God the glory: and he was eaten of worms, and gave up the ghost" (Acts 12:23).

2. *Angels guide believers.* The Ethiopian eunuch wanted salvation. Men did not understand the desire of his heart, but God did. An angel led Philip to the Ethiopian and when the gospel was proclaimed the Ethiopian was saved: "And the angel of the Lord spake unto Philip, saying, Arise, and go toward the south unto the way that goeth down from Jerusalem unto Gaza, which is desert" (Acts 8:26).

3. *Angels assist, protect and strengthen God's people.* Elijah was cared for by an angel when Jezebel sought his life: "And as he lay and slept under a juniper tree, behold, then an angel touched him, and said unto him, Arise and eat" (1 Kings 19:5). Daniel went through the experience of the lions' den and testified, "My God hath sent his angel, and hath shut the lions' mouths, that they have not hurt me" (Dan. 6:22).

4. *Angels will accompany our Lord at His second advent.* "When the Son of man shall come in his glory, and all the holy angels with him, then shall he sit upon the throne of his glory" (Matt. 25:31); "And to you who are troubled rest with us, when the Lord Jesus shall be revealed from heaven with his mighty angels, in flaming fire taking vengeance on them that know not God, and that obey not the gospel of our Lord Jesus Christ" (2 Thess. 1:7,8).

5. *Angels bear God's children to heaven.* Jesus draws apart the curtains separating this world from the next and reveals that angels participate in the act of bringing the sons of God from this world to glory: "And it came to pass, that the beggar died, and was carried by the angels into Abraham's bosom" (Luke 16:22).

## D. The Superiority of Men over Angels.

Despite the fact that angels are superior to men in holiness, might and wisdom, the children of God are actually superior to angels in that they occupy positions and enjoy privileges which angels cannot share.

1. *Angels, for example, do not preach the gospel.* This is

reserved for the sons of God. Nowhere in the Bible is it recorded that an angel gave out the good news of salvation. Even the angel who was responsible for the eunuch's salvation utilized a man in the process. When Cornelius wanted to find salvation an angel directed him to send for Peter but did not himself preach to Cornelius. Men have the rare privilege which even angels do not enjoy—that of preaching the gospel and beseeching men everywhere to be reconciled to God.

2. *Moreover, men will judge angels.* An isolated verse gives us insight into an amazing truth—a truth not fully delineated, but nevertheless a fact: "Know ye not that we shall judge angels" (1 Cor. 6:3)? What a glorious and humbling thought it is that the redeemed sons of men will have the privilege of judging angels! How careful Christians should be to judge and to put away their own transgressions in the light of this solemn and holy prerogative.

# 10

## The Devil

In the drama of redemption the devil has been the persistent foe of God from the beginning. One must know the teaching of the Bible concerning this arch-enemy of the soul if he is to understand the distressing conditions around him and if he is to meet the adversary's attacks victoriously.

Three errors which the devil uses to his own advantage must be studiously avoided. The first error is the popular belief that there is no personal devil. The second is that, if the devil does exist, he is nothing but a fantastic, long-eared, impish, mischievous Miltonic creation. The third error is that the devil's sole residence is hell. To hold any of these views is anti-Scriptural. To ignore or to minimize the devil's power is to reduce one's resistance to his wiles.

### A. The Biblical Designations of the Devil.

The enemy of God is characterized in the Bible in many ways. "He is a liar, and the father of it" (John 8:44); "the prince of this world" (John 14:30); "the god of this world" (2 Cor. 4:4); "the prince of the power of the air, the spirit that now worketh in the children of disobedience" (Eph. 2:2); "your adversary the devil" (1 Pet. 5:8); "the dragon, that old serpent, which is the Devil, and Satan" (Rev. 20:2).

## B. The Origin of the Devil.

At least two passages of Scripture suggest the original nature of Satan and depict his fall from heaven.

1. *Ezekiel 28:12-19.* These words refer to the king of Tyre, first as a historical personage, and second, as a type of the devil prior to the latter's expulsion from the presence of God. Note the phrases: "The anointed cherub" (verse 14), "full of wisdom, and perfect in beauty" (verse 12), "Thou wast perfect in thy ways from the day thou wast created" (verse 15). But "iniquity was found in thee" (verse 15); "thine heart was lifted up because of thy beauty" (verse 17); therefore "I will cast thee to the ground" (verse 17).

The devil was originally a created being of wisdom, beauty and perfection. Because of pride he was debased from his pristine position. As the prince and god of this age he is extremely busy opposing the purposes of God.

2. *Isaiah 14:12-15.* The fall of Lucifer ("light-bearer") is here described. Observe the five-fold occurrence of the words "I will" in verses 13 and 14. The cherub lifted up his heart in self-will against God and was punished for his rebellion. "How art thou fallen from heaven, O Lucifer, son of the morning! how art thou cut down to the ground, which didst weaken the nations!" Is not this fact reiterated in our Lord's statement "I beheld Satan as lightning fall from heaven (Luke 10:18)?" (Compare Rev. 12:7-9.)

## C. The Character of the Devil.

1. *Satan is the mighty enemy of the Lord.* Our wrestling is "not against flesh and blood, but against the principalities, against the powers, against the world-rulers of this darkness" (Eph. 6:12 R.V.). The devil has unseen assistants. As Beelzebub he is "chief of the devils" (Luke 11:15), whose number is "legion" (Luke 8:30). He and his cohorts constitute a powerful host.

2. *The devil is remarkably shrewd and cunning.* He is the one who "deceiveth the whole world" (Rev. 12:9). Paul appreciated his treachery. "But I fear, lest by any means, as the serpent beguiled Eve through his subtilty, so your minds should be corrupted from the simplicity that is in Christ" (2 Cor. 11:3). Satan is a master at disguise, a "fifth columnist" of the first rank, a fabricator of counterfeits. (Study 2 Cor. 11: 13-15.)

3. *He is extremely wicked.* "He that committeth sin is of the devil; for the devil sinneth from the beginning" (1 John 3:8).

## D. The Works of the Devil.

God allows the devil for a time to do many terrible things. Satan is bruising the heel of the woman's seed (Gen. 3:15). He and his allies stand in direct opposition to anything that savors of truth, beauty, or goodness.

1. The devil despises the Word of God and is determined that it will find no permanent abode in the hearts of men. When the seed is sown by the wayside "Satan cometh immediately, and taketh away the word that was sown in their hearts" (Mark 4:15).

2. He blinds men's eyes, that they might not see Christ as their Saviour. "But if our gospel be hid, it is hid to them that are lost: In whom the god of this world hath blinded the minds of them which believe not, lest the light of the glorious gospel of Christ, who is the image of God, should shine unto them" (2 Cor. 4:3,4).

3. Paul dubs him "the tempter" (1 Thess. 3:5). Nothing seems to please the devil more than to seduce the servants of Christ. As he tempted the Saviour, so he levels his attack at believers. He has his areas of temptation (see 1 Cor. 7:5) and his ingenious "devices" (2 Cor. 2:11). The children of God must not be ignorant of these.

4. Satan molests and harasses the followers of Christ in

countless ways. He induces them to become discouraged. He resists them in their Christian work. Paul, for example, wrote to the Thessalonian church: "Wherefore we would have come unto you, even I Paul, once and again; but Satan hindered us" (1 Thess. 2:18). The devil is always on the alert. He loves to stir up trouble. As a roaring lion he "walketh about, seeking whom he may devour" (1 Pet. 5:8).

5. In carrying out his wicked purposes Satan often enters into men and uses them as his tools. Judas' betrayal of Christ was the result of the devil's indwelling power. "After the sop," it is written, "Satan entered into him" (John 13:27). The exorcisms described in the Gospels were necessitated because demons had taken up their residence in human hearts. (See Matt. 12:27,28,43-45.)

6. The devil accuses men before God. The apostle John calls him "the accuser of our brethren . . . which accused them before our God day and night" (Rev. 12:10). Whenever a believer sins, it is as though Satan appeared before the court of heaven with the finger of accusation. In the face of this effrontery the Lord Jesus, our "Advocate with the Father" (1 John 2:1), pleads the merits of His wounds on our behalf; the indwelling Holy Spirit convicts the sinner; repentance, confession, and forgiveness follow (1 John 1:9) and one is restored to fellowship with the Father. (Memorize 1 John 1:9.)

7. In general, Satan's supreme effort is directed toward disrupting the purposes of God. This effort will continue with unabated force until he is overthrown. Some day, thank God, our omnipotent Saviour will "destroy him that had the power of death, that is, the devil" (Heb. 2:14).

## E. THE SPHERE OF THE DEVIL'S ACTIVITIES.

The partial record of Satan's works listed above indicates that our adversary's area of operations is by no means limited to hell. He does not hesitate to invade the hearts of men or the courts of heaven. Assisted as he is by his cohorts of evil, the devil is potentially ubiquitous. Whenever an opportunity presents itself to incite to sin or to oppose the good, he is not slow to avail himself of it. As the god and the prince of this age, he exerts a constant, iniquitous, universal pressure upon the children of men.

## F. The Destiny of the Devil.

One purpose of Christ's incarnation was the destruction of the devil. This destruction will be in fulfillment of the prophecy of Gen. 3:15, in which God warned Satan that some day the seed of the woman, Christ (study Gal. 3:16), "shall bruise thy head." No matter how foul the devil's intentions or how ruthlessly diabolical his machinations, believers may strengthen their hearts in the knowledge that some day he will be permanently eliminated from the scene. Satan is very active indeed today. But his doom is sure, and he knows it.

On Calvary the serpent received, as it were, his deathblow (see John 12:31,32). But he continues to writhe, determined to involve as many souls as possible in his ultimate catastrophe. The climax will be reached when the arch-deceiver is "cast into the lake of fire and brimstone" to be "tormented day and night for ever and ever" (Rev. 20:10).

## G. The Secret of Victory over the Devil.

1. Do not succumb to the illusion that the devil is a mythological character. Appreciate the fact that he is a person of great power and malice, that he is intent on deceiving you and causing you to fall, and that he knows the weakest link in your character. That link may be pride, or lust, or covetousness, or lovelessness. Whatever it may be, he is on the alert to break it and to bring you down to defeat.

2. Remember that victory is possible, but that in your own strength you are totally unable to conquer an adversary who is stronger than you.

3. Believe that God has made provision for your victory over the devil. He has given you the example of Christ for your encouragement and guidance. (See Matt. 4:1-11.) Jesus triumphed over the tempter in the wilderness of Judea. Through Him you too may prevail. Further, God has supplied you with all the spiritual armor you need. (See Eph. 6:11-17.) He has taught you to watch and pray for strength. (See Matt. 26:41.) He has beaten out for you on the anvil of His purposes your one offensive weapon, the Word of God. Learn to wield it effectively, even as your Saviour did. Above all, God has given you a divine Ally, the Holy Spirit, who will never let you down.

Therefore, "resist the devil, and he will flee from you" (James 4:7). Successful resistance is possible. Notice carefully the command which introduces this text: "Submit yourselves therefore to God." Only the yielded soul may expect to be victorious, not the one who tries in his own strength to overcome. He will triumph who remains steadfast in the attitude of submission, and permits and expects the Holy Spirit to work out the victory in and through him.

# PART THREE

# The Human Predicament and Its Solution

---

The conflict which rages between the unseen powers of good and evil is projected into the world of men. This projection is seen in the human predicament, and eventuates in the problem which finds its solution in the gospel of grace.

Today's world is one of disjunction, tension, internal strife, frustration and an individual awareness that Paul was right when he said: "the whole creation groaneth and travaileth in pain together until now." (Rom. 8:22; see also v. 23.) On every hand sin is rampant, selfishness abounds, and men substitute the ego for God.

In Eden's Paradise no human predicament existed. Created after the image of God, man walked in fellowship and harmony with and in obedience to his Creator. But Adam chose his own will instead of God's and plunged the entire human race into moral and spiritual degradation. This evil choice created the human predicament. Sowing the wind of disobedience, man reaped the whirlwind of spiritual suicide. Today he is totally unable to solve the mass of problems occasioned by his initial revolt. He is morally and spiritually incapable of lifting himself back to fellowship with God. Restless, searching, striving—he seeks the Paradise he lost, but always finds it elusively beyond his reach.

What man by seeking God cannot do, God by seeking man has done. The problem, insoluble by human effort, has been divinely and forever solved. This section has to do with the human predicament in all its implications and the divine solution in all its glory.

# 11

## The Story of Creation

The mind of man has grappled with the questions: Who is
man; whence did he come; and whither is he going? And what
is the universe; what is its origin; and what will be its destiny?

### A. WHO CREATED THE UNIVERSE?

Science is able to trace things back many years. Its discoveries reveal the wisdom and power of God. When it comes to
origins, science may hazard its guesses but it can furnish no
satisfactory reply. The Bible is explicit: "Through faith we
understand that the worlds were framed by the word of God,
so that things which are seen were not made of things which
do appear" (Heb. 11:3).

God brought all things into being by His own fiat, His own
word of power. "In the beginning God created the heaven
and the earth" (Gen. 1:1). He is the Creator whom we are to
remember. (See Eccl. 12: 1.) He is the sovereign Lord of His
creation. As a matter of fact, the entire Trinity was active in
creation. God "created" (Gen. 1:1); and the church recites,
"I believe in God the Father Almighty, Maker of heaven and
earth." The Spirit of God "was brooding upon the face of the
waters" (Gen. 1:2 R.V.). The Son, eternally existent in the
bosom of the Father, did His part; "All things were made by

him; and without him was not any thing made that was made" (John 1:3). The persons of the Godhead worked together: God "created all things by Jesus Christ" (Eph. 3:9). (The majesty of His creative work is described in such passages as Isaiah 40:12,22,26-28; Acts 17:24; Rev. 10:6.)

## B. When Was the Universe Created?

The first chapter of Genesis seems to teach that the universe is only a few thousand years old. Geologists insist that it is millions of years old. Hence findings of science appear to contradict the Biblical record. Many students claim to have lost their faith in God because of this seeming contradiction.

But Genesis does not teach anything that contradicts true science. Gen. 1:1 describes the original creation of material substance which occurred in the distant past. Gen. 1:2 reads: "And the earth was without form, and void." The Hebrew word "was" in this text may be translated "became." The world may have become waste and void as the result of some cataclysmic judgment of God. Atomic energy was stored in the original mass, and such a vast destruction is by no means inconceivable. Nothing is said in Genesis about the length of time which elapsed between the first creative work of God (1:1) and the commencement of His work of re-creation (1:2). An indefinite period may have intervened.

Again, in referring to the various "days" of creation, which many have interpreted as "creative periods," the indefinite article "a" is suggested in the Hebrew in each case: e.g. "a first day," "a second day." (See Genesis 1:5,8,13, etc.) No intimation is given of the length of time which may have occurred between these creative periods.

The Genesis record leaves ample time for all truly scientific eras. One need not be alarmed nor deceived when he hears pseudo-scientists attack the Bible on the ground that it denies the findings of geology. Genesis and true geology are in full accord.

## C. How Were the Universe and Life Created?

Man and his environment did not come into being by chance, by any "fortuitous concatenation of atoms." The first Cause of all things is God. But what method did He employ in executing His creative purposes? Was there a gradual emergence of life, a steady biological development from species to species, an advance upward from lower to higher forms of life?

The Bible teaches that God created *ex nihilo*, "out of nothing." The universe was brought into being, not out of "things which do appear" (Heb. 11:3), but solely as the result of God's creative will and activity.

In examining the claims of biological evolutionists, Christians do not dispute the fact that growth and development to a limited degree within species do occur. What they will not admit is that there can be natural transition from:

1. Nothing to the inorganic (matter); or from
2. The inorganic to the organic (life); or from
3. The organic to man.

At these crucial points the Christian faith takes issue with certain forms of the evolutionary hypothesis. Scientific grounds exist for this disagreement. Neither biology, geology, nor paleontology has proved the theory of natural transition. But the Christian takes issue also on religious grounds. The theory of evolution, whether it be of the gradual or the emergent type, leads to two conclusions which are contrary to the teaching of the Scriptures. The first conclusion is that man is evolving in the direction of perfection and needs no regeneration. The second conclusion is that Jesus, far from being perfect God and Man, was simply a stepping-stone in the human advance, splendid for His own day but long since out-distanced, out-moded, and thus no "Saviour" at all. Here the Christian disagrees sharply.

The Genesis story of creation is fascinating because precisely at the three controversial junction points the Hebrew word "bara," "create," occurs. *Between* these points God "caused things to appear," utilizing, for example, the natural processes of evaporation, condensation, or re-arrangement. But *at* each crisis He stepped in with a creative act. He brought into being that which had not previously existed:

1. *Creation of something from nothing.* "In the beginning God created the heaven and the earth" (Gen. 1:1).

2. *Creation of life.* When the earth was ready for living creatures, "God created great whales, and every living creature that moveth . . ." (Gen. 1:21).

3. *Creation of human life.* When God was ready to produce man, He did not cause him gradually to evolve from some lower form of life. His creation was something new. "So God created man in his own image, in the image of God created he him; male and female created he them" (Gen. 1:27).

## D. WHY DID GOD CREATE MAN AND THE UNIVERSE?

The Scriptures reveal at least three reasons why God brought His creation into being.

1. *For His own pleasure.* He saw fit to create. He delighted in the act. Something in His nature elicited the desire to create and brought it to fruition. In John's apocalyptic vision he beheld the four and twenty elders fall down before the throne of God, saying, "Thou art worthy, O Lord, to receive glory and honour and power: for thou hast created all things, and for thy pleasure they are and were created" (Rev. 4:11).

2. *For His own glory.* The original creation sang its Creator's praise. (See Job 38:7; study the entire chapter.) The universe was an adornment to God's being, a revelation of His perfections. And concerning man the Almighty declares: "I have created him for my glory, I have formed him; yea, I have made him" (Isaiah 43:7).

3. *For fellowship with man.* God placed the first man and woman amid surroundings conducive to perfect communion. God is a Spirit. In order that man might have true fellowship

with Him, it was essential that man be a spirit too. Accordingly, God created man "in his own image." This means, among other things, that from the first, man was a free moral agent. He had freedom of choice. Otherwise he would have been an automaton, incapable of fellowship with deity. He was able to choose between good and evil. This ability to choose eventuated in the fall of man and the curse of God upon creation. Fellowship between God and man was broken. This precipitated the Bible drama of redemption. Fellowship is restored through the "new creation."

## E. WHAT IS "THE NEW CREATION"?

1. For man, "the new creation" means the restoration of that which he lost in Eden. Man is by nature and choice a fallen creature. He cannot please God. He no longer reflects God's glory. He stands in desperate need of a new creation. God alone could rectify the situation.

He who miraculously fashioned man of dust is still omnipotent. To bring men back into fellowship with Himself He sent His dearly beloved Son to be their Saviour. Those who put their faith in Christ His Son experience His mighty power. God creates them anew. "Therefore if any man be in Christ, he is a new creature: old things are passed away; behold, all things are become new" (2 Cor. 5:17). "For we are his workmanship, created in Christ Jesus unto good works . . ." (Eph. 2:10).

2. For the universe, the "new creation" means a new heaven and a new earth. Since the fall of man, creation has been under the curse of God. (See Gen. 3:17-19.) "For we know that the whole creation groaneth and travaileth in pain together until now" (Rom. 8:22). It has been subjected to vanity. (See Rom. 8:20.) Yet some day "the creation itself also shall be delivered from the bondage of corruption . . ." (Rom. 8:21 R.V.). Earth's miseries will not endure forever. Nature, "red in tooth and claw," will not always be fettered with the divine curse.

Some day God will once more act in creative power. He will do something *new*. "For, behold, I create new heavens and a new earth: and the former shall not be remembered, nor come into mind" (Isaiah 65:17). "The earth also and the works that are therein shall be burned up." "Nevertheless we, according to his promise, look for new heavens and a new earth, wherein dwelleth righteousness" (2 Peter 3:10,13). And this creation will endure forever.

# 12

# The Problem of Sin

---

SIN—a three letter word that spells the difference between happiness and misery, freedom and bondage, Heaven and Hell. Men may deny its existence, minimize its influence, or try to evade its consequences. But it remains a cold, stubborn, hideous reality, separating the soul from God Almighty.

The fact of sin is proved in three ways. First, history bears eloquent testimony to its existence and influence. As long as man has been on earth wars, tumults, disease, and death have been rampant. All creation bears unmistakably the marks of evil. The pages of history are blackened by its effects. Secondly, the conscience of man bears witness to his own sinful nature. No man, however good he may appear to be, can rightfully claim to be free from envy, pride, lust, greed, malice, or hate. An honest man who calls things by their right names will not hesitate to admit his own sinful nature and acts. Thirdly, the Scriptures bear repeated testimony to sin's reality. From beginning to end the Word of God realistically faces the problem and solves it. Because the Bible traces the rise of sin it is possible for it to trace the drama of redemption in which men are delivered from the curse of sin.

## A. The Nature of Sin.

1. Sin is failure to conform to the law of God either negatively or positively, by omission or commission. It can be understood only in the light of the law of God—an imperial, sovereign, external standard of right and wrong given to humanity by God himself. The law is in itself an expression of the nature and the attributes of God. Thus when men fail to live up to the law of God, or when they transgress it, they are committing an act of hostility toward the Almighty. Sin is reprehensible, deserving the punishment it entails.

The Biblical concept of sin is indicated in the words used to portray it. The Hebrew term means "to deviate from the way"; the Greek terms imply a "missing of the mark," a "going aside from." The very existence of sin reveals that there is a norm or a standard against which the acts of men may be measured. Paul puts it bluntly: "Because the law worketh wrath: for where no law is, there is no transgression" (Rom. 4:15). And John defines sin as lawlessness (see 1 John 3:4), i.e. a breach of the law.

2. Sin appears in two forms:

a. *Overt acts.* For example, one tells a lie, steals what does not belong to him, cheats for personal gain, kills in hatred, or exhibits pride. These are individual acts which separate man from God as well as from his neighbor.

b. *Heart sinfulness.* Behind and beneath all man's overt acts lies a nature in man which is basically sinful. The heart is the source of his evil deeds. The moral depravity of his heart and his corrupt disposition are the spring out of which overt acts arise. Sin itself springs from the innate tendency to sin. Sin "reigns" (Rom. 6:12) in the unregenerate heart. The flesh (one's tendency to sin) "lusteth against the Spirit" (Gal. 5:17). A "law (rules) in my members," Paul writes (Rom. 7: 23), "warring against the law of my mind."

## B. THE SIN OF ADAM.

The questions arise: "Why do we so often sin? Why are we so constantly aware of our sinful disposition? Did something happen to plunge the entire race of men into their sinful estate?" The answer to these questions is found in the record of Adam's sin and in the Biblical revelation of the effect of that sin upon humanity.

1. Adam, created in the image of God, was a free moral agent. Granted the liberty of choice in a context which involved a specific commandment of God, he sinned. His transgression consisted in unbelief—he refused to believe God's word and listened to the devil's lie; and in disobedience—he substituted his own will for the will of God.

2. The consequences of Adam's sin are guilt before God; moral corruption, together with a lack of original righteousness and a total inability to restore his first estate; and separation from God—bodily, spiritual, and eternal death (apart from the life-giving work of Christ).

3. Adam was the federal head of the race. The principle of representation obtained in his Fall. (See Rom. 5:12-21; 1 Cor. 15:22.) You and I were in Adam when he sinned and fell.

4. Adam's sin and its dread results have therefore been imputed to his descendants, put to their account, charged legally to them. (See Rom. 5:12,15,18,19.) All men today have mortal bodies, corrupted souls, inborn tendencies to sin, and the sentence of everlasting death upon them apart from Christ.

5. While men are born in sin and are guilty before God from birth, it is also true that all men reaching the age of responsibility sin overtly themselves. Even though men had not had guilt imputed to them through Adam, they would still become guilty as the result of overt acts of sin and would fall under the condemnation of God.

## C. THE UNIVERSALITY OF SIN.

Adam represented the entire race of men without distinction as to color, condition, circumstance, clime, or culture. Sin is the great leveler. All men everywhere, and in every age, are confronted with the ghastly spectre of iniquity. The heart of the untutored savage, like the heart of the cosmopolite, condemns him. Of sin in relation to men the Bible declares that:

1. No one may escape sin's guilt. "All we like sheep have gone astray; we have turned everyone to his own way" (Isa. 53:6a). The whole argument of Romans 1:18-3:23 is to the effect that all men, Gentiles and Jews alike, are steeped in sin. Paul's conclusion is definitive: "For there is no difference: For all have sinned, and come short of the glory of God" (Rom. 3:22,23).

2. Sin is no respecter of age. Every child is born in sin. David exclaims: "Behold, I was shapen in iniquity; and in sin did my mother conceive me" (Psalm 51:5). The adult knows in the innermost recesses of his heart that sin has been his constant obstacle. The aged look back across the years and marvel that God has spared them in spite of their hardness of heart.

3. Sin embraces EACH because it embraces ALL. This means that it includes YOU and ME. Shall we refuse to acknowledge its presence; shall we explain it away, or condone it? Or shall we confess it, forsake it, and as David did, plead the mercy of the Lord for pardon and cleansing? (See Psalm 51:1-3.)

## D. THE EXTENT OF SIN IN THE HUMAN HEART.

The Scriptures describe the universality of sin. But they do more than that. They speak to men about the totality of sin and the extent of its control over human beings. Invading every heart, it corrupts and mars every life. Men are in rebellion against their Creator.

This depravity must be defined lest one misunderstand it. It does not mean that a man cannot be relatively moral; nor that he cannot be a "good" citizen or father. It does not mean that all men are equally sinful in overt action or inward thought. Great are the numbers of respectable sinners! Human depravity means that man looks upon God as irrelevant. He will not subject himself to his Creator nor pay Him the homage which is His due. By choice he is alienated from God, no matter how good he may seem externally; he has broken his fellowship with his Creator. He has made his choice. "The carnal mind is enmity against God: for it is not subject to the law of God, neither indeed can be" (Rom. 8:7).

### E. The Consequences of Sin.

1. *Degradation.* All the faculties of man's soul and body are morally perverted. His nature is corrupted, his desires polluted, his spiritual sight blinded, his will directed away from God. (See Rom. 1:29-32.)

2. *Condemnation.* A breach of the law brings guilt. Every sin ever committed merits condemnation and demands that a penalty be meted out. This is the irrevocable law of God. (See Rom. 3:19.)

3. *Separation from God, which is death.* The Lord is altogether Holy. He cannot have communion with unholy creatures. For "can two walk together, except they be agreed?" (Amos 3:3). To be separated from God spells death. By nature man is "dead in trespasses and sins" (Eph. 2:1). "Sin hath reigned unto death" (Rom. 5:21). "For the wages of sin is death" (Rom. 6:23). "The soul that sinneth, it shall die" (Ezek. 18:4). (And even the physical death which men experience, the separation of spirit from body, is the result of sin.)

### F. The Solution to the Problem of Sin.

1. Unless something is done to rescue man from the consequences of his sin, his plight will be woeful in the extreme. His separation from God will be eternal; his degradation will be complete; he will spend eternity in hell, "where their worm

dieth not, and the fire is not quenched" (Mark 9:44). But man is unable to remedy the situation. He is incapable of redeeming himself from sin, of extricating himself from his predicament, of saving himself from destruction. Unless God intervenes he is doomed forever.

2. If man is to be saved from sin, the only way in which he can be saved is through Jesus Christ. Thank God for the Son of God who is able to save "to the uttermost" (Heb. 7:25) the foulest wretch and to make him a child of God.

# 13

# The Law of God

Salvation is all of grace. The law cannot save. Yet the Scriptures teach that the law has a place in the perfect economy of God.

## A. THE NATURE OF THE LAW.

1. The law of God is the revealed expression of the will of God. That will is manifested in the human conscience (see Rom. 2:14-16), but chiefly, and more clearly, in the Scriptures.

2. The moral law is comprehended in the Ten Commandments and recorded in Exodus 20 and Deuteronomy 5:6-21. In the New Testament, particularly in Christ's Sermon on the Mount (Matt. 5-7), this law is divinely explained, interpreted, and applied to the internal motives, as well as to the external deeds, of men. The Ten Commandments may be sub-divided into two groups: the first four, which relate to man and his God; and the last six, which relate to man and his neighbor. They are based upon the nature of God and the constitution of man as a fallen creature of God.

3. The judicial and ceremonial laws of the Old Testament are in a different category from that of the moral law. They have to do with a specific people, the Jews, in a specific period

in their history; whereas the moral law concerns the permanent relations of man with regard, for example, to property,
marriage and filial obedience.

4. The law of God is not to be lightly esteemed. The apostle
Paul declares that "the law is holy, and the commandment
holy, and just, and good" (Rom. 7:12). Faith in Christ does
not "make void the law" (Rom. 3:31). It "establishes" the
law.

## B. The Inability of the Law to Save.

1. Salvation is not by the law. The law of God sets before
men a divine standard of conduct. This standard, especially
as emphasized and particularized by Jesus, is precise and demanding. Its "thou shalt nots" are totalitarian. Its "thou shalts"
are all-embracing. Yet the law in itself cannot save a sinner.
Historically, "the law made nothing perfect" (Heb. 7:19).

This truth is repeatedly emphasized in the Word of God.
"By the deeds of the law," Paul writes, "there shall no flesh be
justified in his sight" (Rom. 3:20). The epistle to the Galatians inveighs against the contrary view. The law was "ordained by angels in the hands of a mediator," but it could not
give a sinner life or righteousness. (Study Gal. 3:19,20.)

2. If law could save we would still be lost because of our
failure to keep it. The difficulty is summarized by Paul: "For
we know that the law is spiritual: but I am carnal, sold under
sin" (Rom. 7:14). The apostle "delights in the law of God
after the inward man." But he sees a different "law in my
members, warring against the law of my mind, and bringing
me into captivity to the law of sin which is in my members"
(Rom. 7:22,23).

3. The law of God *enlightens* man concerning the nature
and will of the Almighty; but it *does not empower* him for
life's struggles. It *shows* him the way but it cannot *save* him.
It *reveals* but it cannot *redeem*. It commands the sinner to fly
but it provides no wings. It is a charter of conduct. But it soon

becomes a counsel of despair. For the flesh is too perverse; the carnal nature of man is too corrupt. It takes far more than the naked dictates of the law to redeem him.

4. Much modern preaching is based on a gospel of works. It tragically urges men to action without showing them the source of divine motivation. People are told to "do this" and to "do that." They are put under the law, which is powerless to save. The glories of the gospel of grace are the only antidote to man's moral frustration.

5. Christ is the answer. "What the law could not do, in that it was weak through the flesh . . ." (Rom. 8:3), God accomplished in the sending of His blessed Son.

## C. THE FUNCTION OF THE LAW.

1. *Law reflects the nature of God.* An exhibition of the will of God, it indicates what sort of being the divine "Willer" is. It is a mirror of God's person. It shows Him to be totally unique, alone worthy of the love and worship of His people. He is "a jealous God." He brooks no rivalry in the realm of adoration. He is absolutely just, and at the same time merciful. He is holiness, purity, honesty. The tables of the law proclaim to the world some of the basic attributes of the Lord.

2. *Law governs men's relationships.* It reinforces the testimony of man's conscience concerning moral values among men. To honor parents is always right; to dishonor them is wrong. To esteem human life highly is virtuous; to fail to do so is vicious. Purity is praiseworthy; impurity is sin. To respect human property is good; to disregard the laws of "mine and thine" is evil. To speak truthfully is commendable; to lie is criminal. God's law is the foundation stone of the moral economy.

3. *Law reveals sin.* "By the law is the knowledge of sin" (Rom. 3:20). Conscience may condemn a wicked deed. But the law specifies the precise area, or category, of the immoral act and thus highlights its heinousness. Paul writes: "I had not known sin, but by the law: for I had not known lust except

the law had said, Thou shalt not covet" (Rom. 7:7). The law thus becomes "the strength of sin" (1 Cor. 15:56). It enters the scene "that the offence might abound" (Rom. 5:20). It is thus "our school-master," pointing out ruthlessly our defects, threatening us with judgment, bringing us to the border of despair, and leading us "unto Christ, that we might be justified by faith." (See Gal. 3:24.)

## D. JESUS CHRIST AND THE LAW OF GOD.

1. The Lord Jesus, "when the fulness of the time was come," was "made of a woman, made under the law, To redeem them that were under the law, that we might receive the adoption of sons" (Gal. 4:4,5). Born into a Hebrew household, He fulfilled the demands of the ceremonial law. As a babe He was taken to the temple for circumcision. When full-grown He presented Himself for baptism and, when John expostulated, He said: "Suffer it to be so now: for thus it becometh us to fulfil all righteousness" (Matt. 3:15). No hostile Pharisee could accuse him of legal irregularities in these spheres.

2. Our Saviour, however, was never in bondage to Pharisaical interpretations of the Law. He asserted: "The Son of man is Lord even of the sabbath day" (Matt. 12:8). He was not in the least perturbed when his enemies accused Him of non-compliance with the law in connection with fasting or eating with unwashed hands. (Study Matt. 15:1-6.)

3. Jesus did not come into the world to abrogate the moral law of God. He said explicitly: "Think not that I am come to destroy the law, or the prophets: I am not come to destroy, but to fulfil" (Matt. 5:17). He explained the law, interpreted it and intensified its application. But He also appealed to it: "Have ye not read in the law?" (Matt. 12:5); or again, "Is it not written in your law?" (John 10:34).

4. But above all our Saviour met all the requirements of the moral law. His foes could convict Him of no wrong. He alone

of all men who ever lived was totally free of moral taint. He lived the life which fallen man is totally unable to live. He was "actively obedient" to His Father's will. As the result of His moral and spiritual perfection He is the "lamb without blemish and without spot" (1 Pet. 1:19), the only acceptable sacrifice for the sin of the world.

## E. THE NEW LAW IMPLANTED IN THE SOUL.

So far as salvation is concerned, the believer is "dead to the law" (Gal. 2:19). When he accepted Christ as his Saviour, he was redeemed from "the curse of the law" (Gal. 3:13). He now has divine life within, and this means an entirely new principle of conduct. He operates henceforth under "the law of Christ" (Gal. 6:2), a law implanted in his soul.

1. This new law is variously characterized. It is "the law of the Spirit of life in Christ Jesus," which has "made me free from the law of sin and death" (Rom. 8:2). It is "the perfect law of liberty" (James 1:25). It is the law written upon the fleshy tables of the heart.

2. We are warned as believers not to put ourselves under the bondage of the Mosaic law. "Christ is become of no effect unto you, whosoever of you are justified by the law; ye are fallen from grace" (Gal. 5:4). The danger in seeking to become right with God through obedience to the law is that one breach of the law brings the whole house of legalism crashing down in judgment upon one's head. "For whosoever shall keep the whole law, and yet offend in one point, he is guilty of all" (James 2:10). The classic affirmation of the Christian's true position is: "Ye are not under the law, but under grace" (Rom. 6:14).

3. The believer is indeed under grace. Yet the moral law has not been abrogated. On the contrary, it still reveals the attributes of God and His will for man; and it still brings sinners to their knees at the foot of Calvary. The convicting power of Sinai's thunders has not ceased.

4. Obedience to the new law of liberty does not mean that the child of God will purposely flaunt the moral law. This possibility is discussed in the sixth chapter of Romans. Sin, revealed as sinful by the law, has brought death. But the believer has now been raised with Christ to a new level of life, a level at which he *desires* to do the will of God, not because he is under bondage to the law, but because, as a child of God, he loves his heavenly Father's will. He obeys, not primarily because he knows that infringement bring penalties, but because *he wants to do what he knows he ought to do.* This is the bondage of true freedom.

5. This new principle of conduct, or pattern of behavior, is the result of the work of the Holy Spirit in the life. Hence it is termed "the law of the Spirit of life" (Rom. 8:2). The Spirit, at regeneration, changes a man's motivations, ambitions and objectives, and enables him to attain to righteousness. The result of Christ's incarnation and atonement is "that the righteousness of the law might be fulfilled in us, who walk not after the flesh, but after the Spirit." (Study Rom. 8:3,4.)

F. The Fulfillment of the Law.

Our Lord declared that all the law and the prophets hang on two commandments: "Thou shalt love the Lord thy God with all thy heart, and with all thy soul, and with all thy mind"; and "Thou shalt love thy neighbor as thyself" (Matt. 22:37-40). Paul echoed this sentiment. So far as one's fellowmen are concerned, "all the law is fulfilled in one word, even in this; Thou shalt love thy neighbour as thyself" (Gal. 5:14).

The apostle analyzes this idea in Romans 13:8-10. "He that loveth another hath fulfilled the law." The items listed in the last five of the Ten Commandments, he writes, are "briefly comprehended in this saying, namely, Thou shalt love thy neighbour as thyself." "Love worketh no ill to his neighbour." The one who truly loves another will prefer his neighbor's good, and will therefore do nothing to harm his neighbor's wife, or body, or property or reputation. Love is indeed "the fulfilling of the law."

But remember that true love, the love that issues in virtue and genuine self-forgetful concern, is the fruit of the Holy Spirit. He sheds abroad the love of Christ within the heart. He enables one really to love others. The believer's constant prayer, therefore, as he strives to fulfill the law of Christian love, should be that the Holy Spirit might fill him and produce His heavenly fruit within his breast.

# 14

# The Judgments of God

---

Two attributes of God stand out in sharp contrast in the Scriptures: love and justice. "God is love" (1 John 4:8). He is the God of mercy and grace, of pity and tenderness. But He is also "the Judge of all the earth" (Gen. 18:25). "Justice and judgment are the habitation of thy throne" (Psalm 89:14). He shows mercy to them that love Him and keep His commandments; but He visits "the iniquity of the fathers upon the children unto the third and fourth generation of them that hate" Him. (See Ex. 20:5,6.) One must bear in mind these two attributes of God. Otherwise his conception is distorted. God is absolute love. He is also absolute justice.

## A. What Does God Judge?

The Bible answers the question bluntly and with solemnity —God judges sin. Whenever and wherever He detects sin, He visits it sooner or later with judgment. He never permanently passes over it. He never compromises with it. He never makes light of it nor minimizes its heinousness. Every sin of thought, word and deed that was ever committed, or will ever be committed, merits and will receive divine judgment. For every transgression of God's holy law and every failure to measure up to His moral requirements, judgment will be meted out.

"It is appointed unto men once to die, and after this the judgment" (Heb. 9:27). No evasions nor excuses will be tolerated; no exonerations nor exceptions will be made. The moral nature of God demands judgment for sin.

But some may say, "I am not interested in this harsh and cruel doctrine. Sin and judgment may have been stark realities in the imagination of my forefathers. But I live in an age of enlightenment. Give me the Sermon on the Mount. Let me live in the light of its moral principles. Why should I bother about any dull and heavy theory of divine retribution?"

He who speaks in this vein should understand that the righteous judgments of the Lord are mentioned, not in isolated sections of the Bible, but in a great many of its pivotal passages. Moreover, in the Sermon on the Mount to which appeal is made our gentle, loving Lord, the teacher of Nazareth, speaks repeatedly and in no uncertain voice concerning judgment. "And if thy right hand offend thee, cut it off, and cast it from thee: for it is profitable for thee that one of thy members should perish, and not that thy whole body should be cast into hell." (Matt. 5:30; see also Matt. 5:21-29; 7:13.) The stark, unpleasant fact of judgment is part of the warp and woof of revelation—it is inescapable.

## B. How Does God Judge?

1. *God judges according to the truth.* "But we are sure that the judgment of God is according to truth . . ." (Rom. 2:2; see Rev. 19:2.) God is omniscient. He is never deceived. He perceives the thoughts of man's heart; He hears the words of man's lips; He observes the deeds of man's hands. His balances are accurate. He judges precisely every infraction of his revealed will. He countenances no deception nor concealment of the facts. Moses' warning to Israel reflects eternal truth: "But if ye will not do so, behold, ye have sinned against the Lord: and be sure your sin will find you out" (Num. 32:23).

2. *God makes no exceptions.* He will "render to every man

according to his deeds" (Rom. 2:6). No man may escape the judicial verdict. This is a universal principle, eternally valid.

3. *Unlike man, God is not swayed in judgment by personal considerations.* "For there is no respect of persons with God" (Rom. 2:11). One may not say: "You know me, Lord; you knew my godly mother and Bible believing father. Surely you will take cognizance of my heritage, or background, or the extenuating circumstances in my case." No, Adam, God's first master-piece of human creation, sinned and was judged: he was expelled from Eden. The antediluvian world sinned and was judged: a flood inundated the earth. The nations sinned at Babel and were judged: they were scattered and their speech was confounded. Israel grieved God and was carried into captivity. The Jews sinned in rejecting their Messiah: His blood is still on their heads. No personal appeal for clemency will prevent the execution of divine judgment.

4. *God judges the inner motives as well as the external conduct of sinners.* "God shall judge the secrets of men by Jesus Christ according to my gospel" (Rom. 2:16). The Lord knows what takes place in the dark as well as in the light. His vision pierces into the chambers of man's imagery. Man beholds the outward trappings of his fellow-man; at best he guesses the thoughts and motives within. But God searches man's reins; He knows and tries the heart. Our most sacred, unexpressed, hidden secrets are an open book to Him. "For there is nothing covered, that shall not be revealed; neither hid, that shall not be known. Therefore whatsoever ye have spoken in darkness shall be heard in the light; and that which ye have spoken in the ear in closets shall be proclaimed upon the housetops" (Luke 12:2,3).

## C. What Judgments Are There?

Many people seem to believe that some day everyone, regardless of his age, color, belief or unbelief—all men universally—will stand before the same bar of justice; verdicts will be declared, judgments decreed, rewards granted and punishments carried out. We read about "the day of wrath and revelation of the righteous judgment of God" (Rom. 2:5). In his Athens address Paul said: "He hath appointed a day, in the which he will judge the world in righteousness" (Acts 17:31). Peter speaks of "the day of judgment and perdition of ungodly men" (2 Pet. 3:7). Jude writes about "the judgment of the great day" (Jude 6).

As the result of such passages earnest Christians sometimes have the vague idea that some day a general judgment is coming for everybody. The term "general judgment," or "universal judgment," implies, not that all sinners will be judged at the same time or under the same circumstances, but simply that *all* sinners are judged. Similarly with the expression "day of judgment." A mountain climber often refers to a distant chain of mountains as a "peak," although he knows that valleys lie between its loftiest summits. So the "day of judgment" has its separate "hours" which must be differentiated. Three judgments concern men individually. These are:

1. *The Judgment of Believers' Sins.* This took place once for all at Calvary. On the cross the eternal Son of God bore the sins of the people of God, carried their guilt, and was judged in their room and stead. The judgment was death. Christ fully paid this penalty. Separated from His Father who is "of purer eyes than to behold evil" and who cannot "look on iniquity" (Hab. 1:13), He cried out in His dying agony, "My God, my God, why hast thou forsaken me" (Matt. 27:46)?

The sins of believers, past, present and future, were borne by Jesus in His death. The judgment was unique, definitive and final. None other but Christ was able to bear it. Nor need the judgment be repeated. It solved the Christian's sin problem forever; it made possible his forgiveness and everlasting life; it set his spirit free; it assured his entrance into Heaven. Our Saviour said: "He that heareth my word, and believeth on him that sent me, hath everlasting life, and shall not come into condemnation; but is passed from death unto life" (John 5:24). This verse is conclusive: no judgment unto death awaits true believers. Paul emphasizes the same truth: "There is therefore now no condemnation to them which are in Christ Jesus . . ." (Rom. 8:1).

2. *The Judgment for Rewards.* The sins of believers have been cast forever behind God's back. Christ paid the penalty and they are remembered no more. Yet in writing to Christians Paul declares: "For we must all appear before the judgment seat of Christ; that every one may receive the things done in his body, according to that he hath done, whether it be good or bad" (2 Cor. 5:10). And again: "For we shall all stand before the judgment seat of Christ" (Rom. 14:10).

Does this mean that some day the sin question will once more be raised in connection with believers? Was the Saviour's work not finished after all? The Scriptures leave no doubt here. The Christian's sins have been judged and permanently dealt with. But a reward awaits him if he has been faithful to his trust. All who trust Christ as Saviour will spend eternity in Heaven. But some Christians have accomplished far more for God than others have: they have prayed, served, worshipped, witnessed, sacrificed. God is not unmindful of their consecration.

Christ is the only foundation (1 Cor. 3:11). Upon Him some have built superstructures of gold, silver and precious stones. The enduring edifice "which he hath built thereupon" will make it possible for him to "receive a reward" (1 Cor. 3:14.). (Study 1 Cor. 3:10-15.) Contrariwise, other Christians have erected upon the foundation of Christ superstructures of "wood, hay, stubble" (1 Cor 3:12). Since fire will test "every man's work of what sort it is," their works will be consumed. Instead of receiving a reward they will suffer loss. They themselves "shall be saved; yet so as by fire" (1 Cor. 3:15). No Christian should presume for a moment that simply because the judgment for sin at Calvary guarantees him an entrance into Heaven, he can live as he pleases or do as he chooses. Let every man who professes Christ be warned that his works will be judged either to his profit or to his loss. (See Luke 12:47,48.)

The judgment seat of Christ is for believers only. It will be set up at our Saviour's coming. John records Jesus' promises: "And, behold, I come quickly; and my reward is with me, to give every man according as his work shall be" (Rev. 22:12). Christ may return at any moment. How careful we should be to look to ourselves, "that we lose not those things which we have wrought, but that we receive a full reward." (2 John 8; see also Matt. 5:12; 16:27; Luke 14:14.)

3. *The Judgment of Unbelievers*. This is the judgment of the Great White Throne. All unbelievers of all ages will stand before this bar of justice. Before the new heavens and the new earth are ushered in, the graves will surrender the bodies and Hades will give up the spirits, of those who died in unbelief. Tremblingly they will stand before the august tribunal of God.

The books will be opened. (Study Rev. 20:11-15.) The miserable record of men's sins in the areas of faith and conduct will be read. No appeal will be heard, no excuses tolerated, no mitigating circumstances presented. The verdict will be announced, the sentence passed. The "second death," the lake of fire, awaits all who persistently turn their backs upon God and spurn the gracious offer of His redeeming love.

A solemn, tragic thought. May we be faithful in our ministry of warning, urging, beseeching men to be reconciled to Christ. Knowing "the terror of the Lord" (2 Cor. 5:11), may we seek to persuade men. And in order that our witness might prove effective, may we be careful to keep our own conduct under strict surveillance. "For if we would judge ourselves" (1 Cor. 11:31) we shall escape the severity of divine chastisement in this present life and be in a position to testify effectively for the Lord we love.

# 15

## The Grace of God

---

Salvation from beginning to end is all of grace. Effective service from start to finish is all of grace. Our hope of an abundant entrance into glory is all of grace. The doctrine of grace, therefore, is exceedingly precious to the believer's heart. No wonder Paul wrote of the "glory" and the "riches" of God's grace (see Eph. 1:6,7). Every instructed Christian will share the apostle's exultation and seek to fathom the depths of the grace of God.

### A. The Nature of Grace.

1. *Grace is an attribute of God*. "I am gracious," saith the Lord (Exodus 22:27). I "will be gracious to whom I will be gracious, and will shew mercy on whom I will shew mercy" (Exodus 33:19). In the days of Nehemiah the Levites uttered a true confession: "Thou art a God ready to pardon, gracious and merciful, slow to anger, and of great kindness . . ." (Neh. 9:17). The prophet Jonah relied upon the fact that God is gracious. (See Jonah 4:2.) The apostle Peter called our heavenly Father "the God of all grace" (1 Pet. 5:10). The justice. righteousness and holiness of the Almighty have their counterpart in His grace, mercy, tender compassion and self-originating love.

2. *Grace is the "unmerited favor" which God shows towards sinful man.* Justice demands the sinner's death. Grace
intervenes to place the penalty upon Christ and thus to meet
the demands of justice and set the sinner free. Man did not
deserve pardon or forgiveness or restoration to fellowship with
God. The "graciousness" of God caused Him to extend *Charis*,
"grace," towards an ill-deserving race, thus bringing it back
from sin, degradation and death to His own heart of love.

3. *Grace is a new realm.* In extending grace to sinful man
God transferred him from the sphere of death to a new realm
of salvation and eternal life. This new realm is occasionally
referred to as the area of grace. (See Rom. 5:2; Gal. 1:6.)

4. *"Grace"* is the word sometimes used to signify the gifts
which God bestows upon His people. An illustration of this
usage is found in a contribution which Paul received for the
needy brethren in Judea. The apostle was charged with the
responsibility of administering the offering which he calls "this
grace," i.e. a free gift (2 Cor. 8:19).

5. *A "grace"* is a Christian virtue. (See 2 Cor. 8:7.) The
matter may be summarized thus: The grace of God causes
Him to act in grace toward man, thus bringing him into a
*position* of grace, endowing him with *gifts* of grace, and in-
stilling within him the *qualities* of grace.

## B. THE CHANNEL OF GRACE.

Since the time of Adam God has been dealing graciously
with His people. But His grace was revealed supremely in the
incarnation, ministry and saving work of the Lord Jesus. Christ
instituted, as it were, a new economy, a new era of grace. "For
the law was given by Moses, but grace and truth came by Jesus
Christ" (John 1:17). The Old Testament looked forward to
this manifestation of grace in Christ. The ancient seers "prophesied of the grace that should come unto you" (1 Peter 1:10).
In Christ their predictions were fulfilled. "The grace of God,

and the gift by grace, which is by one man, Jesus Christ, hath abounded unto many" (Rom. 5:15).

The character, teaching and passion of Christ were a revelation of the grace of God. When "the Word was made flesh," He was "full of grace and truth" (John 1:14). The grace of God was upon Him even in His childhood. (See Luke 2:40.) The Psalmist prophesied concerning the coming Messiah: "grace is poured into thy lips" (Psalm 45:2); and when Christ preached, "all bare him witness, and wondered at the gracious words which proceeded out of his mouth" (Luke 4:22). But, of course, His saving death was the most amazing exhibition of divine grace. "But we see Jesus . . . that he by the grace of God should taste death for every man" (Heb. 2:9).

As the consequence of Christ's redemptive work grace now abounds (see Rom. 5:17,20). It reigns "through righteousness unto eternal life by Jesus Christ our Lord" (Rom. 5:21). In the plan of God a new administration has begun. The good news to be proclaimed is "the gospel of the grace of God" (Acts 20:24). The Lord gives testimony "unto the word of his grace" (Acts 14:3; see Acts 20:32). The Holy Spirit is revealed as "the Spirit of grace" (Heb. 10:29).

The contrast between the operations of the law and of grace is sharply drawn. The law challenges the sinner, reveals his iniquity, condemns him to death; grace steps in and provides a righteousness to which the sinner could not otherwise attain. (See John 1:17; Rom. 6:14.) The fact is repeatedly emphasized that the works of the law cannot save; that the grace of God in Christ alone avails for man's redemption. (Study carefully Romans 11:6; Eph. 2:8,9; Titus 3:5.) Jesus Christ is the only channel of divine grace.

## C. The Recipients of Grace.

1. The leaders of the early church experienced the grace of God. "And with great power gave the apostles witness of the

resurrection of the Lord Jesus: and great grace was upon them all" (Acts 4:33). Paul often asserted that he was a recipient of grace and that his effectiveness was solely due to the unmerited favor of God. He spoke and wrote "through the grace given unto me" (Rom. 12:3; see Rom. 15:15); he was "a wise masterbuilder," "according to the grace of God which is given unto me" (1 Cor. 3:10); his abundant labors were the result of grace (see 1 Cor. 15:10; Gal. 2:9); his ministry to the Gentiles was of grace. (See Eph. 3:8.) Indeed, as regards his entire life Paul could say: "But by the grace of God I am what I am" (1 Cor. 15:10). He never ceased to thank his God that to one who had been "a blasphemer, and a persecutor, and injurious," "the grace of our Lord was exceeding abundant with faith and love which is in Christ Jesus" (1 Tim. 1:13,14).

2. The members of the apostolic churches also received manifestations of the grace of the Lord. Paul wrote to the Corinthian church: "And God is able to make all grace abound toward you" (2 Cor. 9:8). In at least ten of his epistles he saluted his addressees with the prayer that grace would abide upon them. "Ye are all partakers with me of grace," he wrote to the Philippians (1:7 R.V.). Why were the Macedonian churches generous? Paul answers the question: the grace of God was bestowed upon them (2 Cor. 8:1,2). Indeed, he told his beloved Ephesian friends, "unto every one of us is given grace according to the measure of the gift of Christ" (Eph. 4:7).

3. All believers of every age and dispensation are recipients of grace. Grace was revealed on Calvary where Christ was a sacrifice for sin. But the shadow of the cross reached backwards to Adam and forwards to the last soul to be saved before Christ's return. All men who have ever been saved, or who ever will be saved, are acceptable to God by virtue of Christ's atoning work. The principle of grace, therefore, extends to all men of every age who are "accepted in the Beloved" (Eph.

1:6 R.V.). Administered in different ways throughout the dispensations, grace is a glorious, changeless principle nonetheless.

## D. THE OUTWORKINGS OF GRACE.

The grace of God is intimately associated with the salvation and service of the believer. The list of God's gracious dealings with men is impressive. Included are the following truths:

1. *The believer's election is of grace.* This is a great mystery, but it is a clear teaching of the Bible. "Even so at this present time also there is a remnant according to the election of grace." (Rom. 11:5; see especially verse 6.)

2. *Salvation is an act of grace.* "The grace of God . . . bringeth salvation . . ." (Titus 2:11). At the Jerusalem Council Peter asserted: "But we believe that through the grace of the Lord Jesus Christ we shall be saved, even as they" (Acts 15:11). Paul has a classic passage on the subject; "For by grace are ye saved through faith . . ." (Eph. 2:8).

3. *Justification is the result of God's merciful favor toward sinners.* We are "justified freely by his grace." (Rom. 3:24; cf. Titus 3:7.) That is, our acceptance with God rests, not upon our character or deeds, but upon God's sovereign, loving, outgoing will.

4. *Every step in man's salvation is the result of unmerited favor.* In Christ "we have redemption through his blood, the forgiveness of sins, according to the riches of his grace; Wherein he hath abounded toward us in all wisdom and prudence" (Eph. 1:7,8).

5. *Faith itself is a gift of God's grace.* The Christians in Achaia "had believed through grace" (Acts 18:27). "Faith-salvation" as over against man's attempted "works-salvation" is of grace. (Study carefully Eph. 2:8,9.)

6. *One's call to Christian life and testimony is all of grace.* Paul is insistent here. God, he declares, "separated me from my mother's womb, and called me by his grace, To reveal his Son

in me, that I might preach him among the heathen" (Gal. 1:15,16).

7. *Spiritual gifts are of grace.* Members of the Christian body have "gifts differing according to the grace that is given to us" (Rom. 12:6). Prophecy, the ministry, the ability to teach or to exhort, the spirit of sacrifice, the capacity to rule or to show mercy—all these are God's gracious gifts to His people.

8. *The believer's daily strength in hours of need, his comfort and hope—all are of grace.* When Paul was troubled by a thorn in the flesh, he heard the words of the Lord: "My grace is sufficient for thee: for my strength is made perfect in weakness" (2 Cor. 12:9). Glorious is the truth: "our Lord Jesus Christ himself, and God, even our Father . . . hath given us everlasting consolation and good hope through grace" (2 Thess. 2:16).

## E. THE CHRISTIAN'S DUTY IN THE LIGHT OF GRACE.

Surrounded as he is by the loving favor of God and sustained constantly by divine grace, the believer is to exhibit in his daily conduct the glories of that grace. He is never to forget for a moment that he is saved, kept and empowered by divine grace.

1. He is to echo the melody which God has put in his heart, "singing with grace" to the Lord (Col. 3:16). The world should be able to recognize a Christian by his happy attitude and demeanor.

2. He is to keep his conversation gracious, even though at times he may be called upon to be emphatic. "Let your speech be alway with grace, seasoned with salt . . ." (Col. 4:6).

3. He is to regard his gifts and his service as promotional agencies of divine grace. Believers are to be "good stewards of the manifold grace of God" (1 Pet 4:10).

4. In return for God's grace vouchsafed to him, the Christian must abound in the grace of generosity toward others (2

Cor. 8:6,7). The "grace of our Lord Jesus Christ" caused Him to become poor for our sakes (2 Cor. 8:9); surely we should respond generously to the needs of our brethren.

5. Rather than remain static in the virtues of the Christian life, the child of God is to "grow in grace, and in the knowledge of our Lord and Saviour Jesus Christ" (2 Pet. 3:18).

6. Above all, the Christian is to be eternally grateful to God for every revelation of divine grace. (See 2 Cor. 4:15.) He owes to God his life, his breath, his health, his preservation, his happiness, his eternal destiny of blessedness. The constant theme of his song should be:

> "O, to grace how great a debtor
> Daily I'm constrained to be;
> Let Thy goodness, like a fetter,
> Bind my wandering heart to Thee."

# 16

## The Forgiveness of Sins

Forgiveness is God's answer to the sin question. It solves the problem of guilt; it heals the sinner's wounded heart; it restores him to fellowship with the Father; it melts his very being with love for the Saviour; it opens before him a new vista of hope and joy. Forgiveness is the pre-requisite to all the blessings and responsibilities of the Christian life.

Our sins, though many and grievous, may be forgiven. This is the glorious dawn that follows the night of despair, the calm after the storm, the peace after the conflict. "I am merciful, saith the Lord, and I will not keep anger for ever" (Jer. 3:12). Our Lord said concerning the sinful woman who kissed His feet and anointed them with ointment: "Her sins, which are many, are forgiven" (Luke 7:47).

### A. THE ALTERNATIVES TO FORGIVENESS.

1. *Ignoring sin.* God might conceivably have dealt with sin by ignoring it. But this would have been a denial of His Word and a disregarding of His holy law. The Almighty will not permanently wink at man's iniquity. He will never enter into collusion with the sinner. Sin merits, and will receive death. From this there is no escape. A God who could ignore sin would not be the God of the Bible.

113

2. *Compromising with sin.* God might presumably solve the sin problem by bargaining with the sinner. He might accept in payment for sin man's offering of character or of deeds well done. Thus God might balance good against evil and on such a basis waive the penalty for sin. But this could never be. To enter into such an agreement with creatures who have rebelled against Him would be to deny His own character of holiness and righteousness.

The penalty for sin must be paid. The sanctity of the law must be upheld. The righteousness of God must be vindicated. In only one way may all these *desiderata* be achieved,—by the forgiveness of sins.

## B. THE NECESSITY OF FORGIVENESS.

1. *Manward.* Unless man's sin problem is dealt with, he remains in his sin, an enemy of God, doomed to an eternity of despair. This fact should be a challenge to every Christian preacher, teacher and personal worker. It is vain to present to one's listeners the virtues and blessings of Christian life and service until first they become right with God. The prisoner in death-row cares little about the sunset. He wants desperately to know how to be free. And if men in general would be free, forgiveness of sin is essential to their freedom.

2. *Godward.* Just as forgiveness is essential to man's freedom from the penalty of sin, so it is essential from God's vantage point. Our heavenly Father's heart of love reaches out to embrace the erring and the lost. But He cannot restore the sinner without forgiveness, for any restoration which is inconsistent with His nature and attributes of holiness and justice is impossible. Therefore if God would have men enter heaven, forgiveness of their sins is necessary.

## C. THE NATURE OF FORGIVENESS.

To forgive means to "give over," or to "give up" resentment for evil or demands for requital. The forgiveness of sins is the very heart of the gospel. Christ's mission was to accomplish the forgiveness of man's sin. The apostles, standing before a hostile council, declared concerning Christ: "Him hath God exalted with his right hand to be a Prince and a Saviour, for to give repentance to Israel, and forgiveness of sins" (Acts 5:31). "Through this man," Paul proclaimed in Antioch of Pisidia, "is preached unto you the forgiveness of sins" (Acts 13:38).

Forgiveness is a divine prerogative. It is an act which the Almighty performs. God "is faithful and just to forgive us our sins" (1 John 1:9). When the Son of God was on earth He healed a palsied wretch and openly associated the miracle with His divine power to forgive sins. Said He: "But that ye may know that the Son of man hath power on earth to forgive sins, (then saith he to the sick of the palsy,) Arise, take up thy bed, and go into thine house" (Matt. 9:6).

## D. The Extent of God's Forgiveness.

When God forgives a sinner the pardon is complete: the sin problem is settled. This fact is illustrated in various ways in the Scriptures.

1. With the exception of the one unpardonable sin even the most heinous iniquity may be forgiven. No greater crime was ever perpetrated than the crucifixion of the Son of God. Yet Jesus prayed for His murderers: "Father, forgive them; for they know not what they do" (Luke 23:34).

2. The number of times our heavenly Father will forgive is limitless. Peter asked the Lord whether he should forgive his brother seven times. "Jesus saith unto him, I say not unto thee, Until seven times: but, Until seventy times seven" (Matt. 18:22). In this reply our Saviour reflected the loving heart of God.

3. The distance God removes our sins from us is infinite. "As far as the east is from the west, so far hath he removed our transgressions from us" (Psalm 103:12). This is a pictur-

esque way of stating that when God forgives sin He banishes it completely from His presence.

4. Our sins are forgiven *wholly*. God does not single out certain particularly flagrant acts and concentrate His forgiveness upon these. He forgives "all trespasses" (Col. 2:13), black, white and gray. The slate is wiped thoroughly clean.

5. Our sins are forgotten. When they are forgiven they are erased, not only from God's book of records, but also from His book of remembrance. "I have blotted out, as a thick cloud, thy transgressions, and, as a cloud, thy sins" (Isa. 44:22) A cloud keeps the sun from shining here below; it discourages the bird from singing; it restrains the rosebud from unfolding its petals. Our sins are clouds: they make life dark and gloomy. But God blots them out! No cloud, obliterated from the heavens, ever forms again in precisely the same fashion. So our sins, once forgiven, are *forgotten*. The heart of the new covenant is in the promise: "I will forgive their iniquity, and I will remember their sin no more" (Jer. 31:34).

### E. THE RATIONALE OF FORGIVENESS.

1. *God's mercy permits it.* The ultimate basis of the sinner's forgiveness rests in the nature of God. Our Father in heaven is holy and righteous. He will see to it that His will is carried out and that justice prevails. But He is also *merciful*. This attribute caused Him to seek out a way to vindicate all the claims of His character and purposes and at the same time to provide for the sinner a way of forgiveness. "To the Lord our God belong mercies and forgivenesses" (Dan. 9:9).

2. *Christ's sacrifice is the ground of it.* The way of forgiveness is through sacrifice. "Without shedding of blood is no remission" (Heb. 9:22). An oblation for sin had to be offered. In the infinite wisdom of God the One chosen for the sacrifice was the eternal Son of God. Paul stated emphatically: "Be it known unto you therefore, men and brethren, that through this man is preached unto you the forgiveness of sins" (Acts

13:38). The sinner's forgiveness is not grounded upon Jesus' character or teaching or example, but upon His shed blood. "We have redemption through his blood, the forgiveness of sins" (Eph. 1:7); for "the blood of Jesus Christ his Son cleanseth us from all sin" (1 John 1:7).

## F. THE CONDITIONS OF FORGIVENESS.

God has already done His part. The Lamb has been slain. The sacrifice has been accepted. But what is man's part in the transaction? Two groups of people need forgiveness:

1. *Those who require forgiveness for salvation.* They are not saved, and if they are to be welcomed into the family of God they must accept Christ's atonement for sin. By faith, the key that unlocks the door to salvation, they must acknowledge their sinful condition and embrace the Son of God as their Saviour. This is the highway to forgiveness and salvation.

2. *Those who require forgiveness for fellowship.* They have been redeemed and their sins have been forgiven but they stand in need of cleansing. Eternally saved, they have picked up, along the dusty road of life, defilements which may mar their fellowship with God. Daily sins need daily repentance, confession and forgiveness. Unconfessed sins are a blight upon Christian effectiveness. Believer, be faithful here. Repent, confess, plead the blood of Christ, maintain the avenue of your communion with God clear and unobstructed. "If we confess our sins, he is faithful and just to forgive us our sins" (1 John 1:9). And "if my people, which are called by my name, shall humble themselves, and pray, and seek my face, and turn from their wicked ways; then will I hear from heaven, and will forgive their sin . . ." (2 Chron. 7:14).

## G. THE UNPARDONABLE SIN.

1. *The reality of the unpardonable sin.* The forgiving grace of God is infinite, but there is "a sin unto death" (1 John 5:16). There is a "blasphemy" which "shall not be forgiven

unto men" (Matt. 12:31). The unforgiven soul "is guilty of
an eternal sin" (Mark 3:29 R.V.). The contrast drawn is ter-
rifying: either one must have his sins forgiven or be everlastingly in disrepute with, and thus separated from, God.

2. *The nature of the unpardonable sin.*

a. NEGATIVELY. It is not some shifting mood, some changing
disposition, some iniquity into which the sinner temporarily
and perhaps inadvertently falls. If one is in agony of spirit
lest he has committed the unpardonable sin, his very sense of
despair is an indication that he has not committed it. When a
man sins unpardonably he does so with no compunction.

b. POSITIVELY. Our Lord speaks to men about the sin that
cannot be forgiven. The context in which He describes this
sin (Matt. 12:31,32; Mark 3:29,30) makes it clear that speaking or blaspheming "against the Holy Ghost" means a definitive, persistent, deliberate, continuous, malicious rejection of
the testimony of the Holy Spirit concerning Christ. This implies, in brief, an utter repudiation, permanently persisted in,
of the gospel of Christ. On what possible ground could such
a heinous denial of the witness of God be forgiven?

## H. THE FORGIVEN SINNER'S DUTY.

Let him rejoice and praise God as long as he draws breath
for the inexhaustible resources of divine forgiveness. Let him
render to the Almighty the gratitude due His holy and com-
passionate name. But let him also translate his thanksgiving for
vertical forgiveness into horizontal forgiveness. "God for
Christ's sake hath forgiven you." Then "be ye kind one to
another, tenderhearted, forgiving one another" (Eph. 4:32).
God has forgiven me. Then let me forgive my brother. God
is pleased when His children show a forgiving spirit. But He
will repay in judgment those who refuse to forgive. As it is
written: "So likewise shall my heavenly Father do also unto
you, if ye from your hearts forgive not every one his brother
their trespasses" (Matt. 18:35).

# PART FOUR

# The Person and Ministry
# of Jesus Christ

---

The human predicament finds its solution in Christ. One might conceivably be a good Confucianist, Buddhist, or Taoist without sustaining any personal relationship whatsoever to the founders of these religions. What Confucius said is determinative, not who he was or what he did. Precisely at this point our Christian faith is totally different from any "religion." The Person, ministry, passion, and continued existence of Jesus Christ are central to Christianity. While we believe and accept all that Jesus taught, the essence of our faith is our personal relationship to Him as the Son of God and Saviour of our souls. Whoever heard of a man being "in Confucius" or "in Buddha" or "in Lao-tze"? But whoever heard of a Christian who was not "in Christ"?

From all eternity Jesus Christ existed in the bosom of the Father, uniquely and generically different from any man who ever lived. To rescue man from everlasting death He laid aside His garments of transcendent light, entered this world of woe as the immortal Son of God, "took upon him the form of a servant, and was made in the likeness of men: And being found in fashion as a man, he humbled himself, and became obedient unto death, even the death of the cross. Wherefore God also hath highly exalted him . . ." (Phil. 2:7-9).

The following section relates exclusively to Jesus, Who He is, what He is like, what He taught, and what He did for man. Along with the rest of this volume it is dedicated to His praise.

# 17

## Jesus Christ and Prophecy

The Old Testament foreshadows the New. Many events and circumstances were foretold long before they occurred. Literally hundreds of specific items might be adduced in proof of this assertion. Prophetic fulfillment is solid evidence that the Bible is the Word of God.

A large number of Old Testament predictions were fulfilled in Jesus' birth, life, and death. These fulfilled prophecies demonstrate to the inquiring mind the validity of God's holy Word. But they do something equally important. They foretell so many things concerning the Messiah to come that the One whose life fulfilled their prophecies could have been none other than the Son of God. The Spirit of God paved the way for honest men to recognize the Redeemer when He should come. They would be able to identify Him inerrantly, for no other life would be marked by the fulfillment of so many prophecies.

No one born in any other place in the world than Bethlehem could be the Messiah. This eliminated most people. No other than a Jew could be the Messiah; He had to be of the tribe of Judah. This eliminated the eleven other tribes. When all the elements of prophecy are taken into account, it can easily be seen that one man and one man alone in the history

121

of the world could have been the Messiah. For those who think that He may yet come and that His birth is still future, the Old Testament even foretells the time of His advent. No one before or after the time indicated by God could be the Messiah. Every man except Jesus of Nazareth must be ruled out.

## A. PROPHECIES CONCERNING CHRIST'S ORIGIN.

1. *He would come out of Israel.* "I shall see him, but not now: I shall behold him, but not nigh: there shall come a Star out of Jacob, and a Sceptre shall rise out of Israel, and shall smite the corners of Moab. . . . Out of Jacob shall come he that shall have dominion, and shall destroy him that remaineth of the city" (Numbers 24:17,19). And, of course, Jesus actually descended from Abraham, Isaac, and Jacob. (See Matt. 1:1-17.)

2. *He would be of the family of David and of the tribe of Judah.* "The sceptre shall not depart from Judah, nor a lawgiver from between his feet, until Shiloh come; and unto him shall the gathering of the people be" (Gen. 49:10). "And there shall come forth a rod out of the stem of Jesse, and a Branch shall grow out of his roots" (Isa. 11:1). Luke tells us that these predictions were fulfilled in Jesus. "And, behold thou shalt conceive in thy womb, and bring forth a son, and shalt call his name JESUS. He shall be great, and shall be called the Son of the Highest: and the Lord God shall give unto him the throne of his father David: and he shall reign over the house of Jacob for ever; and of his kingdom there shall be no end" (Luke 1:31-33).

3. *He would be born in Bethlehem.* "But thou, Bethlehem Ephratah, though thou be little among the thousands of Judah, yet out of thee shall he come forth unto me that is to be ruler in Israel; whose goings forth have been from of old, from everlasting" (Micah 5:2). "And Joseph also went up from Galilee.

out of the city of Nazareth, unto Judaea, unto the city of David, which is called Bethlehem; (because he was of the house and lineage of David:) . . . And so it was, that, while they were there, the days were accomplished that she should be delivered. And she brought forth her firstborn son . . ." (Luke 2:4,6,7). Today no one denies that Jesus was born in Bethlehem.

4. *He would be born of a virgin.* "Therefore the Lord himself shall give you a sign; Behold a virgin shall conceive, and bear a son, and shall call his name Immanuel" (Isa. 7:14). "Now the birth of Jesus Christ was on this wise: When as his mother Mary was espoused to Joseph, before they came together, she was found with child of the Holy Ghost . . . Now all this was done, that it might be fulfilled which was spoken of the Lord by the prophet . . ." (Matt. 1:18,22).

5. *The time of His coming is specified.* "Seventy weeks are determined upon thy people and upon thy holy city, to finish the transgression, and to make an end of sins, and to make reconciliation for iniquity, and to bring in everlasting righteousness, and to seal up the vision and prophecy, and to anoint the most Holy. Know therefore and understand, that from the going forth of the commandment to restore and to build Jerusalem unto the Messiah the Prince shall be seven weeks, and threescore and two weeks: the street shall be built again, and the wall, even in troublous times. And after threescore and two weeks shall Messiah be cut off, but not for himself . . ." (Daniel 9:24-26). The Messiah was to be cut off 490 years following the rebuilding of Jerusalem. This was the time when Jesus died on the cross for our sins. No one before or after that year could have been the Messiah.

6. *His coming would be announced by a forerunner, who proved to be John the Baptist.* "The voice of him that crieth in the wilderness, Prepare ye the way of the Lord, make straight in the desert a highway for our God" (Isa. 40:3). "For

this is he that was spoken of by the prophet Esaias, saying, The voice of one crying in the wilderness, Prepare ye the way of the Lord, make his paths straight" (Matt. 3:3).

7. *The Messiah would be God.* "For unto us a child is born, unto us a son is given: and the government shall be upon his shoulder: and his name shall be called Wonderful, Counsellor, The mighty God, The everlasting Father, The Prince of Peace" (Isa. 9:6). "And the Word" who, according to John 1:1 is God, "was made flesh, and dwelt among us, (and we beheld his glory, the glory as of the only begotten of the Father,) full of grace and truth" (John 1:14).

## B. PROPHECIES CONCERNING CHRIST'S CAREER.

1. *He would spend part of his childhood in Egypt.* "When Israel was a child, then I loved him, and called my son out of Egypt" (Hosea 11:1). "And was there until the death of Herod: that it might be fulfilled which was spoken of the Lord by the prophet, saying, Out of Egypt have I called my son" (Matt. 2:15).

2. *He would suffer and make atonement for sins.* "Surely he hath borne our griefs, and carried our sorrows: yet we did esteem him stricken, smitten of God, and afflicted. But he was wounded for our transgressions, he was bruised for our iniquities: the chastisement of our peace was upon him; and with his stripes we are healed. All we like sheep have gone astray; we have turned every one to his own way; and the Lord hath laid on him the iniquity of us all" (Isa. 53:4-6). And this is just what happened. As it is written: "For he hath made him to be sin for us, who knew no sin; that we might be made the righteousness of God in him" (2 Cor. 5:21).

3. *He would ride into Jerusalem on a colt.* "Rejoice greatly, O daughter of Zion; shout, O daughter of Jerusalem: behold, thy King cometh unto thee: he is just, and having salvation; lowly, and riding upon an ass, and upon a colt the foal of an ass" (Zech. 9:9). And Jesus said, "Go into the village over

against you, and straightway ye shall find an ass tied, and a colt with her; loose them, and bring them unto me . . . All this was done, that it might be fulfilled which was spoken by the prophet, saying, Tell ye the daughter of Sion, Behold, thy King cometh unto thee, meek, and sitting upon an ass, and a colt the foal of an ass" (Matt. 21:2,4,5).

4. *He would be given gall and vinegar in His agony on the cross.* "They gave me also gall for my meat; and in my thirst they gave me vinegar to drink" (Psalm 69:21). The fulfillment: "They gave him vinegar to drink mingled with gall: and when he had tasted thereof, he would not drink" (Matt. 27:34).

5. *He would not have a bone broken, contrary to the customary procedure in connection with crucifixion.* The Psalmist foretold, "He keepeth all his bones: not one of them is broken" (Psalm 34:20). The passover lamb, a perfect type of Christ our Paschal lamb, was not to have a bone broken: "In one house it shall be eaten; thou shalt not carry forth ought of the flesh abroad out of the house; neither shall ye break a bone thereof" (Exod. 12:46). What actually happened when the Lamb of God was slain? "When they came to Jesus, and saw that he was dead already, they brake not his legs. . . . For these things were done, that the scripture should be fulfilled, A bone of him shall not be broken" (John 19:33,36).

6. *Men would cast lots for his garments.* The prediction is in the words: "They part my garments among them, and cast lots upon my vesture" (Psalm 22:18). The fulfillment is precise: "And they crucified him, and parted his garments, casting lots: that it might be fulfilled which was spoken by the prophet, They parted my garments among them, and upon my vesture did they cast lots" (Matt. 27:35).

7. *He would utter certain words in His dying agony:* "My God, my God, why hast thou forsaken me" (Psalm 22:1)? The prediction was fulfilled: "And at the ninth hour Jesus cried with a loud voice, saying, Eloi, Eloi, lama sabachthani?

which is, being interpreted, My God, my God, why hast thou forsaken me" (Mark 15:34)?

8. *He would rise again from the dead.* The Psalmist exultingly declared: "Therefore my heart is glad, and my glory rejoiceth: my flesh also shall rest in hope. For thou wilt not leave my soul in hell; neither wilt thou suffer thine Holy One to see corruption" (Psalm 16:9,10). Simon Peter, filled with the Spirit and speaking as He gave him utterance, asserted that these words were fulfilled in Christ's resurrection. (See Acts 2:31.)

## C. The Implications of These Fulfilled Prophecies.

Either the fulfilled predictions give added proof to the assertions of the Bible and of Jesus or else they are part of a record which is a gigantic fraud designed to deceive men. The child of God, prompted by the Holy Spirit, accepts with joy their testimony and bows with Thomas before the feet of Jesus saying, "My Lord and my God." The faith of our fathers, credible and reasonable as it is, and undergirded by the witness of fulfilled prophecy, stands everlastingly firm.

# 18

# The Earthly Career of Christ

---

## A. His Life.

The career of our Lord is reported chiefly in the four Gospels, although additional isolated items in connection with His life are described in other books of the New Testament. The Gospels do not always follow a chronological pattern in telling the story. Moreover, some aspects of His life are recounted by all four writers, and some by only one. However, scholars have worked out the chronology of Jesus' life; and to a fair degree the various Gospels have been coordinated in such a way as to give us a clear outline of His ministry.

1. *The Life of Christ Prior to His Public Ministry.* This period covers the first thirty years of our Saviour's career. It was a time of preparation in which the Son of God was getting ready for the work for which the Father had sent Him. Few written accounts describe this period. The Gospels concern themselves chiefly with Christ's later life and ministry. Yet the thirty years are extremely important. They may be divided into four parts:

a. *Jesus' pre-incarnate state, birth and infancy.* John speaks of the *logos* as existing before all things and as eternal God. Matthew and Luke give the genealogical background of Jesus' ancestors. They also speak concerning His mother, John the

127

Baptist, the annunciations, the birth, circumcision, flight into Egypt and visit of the wise men. Mark and John say nothing about the historical circumstances surrounding the birth of our Lord.

b. *The childhood of Jesus.* Few facts are recorded. Matthew and Luke provide the only information. Jesus lives in Nazareth and grows as a normal child.

c. *Jesus at the age of twelve.* The curtains are lifted and the boy Jesus is revealed in the temple as conscious of His relationship to God and of the need for being about His Father's business. He is obedient to His parents, inquiring of mind, and developing normally.

d. *The young manhood of Jesus.* He is now approaching thirty. His public ministry is soon to begin. He is baptized, tempted, and He begins to make converts. He attends the wedding feast at Cana with His disciples.

2. *The Public Ministry of Christ.* This covers a period of approximately three years, from his thirtieth to thirty-third year, to the closing days of His life, His death and resurrection.

a. *The opening phases* (about six months in length) take place in Judaea, Samaria and Galilee. John describes more of this period than the other Gospels do. It includes the discourse with Nicodemus on the new birth, the conversation with the woman at the well in Samaria, and our Lord's work in Galilee. Matthew, Mark and Luke say little about this stage.

b. *The earlier Galilean ministry.* This covers a period of approximately 6 to 8 months. Capernaum and Galilee are the areas in which the events transpire. The first three Gospels deal with a large part of this phase of Jesus' life, particularly with His miracles.

c. *The later Galilean ministry.* For about a year the Lord moves in and about Galilee. Crowds still attend Him; miracles are being performed. The Sermon on the Mount is preached, the disciples are sent forth, John the Baptist is decapitated.

**d.** *The specialized ministry*. For about six months the Pharisees and Scribes are seeking Jesus' life. Our Lord's enemies are trailing Him, seeking for grounds on which to persecute Him. The scene is no longer laid in Galilee: Jesus travels to Capernaum, Phoenicia, Magadan, Bethsaida, Cesarea-Philippi and finally re-enters Galilee, but only to leave it again forever. He tells His disciples about His coming death and resurrection. His transfiguration takes place. Matthew and Mark devote more space to this period than Luke does; and John says almost nothing about it.

**e.** *The completion of His public ministry*. This covers a period of six months. It embraces our Lord's later Judaean and Perean ministries. It comes to a close just prior to His triumphal entry into Jerusalem as king. Luke and John describe this period in some detail. It concludes Christ's three years of public ministry.

**3.** *The Conclusion of Christ's Life*. This final period lasts approximately two months. It begins with His entry into Jerusalem and ends with His ascension into heaven. Large portions of all the Gospels recount the events of this period, which may be divided as follows:

**a.** *Conflicts and warnings*. The early days of Jesus' last week before His crucifixion witness His conflict with the Jews and involve His relationship to the Roman government. He laments over Jerusalem, answers questions, performs miracles, but more than anything else devotes time to teaching His disciples concerning the future. Here we have the Olivet Discourse which is of sufficient importance to be recorded in all the first three Gospels. This is followed by a number of parables most of which are narrated only by Matthew.

**b.** *Final teaching and passion*. Most of this material is given by all four Gospel writers, although John alone (Chapters 14-17) presents events and teaching not mentioned by the other writers. These chapters in John cover Jesus' remarks about heaven, His teaching concerning His relationship to the Father, the beautiful portrayal of the vine and the branches, the description of the Holy Spirit, and the high priestly prayer of our Lord. All the evangelists give us the details of our Saviour's arrest, trial, sufferings and crucifixion. The section ends with Jesus' death and burial, with the disciples frightened, baffled and defeated. The tomb is sealed, the soldiers are on guard, and the end appears near.

c. *The resurrection and ascension.* Jesus now rises from the dead. He appears again and again to give evidence of His resurrection. No one is able to dispute His claim or produce His dead body. On five occasions during the period between the resurrection and ascension He proclaims the Great Commission. He repeatedly reveals His concern for the spread of His gospel into all the world. The period concludes, not only with the ascension, but with the promise that Jesus will come again. "This same Jesus . . . shall so come in like manner . . ." (Acts 1:11).

## B. His Miracles.

An entire chapter of this book is devoted to miracles. Suffice it to say at this point that nothing stands out more clearly in the Gospels than Jesus' acts of supernatural power. These divine credentials attest to the fact that He is God. They embrace every conceivable relationship of life. He healed the sick and raised the dead to demonstrate that he had power over sickness, disease and death. He stilled the waves and turned water into wine to show His power over nature. He cast out demons and rebuked them to show His control over the spirit world as well as over the destiny of created spirits. None other but God incarnate could have performed such stupendous acts

## C. His Teaching.

Throughout this volume repeated reference is made to our Lord's teachings. But His teachings are often elevated to a supreme place so that His death and resurrection are decentralized. This is most unfortunate. As much as the Christian believes in and seeks to practice the teachings of Jesus, he must not limit the Christian faith to these ethical and moral principles of conduct. He must not overlook or minimize Christ's atonement for sin and bodily resurrection.

The Sermon on the Mount, embracing as it does the Golden Rule and other basic truths of life and conduct, includes many of our Lord's primary ethical requirements. They may be subdivided thus:

1. *The relation of man to God.* Jesus requires us to love God, trust and place our faith in Him, and pray faithfully to Him. God must be man's central framework of reference. All of life finds its meaning in the relationship which a man has to God.

2. *The relation of man to man.* Christ states that men should do to others what they would have others do to them. They are to love one another, to forgive one another, and in general to exercise restraint and charity towards all men.

3. *The relation of man to himself.* The basic requirements for any man in relation to himself are humility and servanthood. Unworthy and undeserving, man must know himself to be utterly without merit. He must depend upon the grace of God and realize that, having done all, he is still an unprofitable servant. He must understand that he is by nature depraved. By humble submission and the assumption of the position of a bond-slave and by saving faith in Christ, he may realize his highest selfhood and reassume the position he lost in Adam.

In all His instruction the Lord Jesus set such a high and holy moral standard that His teachings should become to the sinner a counsel of despair, driving him for forgiveness and salvation to the cross of Calvary.

# 19

## The Deity of Jesus Christ

For twenty centuries the doctrine of Christ's Person has been a stumbling block. Even in the first century after Christ His deity was disputed. Undoubtedly this is the reason the apostle John proclaimed so insistently that the historical Jesus is the Son of God. (See John 20:31.) In his epistles John fulminates against those who reject the deity of Christ.

Before the Christian faith was four centuries old, Arius engaged in a long controversy with Athanasius. The center of the conflict was the problem of the pre-incarnate Christ. Arius denied the true deity of our Lord. He held that there was a time before creation when Christ did not exist. Athanasius, on the other hand, maintained that there never was a time when Christ did not exist; that He was in the bosom of the Father throughout all the ages of eternity; that He was co-eternal with the Father. The Church Council of Nicea in 325 A.D. proclaimed that Jesus had neither beginning nor end of days. At Chalcedon in 451 A.D. the doctrine was affirmed: He is very God of very God, one with God, co-eternal and consubstantial with the Father.

To this hour men are divided on the question, "Who is this Jesus?" If He is God manifest in the flesh, the effect of such a self-disclosure of God to men is profound; if He is not God, the implications are devastating and the total fabric of the Christian faith is jeopardized.

## A. THE ETERNAL PRE-EXISTENCE OF CHRIST.

Any honest man must conclude, after a search of the Word of God, that the written record asserts that Jesus existed eternally. Thus the prophet Isaiah when speaking of the coming Redeemer describes Him in terms of an eternally pre-existent Being. "For unto us a child is born, unto us a son is given: and the government shall be upon his shoulder: and his name shall be called Wonderful, Counsellor, the Mighty God, The *everlasting* Father, the Prince of Peace" (Isa. 9:6). John, too, says that "in the beginning was the Word, and the Word was with God, and the Word was God. The same was in the beginning with God" (John 1:1,2). The apostle also quotes Christ as saying: "I am Alpha and Omega, the beginning and the end, the first and the last" (Rev. 22:13). The author of Hebrews affirms the same truth: "Jesus Christ the same yesterday, and today, and forever" (Heb. 13:8). Paul assumes the Saviour's pre-existence: "And without controversy great is the mystery of godliness: God was manifest in the flesh . . ." (1 Tim. 3:16; see John 8:14,16,58; John 16:28; John 17:5.)

## B. JESUS' TESTIMONY CONCERNING HIS DEITY.

He declared, "I and my Father are one." (John 10:30); "He that hath seen me hath seen the Father . . ." (John 14:9); "All things are delivered unto me of my Father: and no man knoweth the Son, but the Father; neither knoweth any man the Father, save the Son, and he to whomsoever the Son will reveal him" (Matt. 11:27).

When our Lord appeared before the high priest the question was asked Him: "Art thou the Christ, the Son of the Blessed?" Boldly Jesus replied, "I am." (See Mark 14:61,62.) The high priest and the scribes and elders knew that the Christ who was to come would be God. Therefore they replied to Jesus' assertion by accusing Him of blasphemy: "Ye have heard the blasphemy: what think ye? And they all condemned him to be guilty of death" (Mark 14:64).

Either Jesus' testimony concerning His deity is true or else He was a liar and a deceiver. Men must either fall at His feet and worship Him or declare Him to be the arch-deceiver of men. Yet how strange it is that those who militantly object to believing that He is God still try to believe that He was the best man and finest spiritual teacher ever known. Far from it! If He is not God, He is an evil seducer and an enemy of the souls of men.

Check these additional portions of the Word of God and be confirmed in the truth that, according to His own testimony, Jesus is indeed God (Matt. 28:18-20; John 5:23; 10:32,33; 19:7). (For further testimony to His deity see Matt. 1:21,22, 23; 2:11; 8:29; 16:16; Luke 1:32,33; John 20:28; Acts 3:6; 9:20; Rom. 9:5; 2 Cor. 5:19; Phil. 2:5-11; Col. 1:15; Heb. 1:1-3; Rev. 21:23.)

## C. The Divine Attributes Ascribed to Jesus.

1. *Holiness.* "For such a high priest became us, who is holy, harmless, undefiled, separate from sinners, and made higher than the heavens" (Heb. 7:26). "Which of you convinceth me of sin?" (John 8:46). "For he hath made him to be sin for us, who knew no sin; that we might be made the righteousness of God in him." (2 Cor. 5:21; see also Luke 4:34; 1 Pet. 2:22.)

2. *Eternity.* "For unto us a child is born . . . and his name shall be called Wonderful, Counsellor, The Mighty God, The everlasting Father, the Prince of Peace" (Isa. 9:6). Micah tells us that whereas the child would be born in Bethlehem, yet the Messiah is from everlasting. "But thou, Bethlehem Ephratah, though thou be little among the thousands of Judah, yet out of thee shall he come forth unto me that is to be ruler in Israel; whose goings forth have been from of old, from everlasting." (Micah 5:2; see also John 1:1; 8:58; 17:5,24; Col. 1:17.)

3. *Omnipotence*. The Great Commission was given by Jesus Himself, and its basis is His stupendous claim, "All power is given unto me . . ." (Matt. 28:18). The writer to the Hebrews announces the superiority of Christ and tells us that He, "being the brightness of his glory, and the express image of his person, and upholding all things by the word of his power, when he had by himself purged our sins, sat down on the right hand of the Majesty on high" (Heb. 1:3). In the Revelation of John we read, "I am Alpha and Omega, the beginning and the ending, saith the Lord, which is, and which was, and which is to come, the Almighty" (1:8).

(See also Matt. 11:27; John 5:28,29; Eph. 1:22. The formula is apparent: Jesus is omnipotent, but only God can be omnipotent; therefore Jesus is God.)

4. *Omniscience*. "Now are we sure," say the disciples, "that thou knowest all things, and needest not that any man should ask thee: by this we believe thou camest forth from God" (John 16:30). Matthew records that Jesus knew what men thought before they expressed themselves: "And Jesus knowing their thoughts said, Wherefore think ye evil in your hearts?" (Matt. 9:4). His omniscience is revealed in the record: "Jesus knew from the beginning who they were that believed not, and who should betray him." (John 6:64; see also John 2:24; 18:4; and Col. 2:3.)

5. *Immutability*. "They shall perish; but thou remainest; and they all shall wax old as doth a garment; And as a vesture shalt thou fold them up, and they shall be changed: but thou art the same, and thy years shall not fail" (Heb. 1:11,12). "Jesus Christ the same yesterday, and today, and for ever" (Heb. 13:8).

6. *Omnipresence*. "No man hath seen God at any time; the only begotten Son, which is in the bosom of the Father, he hath declared him" (John 1:18). The Holy Spirit prompted John to write that the God-man, Jesus, is still in the bosom of the Father. This is a wonderful mystery of faith. Our Lord Him-

self emphasized it when He declared, "And no man hath ascended up to heaven, but he that came down from heaven. even the Son of man which is in heaven" (John 3:13). He was in the flesh and upon the earth, but He is also in heaven.

The glory of foreign missions is the covenant of our Lord who says "Lo, I am with you alway, even unto the end of the world" (Matt. 28:20). Any true missionary of the gospel, at all times and under all conditions, may rest assured of the unfailing presence of the omnipresent Redeemer. (See also Matt. 18:20 and Eph. 1:23.)

7. *Creative activity.* "By him," writes the apostle Paul, "were all things created, that are in heaven, and that are in earth, visible and invisible, whether they be thrones, or dominions, or principalities, or powers: all things were created by him, and for him: And he is before all things, and by him all things consist" (Col. 1:16,17). John does not hesitate to affirm, "All things were made by him; and without him was not anything made that was made." (John 1:3; see also 1 Cor. 8:6 and Heb. 1:8,10.)

8. *Ability to forgive sins.* When the palsied man came to Jesus for physical healing the question of forgiveness arose. Jesus said, "Son, thy sins be forgiven thee." The scribes reasoned about these words and thought, "Why does this man thus speak blasphemies? who can forgive sins but God only?" They knew that only God can forgive sins; and they did not believe that Jesus was God. Consequently they were persuaded that He was guilty of blasphemy in claiming to be able to forgive sins. Our Lord answered their inward questionings categorically: "Whether is it easier to say to the sick of the palsy, Thy sins be forgiven thee; or to say, Arise, and take up thy bed and walk? But that ye may know that the Son of man hath power on earth to forgive sins . . ." (Mark 2:5,7,9,10; see also Luke 24:47; John 1:29; Acts 10:43; 1 John 1:7.)

9. *Right to be worshipped.* Worship is due only to God. The worship of any thing or any person other than God is

idolatry. This is an awful sin and carries with it all the consequences of sin. Yet the Bible declares that we are to have faith in Jesus and to worship Him. In the days of His flesh He did not hesitate to accept the worship of men. (See Matt. 8:2.) And some day, Paul tells us, "at the name of Jesus every knee shall bow . . ." (Phil. 2:10).

## D. THE CONSEQUENCES OF DENYING CHRIST'S DEITY.

Everyone should be conscious of the implications of denying the deity of Jesus Christ. Unfortunately some believe that His deity is of little importance and are naïve enough to think that the Christian faith is coherent, sufficient, and satisfactory even if Jesus is not God. They would remove the structure of the faith but retain the outward façade. A denial of Christ's deity leaves a mere religious externalism with meaningless rites and ceremonies. This is religion which has "a form of godliness, but denying the power thereof: from such turn away" (2 Tim. 3:5). If Jesus is not God, then:

1. He bore false witness. He was a liar and thus a sinner Himself. He would then have needed someone to atone for His sins; and obviously could not have atoned for ours. The doctrines of His sinlessness and atonement would have to be scrapped.

2. The Bible itself would be an unreliable witness, and it would purport to reveal a system of religion founded on error rather than on truth. It would lose its authoritative note and become just another book and not a very good one at that.

3. Usually the denial of Christ's deity leads to a denial of the supernatural in general. This, of course, eliminates the virgin birth of Christ, His physical resurrection, and His miracles. The Christian faith cannot be separated from its component parts without destroying the whole. It stands or falls in its entirety. Remove one vital pillar and the entire structure tumbles to the ground. The deity of Christ is a pillar, the absence of which effectively invalidates the faith.

# 20

# The Virgin Birth

Perhaps no other doctrine in the Word of God has caused more intellectual and spiritual difficulty than that of the Virgin Birth of our Lord. Certainly no other doctrine has made it possible to detect more readily whether a man is a theological "conservative" or a "liberal." Other doctrines, such as the resurrection or the atonement may be "interpreted" or "explained" in language that confuses; but the Virgin Birth is either a fact or it is not a fact. It is a touchstone dividing the true from the false.

In bygone years the greatest danger to the church of Christ was caused by attacks from without. Today the menace which confronts the church is caused by attacks from within. Unfortunately some of the strongest opponents of the Biblical teaching of the Virgin Birth are found WITHIN the churches —men who profess to be Christians.

A. THE IMPORTANCE OF THE VIRGIN BIRTH.

1. *The miraculous birth of our Lord relates to the authority of the Word of God.* The Bible clearly and specifically teaches the Virgin Birth. No serious question should arise with regard to interpretation here. Even the rankest infidel must confess that the Bible itself represents Jesus Christ as having been con-

ceived by the Holy Ghost and born of the Virgin Mary. If one denies the Bible teaching on this subject he has rejected the authority of the Book. In such circumstances to speak of the Bible as an adequate and accurate source of spiritual truth is illogical and irrational. One can no longer believe in the infallibility of the Book as such even if he professes to believe some parts of it.

2. *The Virgin Birth raises the question of supernaturalism.* Practically every person who denies the doctrine rejects the supernatural as such. The heart of Christianity is its supernaturalness. A valid test of one's attitude toward the supernatural is his acceptance or rejection of the doctrine of the Virgin Birth. Sometimes one who denies the doctrine outwardly professes to believe in the resurrection or the deity of Christ. If he does believe these other great truths, his concept of them is not likely to be the supernatural one taught in the Scriptures.

3. *The negation of the Virgin Birth is destructive of the whole fabric of the Christian faith.* It leaves us with surmise rather than fact concerning Christ's birth and deprives us of knowledge as to the manner in which He entered the world. It seriously weakens, if it does not destroy, the doctrine of the incarnation (God manifest in the flesh) upon which our confidence rests and without which the Christian faith cannot survive.

### B. The Fact of the Virgin Birth.

Ultimately the question of the Virgin Birth is a question of fact. Jesus Christ either was virgin born or He was not. The belief in the Virgin Birth followed the FACT; the "fact" did not rise out of the belief. To decide this question of fact we must have recourse to the sources relating to the life and ministry of our Lord.

Preserving the stainless integrity and the virginal purity of Mary, Matthew (1:18) says, "When as His mother Mary was espoused to Joseph, before they came together, she was found with child of the Holy Ghost." How graciously God kept Jesus from the shame of illegitimacy! How wonderfully He proclaims that Mary was not a fallen woman!

Joseph believed that Jesus was the Son of God. He knew that the Holy Ghost was the One by whom his child was conceived. This knowledge changed his mind and altered his course of action. He had contemplated putting Mary away; but when God spoke to him he did not hesitate to obey the divine directive. (See Matt. 1:20.)

Luke supplies details about the birth of Jesus that Matthew does not mention. He tells us in a beautiful way how the angel prepared Mary (cf. Luke 1:28-33) for the great event. He reiterates Matthew's statement that the Holy Ghost should beget the child, and that the child should be the Son of God (cf. Luke 1:35).

The Spirit of God carefully informs us that the people of Jesus' day did not understand the Virgin Birth and the incarnation of the Son of God. Yet He does not permit the reader of the Scriptures to be misled. When tracing the genealogy of our Lord, Luke says (3:23): "And Jesus himself began to be about thirty years of age, being (as was supposed) the son of Joseph . . ." Son of Mary, according to the flesh, yes! But Son of God, conceived by the Holy Ghost!

The fact of the Virgin Birth, which the Bible teaches and substantiates, was not invented in order to explain the belief in the Virgin Birth. Rather belief in the Virgin Birth arose as the result of the fact of the Virgin Birth. The Christian Church throughout all the ages of its history has borne witness to its belief in the Virgin Birth based upon the solid, changeless fact.

## C. PROPHECIES CONCERNING THE VIRGIN BIRTH.

More than seven hundred years before the birth of Jesus Christ, Isaiah the prophet foretold His Virgin Birth: "Therefore the Lord himself shall give you a sign; Behold a virgin shall conceive, and bear a son, and shall call his name Immanuel" (Isa. 7:14).

Skeptics have tried to reinterpret the prophecy of Isaiah and to take from it the significance attached to a real virgin birth. They have tried to demonstrate that the "virgin" was not really a virgin, and that the prophecy has no bearing upon the birth of our Lord. But they have failed. Matthew succinctly tells us (for Matthew is the Gospel of fulfillment): "Now all this was done, that it might be fulfilled which was spoken of the Lord by the prophet, saying, Behold, a virgin shall be with child, and shall bring forth a son, and they shall call his name Emmanuel, which being interpreted is, God with us" (Matt. 1:22,23). No matter what men may say, the Spirit of God declares that the Virgin Birth was actually and literally the fulfilment of the prophecy uttered by Isaiah hundreds of years before the event occurred in history.

Thus the Bible teaches that the Son of God would be virgin born, and that the historical Jesus fulfilled the prophetic utterance of Isaiah. We have an authoritative Word and a supernatural Christ who is uniquely the Son of God in a way no other man could be: Jesus is God manifest in the flesh—born of the Virgin.

## D. The Significance of the Virgin Birth.

The significance of the Virgin Birth of Christ pertains both to His person and to His work.

1. *His Person.* Jesus Christ was no phantom; He was a real human being. He was truly man—bone of our bone, and flesh of our flesh. The fact that He was born of Mary assures us of this truth. He "made himself of no reputation, and took upon him the form of a servant, and was made in the likeness of men" (Phil. 2:7).

But Jesus Christ was not man alone. He is also God. He is both God and man—one person in two natures. He had a human nature, but He also had a divine nature. Therefore this virgin born Son of God was called Emmanuel. (See Isa. 7:14; Matt. 1:23.) The word "Emmanuel" is derived from the Hebrew and means "God (is) with us." God Himself has taken the form of sinful flesh; God has tabernacled among men; God has become incarnate in the flesh; God Himself is with us! The Virgin Birth of Jesus witnesses to His deity. He is God Himself!

Jesus was sinless. His birth of a virgin testifies to this fact. He was born of a woman, having no earthly father. He was made under the law; but like Adam before the fall, He was without original sin. He came to fulfill the law. His life, which began without sin, was preserved sinless. As God He was not able to sin, but as man He was able not to sin. By choice He ever remained the One true human being who committed no transgression and whom the law could not rightly accuse of guilt. He could ask without fear of contradiction, "Which of you convinceth me of sin?" (John 8:46); and Pilate said, "I find no fault in this man." (Luke 23:4; cf. John 18:38; 19:4,6.)

2. *His Work.* The Virgin Birth of Jesus gave to us a divine Redeemer whose life became a ransom and a propitiation for sin. A Jesus born in sin or subsequently guilty of sin could not have atoned for sin. The very nature of redemption demands that the offering for sin be sinless and without spot or blemish. "For he hath made him to be sin for us, who knew no sin; that we might become the righteousness of God in him" (2 Cor. 5:21).

Impregnable fortress of the faith, faithful guardian of the incarnation and the sinlessness of our Lord—The Virgin Birth!

# 21

# The Sinlessness of Jesus

---

The sinlessness of the Lord Jesus is indisputably in the warp and woof of the Christian faith. It is impossible to remove it without destroying the pattern of Christianity. Only unbelief will deny it and sinful man try to refute it.

## A. THE MEANING OF SINLESSNESS.

One may know what sinlessness is when he understands its opposite, sinfulness. Sinfulness is a want of conformity to, or antagonism towards the will of God; it implies deviating from the right order of life and choosing the path of evil. Sin is by no means merely an external thing, although men frequently express it outwardly in overt acts such as cheating, lying, stealing or adultery. But all external actions originate from within. The inward motive determines the wickedness of the outward act. Sometimes deeds which appear to be only slightly unworthy actually find their roots in deep and horrible depravity. On the other hand, even so heinous a crime as murder might, under certain circumstances, be less awful than the word of gossip which kills a reputation. But whatever one's motive might be, sinfulness has its roots in the heart.

The Scriptural teaching about sinlessness must be understood against this background. Sinlessness is conformity to all that is good and holy. It may be defined as that state of life in which God is the center of one's being. It does not preclude the possibility of sinning. The man Jesus was sinless in that, although the possibility of His sinning existed and although He was tempted in all points like as we are, He resisted temptation and perfectly fulfilled the law of God.

## B. TESTIMONY TO THE SINLESSNESS OF JESUS.

1. *Jesus' testimony concerning His own sinlessness.* Our Lord had a keen sense of sin in others. His sense of sin with reference to Himself was no less keen. All men admit that they have some faults; Jesus neither admitted to any fault nor ever asked forgiveness for any sin. He never indicated a need for repentance or regeneration in connection with His own life, although He spoke of both constantly so far as others were concerned. His life was pure. He had no evil thought or deed of which to repent. He needed not to be born again into the kingdom of God of which He was Himself the sinless King.

"Which of you convinceth me of sin" (John 8:46)? What other man could ever ask that question with impunity? Christ Himself testified to His complete sinlessness. (See also John 8:29; 17:19.)

2. *Testimony from the lips of others.* People will gladly bear witness to the good lives of their friends. In the nature of the case they are likely to be biased because of their friendship. Friendship overlooks defects. In the case of our Lord, however, we shall not advert to the testimony of His closest friends. Instead, we shall present the testimony of men who were either openly hostile to Him or who had no reason to be either favorable or unfavorable to Him.

a. *Pontius Pilate.* This Roman procurator, who represented the full authority of a mighty empire, sat in judgment upon our Lord Jesus. He heard the witnesses, examined the testimony and reached the verdict: "I find in him no fault at all" (John 18:38).

b. *The wife of Pontius Pilate.* Clearly this woman had no interest one way or the other in Jesus' fate; but tortured in a dream by reason of her assurance that a crime was about to be perpetrated and that justice was to be violated, she sent the message to her husband: "Have thou nothing to do with that just man" (Matt. 27:19).

c. *A thief on the cross.* The wretched malefactor, who was patently guilty and whose own lips had borne testimony to his guilt, spent his dying hours in the presence of the Son of God. In reply to the taunts of his partner in crime he exclaimed: "This man hath done nothing amiss" (Luke 23:41).

d. *Judas Iscariot.* Who could have detected sin more readily than the man who betrayed the Son of God? For two and a half years Judas had opportunity to observe Jesus. He walked with the Lord, he talked with Him, he heard the words of grace which flowed from His spotless lips. Seeing Jesus perform miracles, sitting at the table by His side, observing Him at prayer and marking His close and intimate fellowship with the Father—this man, when he finally pointed the finger of accusation, he pointed at himself because of his own misdeeds and in complete vindication of the Saviour. He cried out: "I have sinned in that I have betrayed the innocent blood" (Matt. 27:4).

e. *The commander of the Roman guard.* The centurion had often witnessed the execution of criminals as a part of his unpleasant task. He had watched men die. At Calvary he beheld the dying agonies of three men, but of only one could he say, as he glorified God, "Certainly this was a righteous man" (Luke 23:47).

3. *Testimony from the Epistles.* Statements about Jesus' sinlessness abound in these letters. "For he hath made him to be sin for us, who knew no sin; that we might be made the righteousness of God in him" (2 Cor. 5:21). "For we have not an high priest which cannot be touched with the feeling of our infirmities; but was in all points tempted like as we are, yet

without sin" (Heb. 4:15). "For even hereunto were ye called: because Christ also suffered for us, leaving us an example, that ye should follow his steps: Who did no sin, neither was guile found in his mouth." (1 Peter 2:21,22; see also Heb. 7:26,27; 1 John 3:5.)

## C. Arguments Against the Sinlessness of Jesus.

1. *Denial of the possibility of sinlessness.* Here all that Christians need to do is to confine themselves to the question of fact. Was Jesus sinless? This is not a matter of theory. Either He was sinless or He was not. The testimony of the Word of God satisfies Bible believers. What is that testimony? The Son of God was sinless!

2. *Denial that Jesus was sinless.* He was good, it is claimed, but not without sin. This argument, like the one above, is refuted by the Bible itself. We are faced once more with the decision as to whether to accept or to deny the Word of God. After all, the only Jesus we know is the Jesus of the Bible, the sinless Son of God.

3. *Denial of the truth that Jesus was tempted as we are tempted, with the basic presupposition that such temptation in itself implies sinfulness.* Now the Bible teaches both the temptation and the sinlessness of Jesus. It maintains that Jesus "was in all points tempted like as we are, yet without sin" (Heb. 4:15). Thus we conclude that despite His temptations He did not sin, and that it was possible for Him to be tempted without sinning. The mere offering of the allurements of the world is not itself sin. Only when the heart submits or capitulates to their enticement is there sin. As a true human being Jesus faced all the temptations we face, but He differed from us in that He resisted them and lived a holy and sinless life.

## D. The Consequences of Denying Jesus' Sinlessness.

1. If Jesus had been sinful, He could not have been the Son

of God of the apostolic faith which for two thousand years has proclaimed His sinlessness.

2. If sinful, Jesus could not have been the Son of Man and the prototype of perfect redeemed man.

3. If sinful, He could not have been our sacrifice for sin; He could not have been the all-sufficient Saviour and Redeemer of sinful men.

4. If Christ had been a sinner, His church would have no secure foundation on which to rest and the Christian faith would have lost its ground for existence.

## E. THE IMPLICATIONS OF THE SINLESSNESS OF JESUS.

1. He was actually the personal revelation of the holy God. This He could never have been had He not been sinless.

2. He is the Mediator between God and man. He is the sinless sacrifice making atonement for the sins of men. He is the guiltless and the innocent offered up for the guilty and the vile. His very sinlessness effected the redemption which all previous offerings had been unable to accomplish. (See 1 Peter 1:18.)

3. He founded a universal fellowship which knows neither space nor bounds. It is the church of redeemed men and women, a heavenly, holy society which sinful men could never have inaugurated, and which only a sinless Savior could have called into being.

# 22

# *Miracles*

---

The subject of miracles has been for centuries a battleground on which men have fought unceasingly. The problem has been debated through the centuries, and of the making of books on the subject there is no end. The so-called "scientific" mind of the twentieth century has grappled vigorously with the problem; with the result that some still believe in miracles and some still deny them.

We can simplify the problem of miracles, to some extent, by admitting that belief or disbelief in them is generally derived from a prior attitude of heart and mind: from the disposition to admit or to deny the possibility of the miraculous. Many scientists have an *a priori* "belief" in the impossibility of miracles. When they are presented with evidence of a miracle they rule it out and explain it away because they have already decided that miracles cannot occur. The Christian also begins with a belief, but his belief is in the possibility of miracles. Because he is a believer the supernatural is not a stumbling block to him; and because he has encountered an Almighty God who can and does do anything He pleases, miracles are no obstacle to his faith. Thus the Christian does not try to explain away or rule out the miracles he finds in the Bible. He simply accepts them.

Now it must be admitted that belief in miracles may lead one to call some events miraculous when they actually may not be miraculous at all. Thus when a man in an automobile accident survives, some people quickly attribute his preservation to a miracle. Undoubtedly in most instances his survival is a matter of divine providence and does not involve the miraculous. Divine providence operates constantly in the lives of men and no aspect of life is free from it. But we must be careful to distinguish between divine providence and miracles, lest our opponents deride our faith in miracles on the ground that we denominate some events miraculous when clearly they are matters of divine providence. It is just as wrong to call something a miracle when it is not a miracle as it is to deny that something is a miracle when it actually is miraculous. In each instance falsity is involved and a lie is a lie even when one may think that he is helping God's cause. But the questions arise: What is a miracle, and how does it differ from divine providence?

## A. THE DEFINITION OF A MIRACLE.

1. A miracle has been defined as "an effect in nature nor attributable to any of the recognized operations of nature, nor to the act of man, but indicative of superhuman power, and serving as a sign or witness thereof; a wonderful work manifesting a power superior to the ordinary forces of nature."

2. Divine providence, on the other hand, includes preservation and government. The universe and all its creatures are subject to the will of God. This subjection includes cause and effect as well as the operations of natural law. The idea of government embraces both design and control and implies that the end and the means of attaining the end are within the scope of divine providence. All these operations are consistent with God's wisdom and holiness; and while miracles may occur in the pattern of providence they are the exception rather than the rule. Thus the man who escapes death in an automo-

bile accident does so because of God's providence but not because of a miracle. (See the definition of miracle given above.)

The providential, preserving power of God is attested by the Scriptures. "Thou, even thou, art Lord alone; thou hast made heaven, the heaven of heavens, with all their host, the earth, and all things that are therein, the seas, and all that is therein, and thou preservest them all" (Neh. 9:6). "By Him all things consist," or "continue to be." (Col. 1:17; see also Heb. 1:3; Psalms 104 and 148.)

## B. The Uniqueness of Jesus' Miracles.

1. Our Lord's miracles were designed to witness to His deity and to accredit His message and His Person. "This beginning of miracles did Jesus in Cana of Galilee, and manifested forth His glory." "But these are written, that ye might believe that Jesus is the Christ, the Son of God; and that believing ye might have life through His name" (John 2:11; 20:31).

2. Jesus' miracles differed from the miracles of the prophets and apostles. The prophets performed miracles by delegated power as they themselves affirmed. The apostles attributed to God's power, and not to their own, the miracles they performed. But Jesus wrought miracles by inherent power; He had the power and the authority within Himself.

Moses attributed the miracles of redemption from the hands of the Egyptians, not to his power, but to that of God: "And Moses said unto the people, Fear ye not, stand still, and see the salvation of the Lord, which He will shew to you today: for the Egyptians whom ye have seen today, ye shall see them again no more for ever" (Exodus 14:13). When Simon Peter was acclaimed as a miracle worker ". . . he answered unto the people, Ye men of Israel, why marvel ye at this? or why look ye so earnestly on us, as though by our own power or holiness we had made this man to walk. The God of Abraham . . . hath glorified his Son Jesus. . . ." (Acts 3:12). Luke declares that "God wrought special miracles by the hands of Paul" (Acts 19:11). These were not the result of any inherent power in Paul but were the result of delegated power. It was God through Paul; not Paul in himself.

Jesus performed, so far as the written record is concerned, somewhere between 35 and 40 miracles. He stilled the waves, made the blind to see, the lame to walk, the dumb to speak. He always acted by His own power. When questioned about the supreme miracle of all, the forgiveness of sins, He openly stated that He had the inherent right and divine power to deal with men's iniquities. Remember that in the Great Commission He claimed that "all power" was given unto Him. (See Matt. 28:18.)

In a real sense the question of miracles is subordinate to another question. Who was Jesus and what was His work? If we see Him as divine and accept Him as the Son of God and Saviour then miracles cause us no trouble. Only when His person and work are called into question do people stumble at His miracles. One should expect miracles from Jesus as tangible evidence that He is the accredited Son of God.

## C. The Scope of Jesus' Miracles.

The signs which our Saviour wrought show His power in many areas:

1. *Over disturbances of nature.* He stilled the tempest. "Then He arose, and rebuked the winds and the sea; and there was a great calm. But the men marvelled, saying, What manner of man is this, that even the winds and the sea obey him!" (Matt. 8:26,27.)

2. *Over devils.* "And all the devils besought him, saying, Send us into the swine, that we may enter into them. And forthwith Jesus gave them leave. And the unclean spirits went out, and entered into the swine. . . ." (Mark 5:12,13; see also Matt. 8:28-32; 9:32,33; 15:22-28; 17:14-18; Mark 1:23-27.)

3. *Over disease.* "And Jesus put forth his hand and touched

him, saying, I will; be thou clean. And immediately his leprosy was cleansed" (Matt. 8:3). "And, behold, there was a man which had his hand withered. . . . Then saith he to the man, Stretch forth thine hand. And he stretched it forth; and it was restored whole, like as the other." (Matt. 12:10-13; see also Matt. 8:5-15; Mark 2:3-12; John 4:46-53.)

4. *Over death.* "Then said Jesus unto them plainly, Lazarus is dead . . . And when he had thus spoken, he cried with a loud voice, Lazarus, come forth. And he that was dead came forth, bound hand and foot with graveclothes . . ." (John 11:14,43,44; see also Matt. 9:18,19, 23-25; Luke 7:12-15.)

## D. The Credibility of Jesus' Miracles.

1. Jesus' miracles are in the warp and woof of the Bible and cannot be separated from it.

2. The records of His miracles are restrained and chaste, and contain nothing unreasonable.

3. Our Lord's miracles were performed openly and in the presence of many witnesses. They were in the realm of the physical and could be studied and appraised by the physical senses. Yet they have never been disproved nor can modern science reproduce them.

4. Christ never used miracles for immoral or unworthy purposes. He had a worthy motive in each case.

5. The miracles of Jesus were effected instantaneously, not over an extended period of time. They were supernatural interventions, not natural processes.

6. Jesus Himself placed great emphasis on miracles. The concept that belief in miracles arose gradually in the church is untrue. In point of fact, miracles became more infrequent toward the end of the Gospel narratives and died out completely in the early church.

7. To explain away miracles by calling them frauds or mythological propaganda, or by attributing them to autosuggestion, or to the credulity of the people, or to natural

causes not immediately discerned,—such explanations pose questions far more difficult than does the Christian view that the miracles actually occurred historically, and that they accomplished the purposes which our Savior had in mind when He performed them.

### E. The Possibility of Miracles Today.

Since miracles died away in the early church, inquiring Christians want to know whether miracles can actually occur today. The answer to this question is twofold:

1. *Miracles are definitely a possibility*. Our God has never changed. His power is the same today as it was in the days of the prophets and of His Son.

2. *But miracles are not a necessity today*. By definition a miracle is a "supernatural event wrought by the immediate power of God in the external world." It is intended to accredit a message or a messenger. God is still doing marvelous things every day. But He is accrediting the gospel first and foremost through the "miracle" of the new birth. Beyond this, God answers the prayers of His children so that when He pleases He can and does perform "miracles," not for any accrediting purpose but for the good of His people and for His own glory.

# 23

# The Resurrection of Christ

The question of the resurrection of Jesus from the dead has elicited many theories and resulted in numerous controversies and differences of opinion. This is undoubtedly due to the fact that the resurrection is a fundamental truth. Remove it from the Scriptures and the Christian faith is emasculated; keep it and a central note in gospel preaching will be "now is Christ risen from the dead."

Countless men for two thousand years have attempted to "explain away" the historical fact of, and the Biblical teaching concerning, the resurrection. Unbelief always remains dissatisfied with a living Jesus; it always covets a dead body. The reason is simple. Once one admits that Jesus Christ arose from the dead, the remainder of the Christian faith is readily established. One is closed up to the acceptance of that faith.

A. THE IMPORTANCE OF THE RESURRECTION.

1. Like the Virgin Birth, the doctrine of the resurrection is connected with the authority of the Bible. As in the case of the former doctrine, to deny the physical resurrection of Jesus means to discount what the Bible teaches. Such a denial deprives one of an infallible record of divine truth. No matter how much he may believe apart from this miracle, he is left

with a fallible record. If one cannot trust the Book in what it says about this important doctrine, how can he trust the record in other areas of its teaching?

2. The belief in the physical resurrection presupposes a belief in the supernatural. These two facts cannot be divorced. In nearly every case those who deny the resurrection do so because they have first denied the supernatural. To rise from the dead is a supernatural act. Thus a denial of the supernatural will always result in a denial of the resurrection; and the denial of the resurrection generally reflects disbelief in the supernatural.

3. Whether or not Jesus rose from the dead is a question the answer to which either validates or invalidates the whole Christian faith. The apostle Paul explores the problem. He deduces certain grave consequences of a denial of the resurrection.

The Pauline argument is as follows: If one starts with the assumption that the dead do not rise, then Christ is not risen. If He is not risen, the gospel is not true and the disciples are false witnesses. A dead Christ means a dead faith; a dead faith means that believers are still unforgiven and unjustified sinners; and that those who fell asleep in Jesus supposing Him to have been raised from the dead have perished. Faith in Christ which has reference only to this life and does not carry with it life and resurrection power beyond the grave leaves man in despair. (See 1 Cor. 15:12-19.)

In short, if Jesus arose from the grave we have a valid faith; if He did not rise we have no faith and no hope.

## B. THE FACT OF THE RESURRECTION.

Like the Virgin Birth of our Lord the resurrection is a question of fact. Either He did rise or He did not rise. We know that whatever the skeptics may say, the apostles and the early church taught and believed that He rose from the dead. The church was established on this basis. Belief in the resurrection sprang out of the fact of the resurrection, and not vice versa.

Indisputable evidence exists to convince the skeptic that Jesus rose from the dead. For example:

a. *The Testimony of Paul.* The apostle to the Gentiles claims to have seen the risen Lord Jesus, and adds that Peter, all of the apostles, and five hundred brethren at once, saw Him. (See 1 Cor. 15:5-8.) The preaching, teaching and theological convictions of Paul were determined by his belief in the historicity of the resurrection.

b. *The Gospel Accounts of the Bodily Resurrection.* The angel said that Christ was risen (see Matt. 28:6); Mary Magdalene saw Him (see John 20:14-18); the women upon their return from telling the disciples saw Him (see Matt. 28:8-10); after his denial Peter saw Him (see 1 Cor. 15:5; Luke 24:34); Thomas the doubter put his finger into the print of the nail and thrust his hand into the riven side (see John 20:24-29); the apostles, with the exception of Thomas, who was not then present, saw Him (see Luke 24:36-43).

The great variety of Jesus' appearances after His resurrection, the circumstances surrounding these appearances, the published evidence which describes the event and the time, all demonstrate that the belief in the resurrection sprang from the fact itself. The disciples did not depend on hearsay; they were eyewitnesses of Christ's post-resurrection presence. To suggest that they were not eyewitnesses is to accuse them of being liars and deceivers.

c. *The Rise and Present Existence of the Church.* The visible churches today are the consequence of the resurrection. They owe their existence to the fact that Christ arose. For two thousand years countless thousands of individual churches, and millions of believing members have proclaimed their faith in the resurrection and their assurance that the historical Jesus rose in the same body in which He suffered. The celebration of Easter; the use of Sunday, the time of Christ's resurrection, as the day of Christian worship; the creedal formulations of the church—these things are outward evidences of the faith of christendom.

## C. Theories Opposing the Resurrection.

Many contrary explanations have been adduced to account for the resurrection of Christ. Men seem determined to undermine the historical account and to explain away evidence that would hold in any court of law. In the main four theories stand out. The first is the historical theory which we have considered under "The Fact of the Resurrection." This we believe to be the true account and the only one that is logically, rationally and Biblically valid. Other theories are:

1. *The Swoon Theory.* Jesus never actually died. He was removed from the cross in a swoon, the soldiers and the multitudes thinking Him to be dead. Consequently He could not possibly have arisen from the dead. A weak, emaciated, dying Jesus came out of the tomb and then subsequently died, only to remain dead.

The facts which contradict this theory are numerous. The record states that the soldiers did not break Jesus' legs because he was already dead; His body was embalmed and linen cloths covered His face; after the resurrection no one was able to produce the body; Jesus was seen by many people after He rose, and He was observed to be healthy, strong and powerful, rather than weak and dying. The swoon theory hardly solves the problem. If it were true, the disciples were false witnesses and died for a belief they knew to be untrue.

2. *The Fraud Theory.* This is also known as "The Stolen Body Theory." It presupposes that the disciples were dishonest. They came during the night and removed the body of their Leader. Then they went forth and proclaimed Him as having risen from the dead. They were thus base deceivers who perpetrated a fraud on men. This is an old, old story. The Jews paid the Roman soldiers to invent the tale. (See Matt.

28:12-15.) How could sleeping soldiers have known who stole the body? And if they had known they could have prevented the theft. Further, no one was able to discover the body. The empty tomb remains an unanswered enigma. How can one believe that Peter, James, John, Andrew, Paul and hosts of others gladly and willingly laid down their lives to support a belief they knew to be false and to perpetuate a lie?

3. *The Hallucination Theory.* This is sometimes known as "The Vision Theory." According to this view the disciples and other people connected with the death of Jesus were highly stirred by the events that transpired. Because they believed that He was going to rise from the dead, their fevered imaginations led them to the conviction that they had seen the risen Lord. Their vision of Christ was like a mirage.

In reality the empty tomb is a rebuke to the chimera view. Had the risen Christ been seen only in the disciples' imagination, the Jews would have punctured the illusion and the Roman soldiers would have produced the dead body. Moreover, to suggest that so many people on so many different occasions had so many hallucinations is to concoct an idea more difficult of acceptance than the supernatural fact of the resurrection itself.

4. *Some alternate views.* Some say that Christ was buried in a different tomb; some say that the women came to the wrong tomb; some say that our Lord "telegraphed" back a vision of Himself to the minds of the apostles; some say that the writers corrupted and falsely represented the truth. In spite of all contrary views, let us remember Paul's affirmation: Christ "rose again the third day according to the scriptures" (1 Cor. 15:4). So we believe and so we teach!

## D. THE RESULT OF THE RESURRECTION.

1. It guarantees the deity of the Lord Jesus. He is "declared to be the Son of God with power, according to the Spirit of holiness, by the resurrection from the dead" (Rom. 1:4).

2. It is essential to our justification. (See Rom. 4:25; 8:34.) Because Jesus rose from the dead all who believe in Him are justified "from all things, from which ye could not be justified by the law of Moses" (Acts 13:39).

3. It makes possible the forgiveness of sins. (See 1 Cor. 15:17.)

4. It makes certain a final judgment "because he hath appointed a day, in the which he will judge the world in righteousness by that man whom he hath ordained; whereof he hath given assurance unto all men, in that he hath raised him from the dead" (Acts 17:31).

5. It furnishes every believer with a deathless hope. "But now is Christ risen from the dead, and become the first-fruits of them that slept" (1 Cor. 15:20). As He rose from the dead and liveth forever, so will the bodies of believers be raised from the tomb. This is the unshakable confidence of the saints.

# 24

## The Ascension of Christ

---

Four great miracles are part of the warp and woof of the Christian faith. These are the incarnation, the resurrection of our Lord, His ascension into heaven and His second advent. All these miracles are matters of fact and do not involve individual judgment. Each is based upon substantial testimony and each must be accepted and believed.

The ascension of our Lord is of more than passing importance. An understanding of all its implications relating to our heritage will help one to live out in the flesh the life that Christ died for him to win.

### A. The Reason Christ's Ascension Was Delayed.

1. Jesus waited for forty days before ascending into heaven to prove beyond doubt that He had risen from the dead. Had He ascended immediately it might have given rise to the conclusion that He had not risen but that His body had disappeared. During the forty days He was seen by numerous people and on different occasions. Through His post-resurrection appearances He gave substance and validity to the truth of the Scriptures, and stopped the mouths of many a gainsayer and scoffer.

2. He tarried before ascending in order to instruct the dis-

ciples in the truths of the Christian faith. Christian theology had its real origin in full and expanded form during this period of instruction. Luke says that "beginning at Moses and all the prophets, he expounded unto them in all the scriptures the things concerning himself" (Luke 24:27). By the time the Holy Spirit came to endue the disciples with power they were already acquainted with the basic doctrines of the revelation of God and were able to witness accurately and intelligently concerning the Christian faith. The historical Jesus whom the disciples knew so well personally taught them all that they needed to know.

3. He delayed His ascent in order to prevent seducing spirits from falsely interpreting His person and work, and from subverting the apostles' faith in the Scriptures. He told His disciples that the Holy Spirit would "teach you all things, and bring all things to your remembrance, whatsoever I have said unto you" (John 14:26). The additional days spent with them made it possible for Him to complete His instructions, and to pave the way for the Spirit's work of confirmation.

B. THE NECESSITY OF THE ASCENSION.

Why was it necessary for the Lord Jesus to ascend into heaven?

1. Heaven was His home and the place from which He came. He said, "I know whence I came . . ." (John 8:14). But heaven is heaven because of His presence, and the resurrected Christ could hardly have remained on a polluted and sinful earth. He went back to the place whence He came, having prophesied, "I go my way, and ye shall seek me, and shall die in your sins: whither I go, ye cannot come . . . Ye are from beneath; I am from above: ye are of this world; I am not of this world" (John 8:21,23).

2. His prophetic statement that He would ascend into heaven had to be fulfilled. "Ye have heard how I said unto you, I go away, and come again unto you. If ye loved me, ye would

ejoice, because I said, I go unto the Father . . ." (John 14: 28). "But now I go my way to him that sent me . . ." (John 16:5). "Touch me not; for I am not yet ascended to my Father: but go to my brethren, and say unto them, I ascend unto my Father, and your Father; and to my God, and your God" (John 20:17).

3. In the divine plan the advent of the Holy Spirit was to be preceded by Christ's ascension into heaven: "Nevertheless 1 tell you the truth; It is expedient for you that I go away; for if I go not away, the Comforter will not come unto you; but if I depart, I will send him unto you" (John 16:7).

4. The ascension of Christ was a prerequisite to His further work. "I go to prepare a place for you. And if I go and prepare a place for you, I will come again, and receive you unto myself; that where I am, there ye may be also" (John 14:2,3). Prior to His second advent He went to heaven to make ready a dwelling place for the saints. This He is now doing.

5. Jesus Christ, as our High Priest, having offered Himself as Sin-bearer, now appears before God on our behalf. Obviously He could not do this until He had ascended into heaven. But now at God's right hand He is our Mediator before the Father. "We have such an high priest, who is set on the right hand of the throne of the Majesty in the heavens; a minister of the sanctuary, and of the true tabernacle, which the Lord pitched, and not man" (Heb. 8:1,2).

## C. The Nature of the Ascension.

1. *The One who ascended is the God-man.* The whole person ascended, not just the divine son or the human man. He went to heaven in a resurrected body, but in a human body that was raised incorruptible. He will never relinquish His human nature, for He is forever God and man.

2. *The ascension was a real departure from this earth and a real entrance into heaven.* Jesus passed from the visible world into the invisible, to the eternal and abiding world. "This same

Jesus, which is taken up from you into heaven, shall so come in like manner as ye have seen him go into heaven" (Acts 1:11). He is gone; He was taken up; heaven is the place to which He went—all this is perfectly apparent.

3. *The ascension was visible, not secret.* It was seen by men and accomplished in their presence. ". . . they looked stedfastly toward heaven as he went up . . ." (Acts 1:10). The transfer of Christ's body from one place to another is not an idea which we accept apart from knowledge. The facts produced the doctrine. What men saw done before their eyes was the substance of their testimony. A similarity obtains between Christ's ascension and His second advent. He went away personally, visibly and in power. He shall so come in like manner as He was seen going into heaven. (See Acts 1:11.)

D. THE ASCENDED CHRIST.

1. Having ascended, Our Lord is now at the Father's right hand. This is a position of power. ". . . by the resurrection of Jesus Christ: Who is gone into heaven, and is on the right hand of God; angels and authorities and powers being made subject unto him" (1 Pet. 3:21,22). It is also a place of dignity. "Which he (God) wrought in Christ, when he raised him from the dead, and set him at his own right hand in the heavenly places, Far above all principality, and power, and might, and dominion, and every name that is named, not only in this world, but also in that which is to come: And hath put all things under his feet, and gave him to be head over all things to the church, Which is his body, the fulness of him that filleth all in all." (Eph. 1:20-23; see also Heb. 1:3; Col. 3:1.) And it is a position of glory. "Ought not Christ to have suffered these things, and to enter into his glory?" (Luke 24:26.)

2. God the Father has given Him a name that is above every name. "Wherefore God hath highly exalted him, and given him a name which is above every name: That at the name of Jesus every knee should bow, of things in heaven, and things in

earth, and things under the earth" (Phil. 2:9,10). The power of Jesus extends to earth as well as to heaven. Christ is Lord of all and over all.

3. The mystery of the exalted God-man is that He is ever God and ever man. As man He still has human sympathies and affections; He still has a feeling for our infirmities; He knows tenderness, love, compassion and forbearance. In Him, however, "dwelleth all the fulness of the Godhead bodily" (Col. 2:9).

4. Having ascended up on high, He is the Head of His body the Church. God "hath put all things under his feet, and gave him to be the head over all things to the church, Which is his body, the fulness of him that filleth all in all." (Eph. 1:22,23; see also Col. 1:18.)

5. Christ now reigns from heaven and will continue this mediatorial, ruling work until His task is finished. "For he must reign, till he hath put all enemies under His feet. The last enemy that shall be destroyed is death" (1 Cor. 15:25,26). "Thou hast put all things in subjection under his feet. For in that he put all in subjection under him, he left nothing that is not put under him. But now we see not yet all things put under him" (Heb. 2:8). Our Lord has already undermined Satan's world. The beast has been wounded fatally and his end is sure. But the final victory of Christ over evil is not yet apparent. It will, however, become a reality before the end of this age. The carpenter is making coffins for all the kings and kingdoms of this world. Kings and kingdoms flourish and are gone, but Christ has an everlasting kingdom and "that alone endures which belongs to Him."

6. Christ intercedes in heaven for the saints. "Who is he that condemneth? It is Christ that died, yea rather, that is risen again, who is even at the right hand of God, who also maketh intercession for us" (Rom. 8:34). "For Christ is not entered into the holy places made with hands, which are the figures of the true; but into heaven itself, now to appear in

the presence of God for us" (Heb. 9:24). At this very moment Jesus is praying for His own and pleading with God on their behalf. This should be a source of profound and continued encouragement to the children of God.

# 25

# The Second Advent of Christ

For two thousand years Christians have believed in the first and second advents of our Lord. They have borne consistent testimony that God was manifest in the flesh in the person of our Lord Jesus. With equal consistency they have witnessed to their belief that Jesus Christ will come again. All Bible believing Christians in all ages have agreed that the first coming was in humiliation but that the second advent will be in power and great glory.

But this statement must be immediately qualified. It must be admitted that within the framework of this general conviction wide differences of opinion have existed and still exist about our Lord's coming. The various schools of thought agree that He will come, but they differ markedly about certain points, one of which has to do with the millennium. Every Christian ought to be careful not to condemn those who disagree with him on the millennial question. Because a brother in Christ differs from him does not necessarily mean that the brother is an unbeliever. Differences of interpretation exist. They are not basic to salvation, but deal with matters which have perplexed countless generations of Christians and about which good men have always differed. Christian liberty and forbearance must be allowed to operate. Discussions on the subject should generate light rather than heat.

## A. The Three Major Viewpoints Respecting Our Lord's Second Coming.

1. *The Post-millennial view.* This view was popular a hundred years ago. It was held by many leading theologians of different denominations. Generally speaking, its major emphasis with regard to the millennium is that the return of our Lord will follow rather than precede the millennial age. Jesus will come at the end of an earthly millennium, which will be a golden age characterized by peace and prosperity. In this view the millennium will not necessarily be man-made. Many post-millenarians believe that the golden age will be ushered in through divine intervention, although not by the actual coming of our Lord. It should be noted that this view accepts and teaches the truth that Christ will come personally at the end of the age.

Post-millennialism is closely identified in the twentieth century with an optimistic view of history and, in a superficial way, may be thought of as an eschatological confidence that "every day in every way things are getting better and better." Two world wars in less than thirty years have largely destroyed the idea of inevitable progress, and post-millennialism has been scrapped by great numbers of people. The major question, however, is whether post-millennialism can stand the scrutiny of Biblical exegesis. At this point the opponents of the view believe that it falls short. The position does not seem to square with the Scriptural view of eschatology.

2. *The A-millennial view.* A-millennialists are sometimes accused of being "disappointed post-millennialists." This is hardly true, for in a number of ways a-millennialism is closer to pre-millennialism than post-millennialism. The a-millennialist believes in the imminent coming of our Lord; he does

not look for a golden age of a thousand years prior to the event; and he often agrees with the pre-millennialist with respect to the signs foretelling the coming. He does not believe, however, that there will be a millennial age of a thousand years either before or after the advent of the Lord. In his opinion the coming of Christ will signify the end of the age and a transition into the everlasting kingdom.

The question whether Christ will reign on earth for a thousand years is an exegetical one, and one's viewpoint must be determined by what he believes the Bible teaches. The book of the Revelation, which speaks definitely of a thousand years (Rev. 20), must be understood either literally or figuratively. The pre-millennialist understands it literally and the a-millennialist figuratively. The latter spiritualizes the words and also many Old Testament passages dealing with the return of Israel to Palestine, etc.

3. *The Pre-millennial view*. This is the view we believe to be correct. It holds to the coming of our Lord to set up an earthly, thousand year kingdom. It claims that conditions on earth will not improve, but will on the contrary grow worse as the end of the age approaches and the time of Christ's coming draws nigh. Many people automatically assume that if a man is a pre-millennialist he is also a dispensationalist. But this is not the case. A man may be both a pre-millennialist and a dispensationalist. But hosts of pre-millennialists are definitely not dispensationalists. In general it may be said that all dispensationalists are pre-millennialists, but that not all pre-millennialists are dispensationalists.

## B. The Pre-millennial View of Our Lord's Second Coming.

1. The events which precede His coming:

a. *The destruction of Jerusalem*. "And when ye shall see Jerusalem compassed with armies, then know that the desolation thereof is nigh . . . and Jerusalem shall be trodden down

of the Gentiles, until the times of the Gentiles be fulfilled"
(Luke 21:20,24).

b. *The calling out of the Gentiles.* "For I would not, brethren, that ye should be ignorant of this mystery, lest ye should
be wise in your own conceits; that blindness in part is happened to Israel, until the fulness of the Gentiles be come in"
(Rom. 11:25).

c. *The preaching of the gospel to the ends of the earth.* "But
ye shall receive power, after that the Holy Ghost is come
upon you: and ye shall be witnesses unto me both in Jerusalem, and in all Judaea, and in Samaria, and unto the uttermost part of the earth" (Acts 1:8). "And this gospel of the
kingdom shall be preached in all the world for a witness unto
all nations; and then shall the end come" (Matt. 24:14).

d. *The coming of the anti-Christ.* "Let no man deceive you
by any means: for that day shall not come, except there come
a falling away first, and that man of sin be revealed, the son
of perdition . . . And then shall that Wicked be revealed,
whom the Lord shall consume with the spirit of his mouth,
and shall destroy with the brightness of his coming" (2 Thess.
2:3-8).

e. *Strange physical phenomena.* "Immediately after the tribulation of those days shall the sun be darkened, and the moon
shall not give her light, and the stars shall fall from heaven,
and the powers of the heavens shall be shaken" (Matt. 24:29).
"And there shall be signs in the sun, and in the moon, and in
the stars; and upon the earth distress of nations, with perplex-
ity; the sea and the waves roaring; Men's hearts failing them
for fear, and for looking after those things which are coming
on the earth: for the powers of heaven shall be shaken"
(Luke 21:25-26).

f. *The rapture of the church.* Many pre-millennialists believe in the pre-tribulation rapture of the church. Other pre-
millennialists believe in the mid-tribulation rapture. Still others
hold that the Church will go through the great tribulation.

And some teach the secret, any-moment rapture, holding that nothing needs to be fulfilled before the advent of our Lord. A pertinent passage is 1 Thess. 4:15-17. Unfortunately this portion of Scripture, while it teaches that believers, dead and living, will be caught up to meet the Lord, does not indicate the time-relationship of the rapture to the second advent. There seems to be no plain statement in the Bible dealing with the precise time of the rapture. One's viewpoint must be determined on the basis of an examination of all the Scripture passages on the subject. He should endeavor to be irenic in approach and objective in treatment. The time of the rapture should never be made a test of orthodoxy, nor should any Christian criticize those who hold views in this area other than his own.

g. *Other signs of Christ's coming.* The list includes, for example, the persecution of the church; the rise of false prophets and false Christs; a deepening apostasy in the professing church; and the return of Israel to the land. (See 2 Tim. 3.)

2. Details of His coming:

a. *The time of Christ's return is unknown.* "Watch therefore: for ye know not what hour your Lord doth come" (Matt. 24:42). Repeating the same admonition Jesus said, "Ye know neither the day nor the hour wherein the Son of man cometh" (Matt. 25:13). "But of that day and that hour knoweth no man, no, not the angels which are in heaven, neither the Son, but the Father" (Mark 13:32).

b. *Our Lord will come personally.* "This same Jesus . . . shall so come in like manner" (Acts 1:11). "For what is our hope, or joy, or crown of rejoicing? Are not even ye in the presence of our Lord Jesus Christ at his coming?" (1 Thess. 2:19). "Henceforth there is laid up for me a crown of righteousness, which the Lord, the righteous judge, shall give me at that day: and not to me only, but unto all them also that love his appearing" (2 Tim. 4:8).

c. *He will come physically and visibly.* "Behold, he cometh with clouds; and every eye shall see him, and they also which pierced him: and all kindreds of the earth shall wail because of him" (Rev. 1:7). "And then shall appear the sign of the Son of man in heaven: and then shall all the tribes of the earth mourn, and they shall see the Son of man coming in the clouds of heaven with power and great glory." (Matt. 24:30; see also Mark 13:26; Luke 21:27; and Titus 2:13.)

d. *He will come suddenly.* "But as the days of Noe were, so shall also the coming of the Son of man be" (Matt. 24:37). Read also the parable of the wise and the foolish virgins concerning the suddenness of His coming (Matt. 25:1-13). "Watch ye therefore: for ye know not when the master of the house cometh, at even, or at midnight, or at the cockcrowing, or in the morning: Lest coming suddenly he find you sleeping" (Mark 13:35,36).

e. *He will come gloriously and triumphantly.* "And to you who are troubled rest with us, when the Lord Jesus shall be revealed from heaven with his mighty angels, In flaming fire taking vengeance on them that know not God, and that obey not the gospel of our Lord Jesus Christ. . . . When he shall come to be glorified in his saints, and to be admired in all them that believe "in that day" (2 Thess. 1:7-10). In the Revelation a description of Christ's coming is given which should stir the heart of every believer. (See Rev. 19:11-16.)

3. The purpose of His coming:

a. *Christ will judge the works of believers.* "So then every one of us shall give account of himself to God" (Rom. 14:12). "Every man's work shall be made manifest: for the day shall declare it, because it shall be revealed by fire; and the fire shall try every man's work of what sort it is. If any man's work abide which he hath built thereupon, he shall receive a reward. If any man's work shall be burned, he shall suffer loss: but he himself shall be saved, yet so as by fire." (1 Cor. 3:13-15; see also Rom. 14:10; 2 Cor. 5:10.)

b. *He will set up His thousand year earthly kingdom.* "He

shall be great, and shall be called the Son of the Highest: and the Lord God shall give unto him the throne of his father David: And he shall reign over the house of Jacob forever; and of his kingdom there shall be no end." (Luke 1:32-33; study Rev. 20:1-6.)

c. *He will judge the nations.* "And before him shall be gathered all nations: and he shall separate them one from another, as a shepherd divideth his sheep from the goats . . . And these shall go away into everlasting punishment: but the righteous into life eternal" (Matt. 25:32,46). "Behold, the Lord cometh with ten thousands of his saints, To execute judgment upon all, and to convince all that are ungodly among them of all their ungodly deeds which they have ungodly committed, and of all their hard speeches which ungodly sinners have spoken against him" (Jude 14,15).

d. *He will destroy death.* "Then cometh the end, when he shall have delivered up the kingdom to God, even the Father; when he shall have put down all rule and all authority and power. For he must reign, till he hath put all enemies under his feet. The last enemy that shall be destroyed is death" (1 Cor. 15:24-26). The devil, his angels, and his followers will be cast into the lake of fire, separated from the presence of God forever.

e. *At His coming He will complete the redemption of believers.* He will be glorified in the saints and admired in all them that believe; we shall participate with Him in the marriage supper of the Lamb; a new heavens and a new earth, following the millennium, will be instituted; the eternal kingdom will come into being wherein dwelleth righteousness forever. (See 2 Peter 3.)

## C. THE RELATIONSHIP OF THE LORD'S ADVENT TO THE BELIEVER TODAY.

1. *We are warned to watch and to be ready.* "Take ye heed, watch and pray: for ye know not when the time is" (Mark

13:33). "Watch therefore: for ye know not what hour your Lord doth come" (Matt. 24:42).

2. *We are warned that we have a stewardship given to us by our Lord and that we are to be found faithful in the execution of His tasks till He come.* We are to be busy in the service of our Saviour, occupying until He comes; we are to suffer for His sake; we are to live for Him and to reflect His glory. (Study the parable of the talents in Matt. 25:14-30.)

3. *We must be extremely careful to maintain a worthy character.* The hope of Christ's return is an incentive to integrity, purity, and holiness. (See 1 John 3:1-3.)

4. *We are to carry out the terms of the Great Commission.* (See Matt. 28:18-20.) Acts 1:8 is a prophetic statement of God's plan. It declares that the gospel shall reach to the ends of the earth during the church age. We must do our utmost to further the cause of missions.

# PART FIVE

# The Doctrines of Salvation

---

This section recounts the blessings of salvation which the Lord Jesus procured for sinful man. Paul declares that Christ "is made unto us wisdom, and righteousness, and sanctification, and redemption" (1 Cor. 1:30). This is but a partial catalog of the benefits our Saviour made available to the people of God.

The following chapters deal with several doctrines of soteriology. The saving work of Christ altered man's state, his standing before God, and his entire spiritual outlook. Each chapter has its particular approach and emphasis. Yet a crimson cord runs throughout the section: the blood of Christ, outpoured on Calvary, is man's only plea. Whether the theme be atonement, redemption, regeneration, or justification, one cannot escape the fact that the cross of Christ is man's refuge from the storm of impending wrath, the basis of his change of condition from death to life, the ground of his eternal confidence and the certainty of his entrance into heaven. No wonder the apostle proclaimed: "For I determined not to know anything among you, save Jesus Christ, and him crucified" (1 Cor. 2:2).

Closely allied with Calvary is the empty tomb. Crucifixion was followed by resurrection. The Father placed His seal forever upon the perfect work of the Son. The work of reconciliation which Christ came to accomplish is completed: He arose from the dead. The contemplation of His utterly selfless achievement for a race at enmity with God should drive us once more to our knees in grateful adoration and homage: "Thou art worthy . . . for thou wast slain, and hast redeemed us to God by thy blood out of every kindred, and tongue, and people, and nation" (Rev. 5:9).

# 26

## Atonement

---

"Christ died for our sins according to the scriptures" (1 Cor. 15:3).

Atonement for sin is at the heart of the gospel. This teaching, however, has often been misunderstood or misinterpreted. This is tragic, for apart from the atonement our Saviour wrought upon the cross, man is hopelessly lost in sin and doomed to eternal separation from God.

The apostle Paul believed that the doctrine of the atonement is essential, and includes it in his classic definition of the gospel in the early verses of 1 Corinthians 15. Despite this, men have tried to evade its implications or at any rate to weaken the force of its impact upon the human heart.

How have they done this? By promulgating "theories" of the atonement which, although they contain elements of truth, are dangerous if not deadly because of their wrong emphases. In almost every instance these "theories" either overlook or deny the basic element in the atonement without which the doctrine loses its real meaning. Beware of these subtle, but soul-destructive devices of men.

One such "theory" asserts that Christ's death on Calvary is "atoning" in that it exerts a "moral influence" upon the spiritually sensitive soul. Man learns of the unselfish suffering of

Jesus and is thereby prompted to emulate the example of the Master. It is true that our Lord left us an example of patience in suffering (1 Peter 4:1). But to make this secondary implication of Calvary primary is to vitiate the Scriptures. On the cross Jesus did far more than teach us unselfish suffering. He atoned for our sins.

Another suggestion is that the blood of Christ shed upon the cruel tree is a spiritual "blood-transfusion" for the Christian, who in turn must pour out his life "redemptively" for others. Do not be misled into thinking that this is the heart of the atonement. Of course the believer has received life as the result of Jesus' death; of course he must live devotedly and unselfishly for others. But this is not the connotation of the text: "Christ died for our sins according to the scriptures."

## A. The Meaning of Christ's Atonement.

Three principles underlie the atonement. These are closely related to, and associated with, the fact of sin.

1. *The principle of "covering."* The blood of Jesus Christ, outpoured upon the cross, covers the believer's sins. Apart from the Saviour's shed blood one's sins stand naked, open, exposed to the displeasure, judgment and wrath of God. But the blood serves as a covering. To be "under the blood," or "beneath the cross of Jesus," is to be in a place of complete security.

2. *The principle of reconciliation through expiation, i.e. through payment of the penalty.* The word "atonement" is used only once in the King James version of the New Testament—"our Lord Jesus Christ, by whom we have now received the atonement" (Rom. 5:11). The literal meaning of the word used here is "reconciliation." The sinner was estranged from his Creator. The visitation of judgment upon God's dearly beloved Son and the satisfaction rendered to divine justice solved the problem of estrangement. This re-

stored the broken divine-human relationship, bringing about perfect reconciliation.

3. *The principle of "substitution."* Christ died, not as a martyr for some "cause," nor as a religious enthusiast, nor merely as a prophet who sealed his testimony with his blood, but as the sinners' substitute. He died "for our sins." He died in our room and stead. Someone had to die the death we deserved. In loving compassion He experienced the lethal stroke. "But he was wounded for our transgressions, he was bruised for our iniquities: the chastisement of our peace was upon him; and with his stripes we are healed" (Isaiah 53:5).

Substitutionary, vicarious atonement: this is what the Bible teaches.

This is the sinner's only plea.

That Christ the Saviour died for me.

## B. The Old Testament Concept of Atonement.

Christ died for our sins "according to the scriptures." Speaking generally, the whole Old Testament sacrificial, priestly system was a foreshadowing of the saving ministry of Christ. The principles already discussed are delineated in the sacrificial worship of the Hebrews. The prefiguration in the Old Testament helps us to understand more fully the significance of Christ's death.

Two illustrations demonstrate this truth:

1. *The Jewish Passover.* (Study Exodus 12:3-14 in the light of 1 Cor. 5:7.) A lamb without blemish was slain. The blood was applied to the two sideposts and the upper doorpost of the house. And God said: "I will pass through the land of Egypt this night, and will smite all the first-born in the land of Egypt . . . and when I see the blood, I will pass over you."

The safety of the Israelites depended solely upon the shedding and application of the lamb's blood and their position beneath its covering. The parallel is obvious. The blood shed on the cross, applied in heaven, and accepted by saving faith, is one's guarantee of entrance into the company of the redeemed.

Notice carefully: it was not the character of the Jews that saved them from destruction; it was the blood of the lamb. "Christ our passover is sacrificed for us" (1 Cor. 5:7). Neither *conduct* nor *character* saves us; the blood of the Lamb of God "taketh away the sin of the world" (John 1:29). When will the proud heart of man confess this and fall in adoration at the feet of the Son of God, who alone is the believer's Surety, Covering, Security and Peace?

2. *The Jewish Day of Atonement.* (Study carefully Leviticus 16, which describes this in detail.) Notice the repeated and intentional use of the words "sin offering" and "atonement." The high priest slew the sacrificial animal as an offering for sin, entered the holy place of the tabernacle "within the vail before the mercy seat," and there sprinkled the blood in the presence of the Lord. By this act the blood covered the sins of the nation. The ideas of "imputation" and "representation" are both important. The sins of the people were transferred to the animal victim, "put to its account," "reckoned" to it; the high priest was the nation's chosen representative in the atoning process.

How great is our amazement that the Lord Jesus is both sacrifice and priest. He is the Lamb of God. His blood was shed for sin. He is today our great High Priest at the right hand of God in the holy of holies, applies the blood and pleads the merits of His wounds on our behalf.

## C. THE UNIQUENESS OF CHRIST'S ATONEMENT.

For two reasons the atonement consummated by our Savior is totally unique:

1. Because it is the only valid method of dealing with the problem of sin. "Without shedding of blood is no remission" (Heb. 9:22). Man in his stubborn rebellion against God may look upon this teaching as revolting But humble hearts, who

realize something of the infinite holiness of God and the awful depths of sin, rejoice that our heavenly Father has conceived and provided a perfect remedy in the saving death of His Son. The rejection of this truth means the denial of God's revelation.

2. Because it differs even from its Old Testament prototype. (Study Hebrews 8 and 9.) Christ has "obtained a more excellent ministry" than that of the ancient priesthood, "by how much also he is the mediator of a better covenant, which was established upon better promises" (Heb. 8:6). The Old Testament priest shed the blood of an animal; Christ shed His own precious blood. The Hebrew priest made atonement first for his own sins and then for the sins of the nation; the sinless Christ needed no personal atonement, but offered His own blood for the iniquities of the human race. No other avenue leads to glory, no other road points the way to heaven. "The way of the cross leads home."

## D. THE FINALITY OF CHRIST'S ATONEMENT.

The Hebrew priest entered into the holiest of all every year. The sacrifice on the Day of Atonement was an annual celebration. Christ offered Himself only once. His one offering was adequate to atone for sin forever. "Now once in the end of the world hath he appeared to put away sin by the sacrifice of himself" (Heb. 9:26). Note three things:

1. The sins of believers prior to Calvary were "covered" by the blood of animal sacrifices, covered until the Lamb of God shed His precious blood for the sins of all believers, past, present, and future. When our blessed Lord cried out on the cross, "It is finished," He was not simply declaring that His human life was ended. Rather, the final sacrifice now had been made. Ultimate expiation for sin now became a fact in history.

2. Any effort to substitute another medium of salvation is contrary to the mind of God; it is a denial of the revelation of the Almighty, and a defiance of His eternal purpose in Christ

Jesus. Our Saviour "washed us from our sins in his own blood" (Rev. 1:5). Calvary is the one altar of atonement. Seek no other.

3. The "once for all" aspect of Christ's sacrifice looks toward the future. Any "repetition" of Calvary, bloodless or otherwise, no matter who tries to celebrate it, or under what mystic circumstances it is performed, is a blasphemous refusal to accept Christ's atonement as eternally complete.

## E. Appropriation of the Benefits of Christ's Atonement.

The atonement which Christ wrought upon the tree was in the mind of God from all eternity. There God demonstrated His inscrutable wisdom and unfathomable love. At Calvary the Creator stooped in infinite mercy to the needs of a sinful race. (See Eph. 2:4-7.)

The question arises, "How may I be sure that Christ's offering for sin was for me?" Understanding a general principle is one thing; making it practical, individual and personal is another.

God declares that the determining factor is one's relationship to Christ. Hear the Word of salvation; open your heart to the Lord Jesus; acknowledge Him as the Son of God whose blood atoned for your sin, and accept Him as your Saviour. One receives the benefits of Christ's atonement through faith. (See John 1:12; 3:16; 5:24; 14:6; Eph. 2:8.)

# 27

# *Redemption*

---

Calvary is central in the divine plan of salvation. A beautiful gem, it has many facets. Each facet represents an aspect of the work of Christ on the cross. Each sparkles with a luster peculiarly its own. One of these facets is redemption.

Christians should study the doctrine of redemption for two reasons because:

1. Redemption is a vital part of God's revelation concerning His eternal purposes for man. He "redeemeth thy life from destruction" (Ps. 103:4). Man must seek to understand what God has done for him in rescuing his soul from the pit.

2. Too much loose thinking exists concerning redemption. The act of redeeming is a precise, technical transaction. It involves parties, prices, payments. Men have sought to convert the term into one of vague, pale sentimentality. "Redemptive living" is a phrase often but falsely applied to a life of generous, sacrificial love. Such a life may be commendable, but it is not "redemptive."

A. THE CONCEPT OF REDEMPTION.

The English word itself is derived from the Latin, "a buying back." This is the terminology of the market place. A person, perhaps originally the possession of the purchaser, is presently under the control of someone else. He has, for example, become a slave. As such he is in a position, or condition, which requires the payment of a price if the ownership is to be transferred. When the price is paid his position is changed. The act of payment, which is not a pious attitude but a definite transaction, is known as "redemption." Bible illustrations of this usage of the word abound.

1. The firstborn of the Jews, the Lord informed Moses, were to be dedicated sacrificially as a token of thanksgiving for their deliverance from Egypt. They were not to be offered up, but were to be "redeemed" (Ex. 13:15). Animal sacrifices were the price of their liberty. Redemption was complete when the animal was offered.

2. A maidservant, "if she please not her master, who hath betrothed her to himself," was not to be sold unto a strange nation, but on the payment of a price could be "redeemed," i.e. bought back by the father who originally sold her. (See Ex. 21:7,8.)

3. God chose the Levites to serve in connection with the sanctuary. They were substituted for the firstborn of Israel. The additional firstborn in the other tribes were relieved from service by the act of redemption, the payment of a price, in this instance five shekels per person. (See Num. 3:46-51.)

4. Boaz "redeemed" his right to a field. The redemption was duly advertised and carried out in formal fashion through certain definite acts including the payment of the proper price. (See Ruth 4:7.)

In every Biblical instance where redemption is involved there is no vagueness. The act is always a well defined, legitimately executed transaction.

B. The Condition of Men Which Requires Redemption.

Man belongs to God by creation. At the Fall he entered into a position of bondage and he is now by nature a slave. Until he is set free he is under a harsh and cruel taskmaster. This

bondage is often mentioned, and variously described in the
Bible as bitter, ruthless, and enduring. Sin is the master whose
whiplash the slave is made to feel. Man's predicament is emphasized by the curse of the law and issues in death. Paul
writes: "Ye were the servants of sin" (Rom. 6:17). This is an
echo of Jesus' words: "Whosoever committeth sin is the servant of sin" (John 8:34). And "the wages of sin is death"
(Rom. 6:23).

### C. The Channel of the Believer's Redemption.

1. *Redemption begins and ends with God and is all of grace.*
David calls the Lord his strength and his Redeemer (Ps. 19:
14). God speaks through Isaiah: "All flesh shall know that I
the Lord am thy Saviour and thy Redeemer, the mighty One
of Jacob" (Isa. 49:26). Job declares prophetically: "I know
that my redeemer liveth, and that he shall stand at the latter
day upon the earth" (Job 19:25). Yes, it is God who redeems!
(See also Ps. 34:22; 130:7,8.)

Nothing brings to the sinner a greater sense of confidence
than the knowledge that the redemptive benefits which flow
from Calvary have their origin, not in the guilty, unreliable
heart of man, but in the loving heart of God; not in the labor
of men's hands, but in the work of our Lord Jesus.

2. *Redemption is by Christ.* "But of him are ye in Christ
Jesus, who of God is made unto us wisdom, and righteousness,
and sanctification, and redemption" (1 Cor. 1:30). He has "redeemed us from the curse of the law, being made a curse for
us" (Gal. 3:13). In Christ "we have redemption through his
blood" (Eph. 1:7).

The goal of the Saviour's incarnation was the redemption of
man. "But when the fulness of the time was come, God sent
forth his Son, made of a woman, made under the law, To
redeem them that were under the law, that we might receive
the adoption of sons" (Gal. 4 4,5). Calvary saw the transaction completed. Christ "gave himself for us, that he might

redeem us from all iniquity" (Tit. 2:14). The divine promise "I will ransom them from the power of the grave; I will redeem them from death" (Hos. 13:14) was perfectly fulfilled at Golgotha.

## D. THE COST OF THE BELIEVER'S REDEMPTION.

Redemption's cost was of staggering proportions. Sin had permeated every area of man's life. It brought him into utter and abject slavery. This bondage extended to all men. Thus the problem of redeeming individuals from the effects of sin as well as buying back the race of men was of colossal dimensions. The potential redemption of all men from bondage demanded a price commensurate with human depravity. In the wisdom and compassion of God the price was available. Nothing but the life-blood of His Son would suffice. This was the price of our redemption. "Forasmuch as ye know that ye were not redeemed with corruptible things, as silver and gold. . . . But with the precious blood of Christ, as of a lamb without blemish and without spot" (1 Pet. 1:18,19).

Four truths need to be emphasized concerning this payment price:

1. The blood, as it coursed through Christ's veins, did not redeem us. The blood, outpoured in death and applied in the holiest of all, is the basis of our redemption. This distinction must be pressed, for many are led astray by incorrect teaching at this point.

2. The blood of Christ is of inestimable value: able to meet the need, valid in the eyes of God, and dear to the believer's heart.

3. The sacrificial lamb had to be perfect, "without blemish." Our blessed Lord met the requirements: the physical, moral, and spiritual aspects of His life were entirely above reproach.

4. It was as a "ransom" from sin and its dread consequences that He laid down His life. Mark 10:45 and 1 Tim. 2:6 make

this clear. His blood sacrifice bought the captive and brought him back to God.

## E. THE COMPLETION OF THE BELIEVER'S REDEMPTION.

The payment price has been forever paid. The spirits of believers are eternally and securely redeemed. The possession has already been purchased. Yet the Scriptures often refer to our redemption as future. "And grieve not the Holy Spirit of God, whereby ye are sealed unto the day of redemption" (Eph. 4:30). We are "waiting for the adoption, to wit, the redemption of our body" (Rom. 8:23). When certain events take place, our Lord declared, men are to look up and lift up their heads, "for your redemption draweth nigh" (Luke 21:28).

No contradiction exists between the passages of Scripture which speak of redemption as past and future. The references to the future relate to the bodily redemption of believers. The price has been paid once for all. Yet we are still in the flesh. We "groan within ourselves, waiting . . ." (Rom. 8:23). These bodies of ours are still tabernacles of clay, susceptible to suffering and decay. They still groan under the pressure of the curse pronounced upon Adam and his seed. But they live in hope. At Christ's appearing their redemption, already potentially achieved, will be consummated. The children of God will put on incorruption. Their vile bodies will be changed. They will be clothed in the flesh of immortality. Anguish and pain will be gone eternally.

This is the "redemption of the body" for which we inwardly yearn.

## F. THE CONSEQUENCE OF THE BELIEVER'S REDEMPTION.

1. Once we belonged to Satan; now we belong to God. This is a comforting truth. Paul asserts that Christians are not their own. "Ye are bought with a price" (1 Cor. 6:20). What a

stupendous price it was! The Lord Himself has bought us. (See 2 Peter 2:1, in which it is suggested that a denial of this redemptive work of Christ is a "damnable heresy.")

2. Life's supreme duty is to glorify the One who bought us (see 1 Cor. 6:20): to magnify Him in thought, word, and deed, and to make His name known and glorious to the ends of the earth.

Let us all ceaselessly praise our Father in heaven that Christ paid it all, that our redemption is sure, that our bodies will soon be transformed into the likeness of the Saviour's glory. Let us in the Spirit seek to glorify our Redeemer daily, hourly, and in every aspect of life.

# 28

# *Repentance*

---

A doctrine of the Bible largely neglected today is that of repentance. Much gospel preaching seems to overlook the truth that repentance is essential to salvation. The Bible teaches that no man can be saved, regenerated, and justified without repentance. Repentance does not earn salvation or forgiveness. But it does put a man in a position in which God, on the ground of the work and merits of the Lord Jesus Christ, is free to pardon his sins and to make him a son of God.

## A. The Importance of Repentance.

No portion of the New Testament neglects repentance. The Gospels, the Acts of the Apostles and the Epistles all stress it. Even a superficial study of God's Word brings to light the importance of the teaching.

1. *The Gospels.* Here repentance is often emphasized. "In those days came John the Baptist, preaching in the wilderness of Judaea, And saying, Repent ye" (Matt. 3:1,2). "From that time Jesus began to preach, and to say, Repent" (Matt. 4:17). "And they (the disciples) went out, and preached that men should repent" (Mark 6:12). Jesus "said unto them; Thus it is written, and thus it behooved Christ to suffer, and to rise from the dead the third day: And that repentance and remis-

sion of sins should be preached in his name among all nations, beginning at Jerusalem" (Luke 24:46,47). Surely if our Lord and His associates proclaimed the doctrine so zealously, we too should declare it.

2. *The Acts of the Apostles.* After Christ's ascension the apostles faithfully proclaimed the same message. "Then Peter said unto them, Repent, and be baptized every one of you in the name of Jesus Christ for the remission of sins, and ye shall receive the gift of the Holy Ghost" (Acts 2:38). "And the times of this ignorance God winked at; but now commandeth all men everywhere to repent" (Acts 17:30). "Testifying both to the Jews, and also to the Greeks, repentance toward God, and faith toward our Lord Jesus Christ" (Acts 20:21).

3. *The Epistles.* The apostolic injunctions to the churches echoed the same refrain. "Or despisest thou the riches of his goodness and forbearance and longsuffering; not knowing that the goodness of God leadeth thee to repentance" (Rom. 2:4)? "Now I rejoice, not that ye were made sorry, but that ye sorrowed to repentance: for that ye were made sorry after a godly manner, that ye might receive damage by us in nothing. For godly sorrow worketh repentance to salvation not to be repented of: but the sorrow of the world worketh death" (2 Cor. 7:9-10). "The Lord is not slack concerning his promise, as some men count slackness; but is longsuffering to us-ward, not willing that any should perish, but that all should come to repentance" (2 Peter 3:9).

## B. THE MEANING OF REPENTANCE.

1. Repentance involves a change of mind and implies an alteration of course. What one has been doing he decides to do no more. This means a change of direction and of conduct. Notice the following illustrations:

a. *The parable of the two sons.* "A certain man had two sons; and he came to the first, and said, Son, go work today

in my vineyard. He answered and said, I will not: but after-
ward he repented, and went" (Matt. 21:28,29). The son who
said he would not go changed his mind and went.

b. *The parable of the prodigal son.* The erring son took his
inheritance and spent it riotously. But he "came to himself"
and said, "I will arise and go to my father . . ." (Luke 15:17,
18). Obviously he repented, changed his mind and acted on
his new decision.

c. *The first apostolic sermon.* Peter preached to the assem-
bled people about Christ. His audience did not believe that
Jesus was the Messiah. But before Peter completed his sermon,
the Holy Spirit wrought conviction in their hearts. They asked
the apostle what they ought to do. He replied, "Repent . . ."
He told them that they had to "change their minds" and to
believe that Jesus was the promised Messiah. This they did and
by faith were born into the kingdom.

2. Repentance involves a deep godly sorrow for sin; a man
sees himself as he is. Contrition and humiliation ensue. The
Bible declares that true conviction of sin is accompanied by
sharp remorse and heart sorrow.

David cried out, "I will declare my iniquity; I will be sorry
for my sin" (Psalm 38:18 R.V.). In the parable of the publican
and the Pharisee, Jesus tells us that the Pharisee experienced
no humbling of heart and knew no real contrition. He was
self-righteous. On the other hand the publican bowed his head
to the ground, as it were, "smote upon his breast, saying, God
be merciful to me a sinner." Our Lord says that the publican
went down to his house justified while the Pharisee did not
(see Luke 18:9-14). Our Saviour warns against a lack of repentance. "Woe unto thee, Chorazin! woe unto thee, Bethsaida! for if the mighty works had been done in Tyre and
Sidon, which have been done in you, they had a great while
ago repented, sitting in sackcloth and ashes" (Luke 10:13).
To "sit in sackcloth and ashes" is evidence of a genuine heart

sorrow for sin. One may feign sorrow by such outward signs; but true repentance is always accompanied by godly sorrow for sin.

3. Repentance involves confession of sin to Almighty God, and sometimes to men if the circumstances require it. The Psalmist cried, "I will declare my iniquity" (Psalm 38:18). The prodigal son confessed, "I have sinned against heaven, and before thee" (Luke 15:18). The publican openly acknowledged that he had transgressed God's law: "God be merciful to me a sinner" (Luke 18:13). Ministers and other Christians do not have the right nor the power to forgive sins, yet under certain conditions confession to them may be helpful. Any Christian has the authority to declare to a repentant sinner that his sins are forgiven for Jesus' sake.

4. Repentance involves forsaking one's sin. The repentant sinner hearkens to the command of Jesus: "Go, and sin no more" (John 8:11). The exhortations of the Scriptures are emphatic: "He that covereth his sins shall not prosper: but whoso confesseth and forsaketh them shall have mercy" (Prov. 28:13); "If ye do return unto the Lord with all your hearts, then put away the strange gods and Ashtaroth from among you . . ." (1 Sam. 7:3); "Let the wicked forsake his way, and the unrighteous man his thoughts . . ." (Isa. 55:7).

5. Repentance involves the turning of the sinner to God. God alone can offer pardon and give peace. The apostle Paul stresses this point. The goal of his preaching to the Gentiles was "To open their eyes, and to turn them from darkness to light, and from the power of Satan unto God, that they may receive forgiveness of sins, and inheritance among them which are sanctified by faith that is in me" (Acts 26:18). His efforts were not in vain. To the Thessalonians, for example, he writes: "For they themselves shew of us what manner of entering in we had unto you, and how ye turned to God from idols . . ." (1 Thess. 1:9).

## C. The Consequences of Repentance.

1. *Pardon and forgiveness follow.* "Let the wicked forsake his way, and the unrighteous man his thoughts: and let him return unto the Lord, and he will have mercy upon him; and to our God, for he will abundantly pardon" (Isa. 55:7). "Repent ye therefore, and be converted, that your sins may be blotted out . . ." (Acts 3:19).

2. *The Holy Spirit is given to those who truly repent.* "Repent, and be baptized every one of you in the name of Jesus Christ for the remission of sins, and ye shall receive the gift of the Holy Ghost" (Acts 2:38).

## D. The Call to Repentance.

All the world is faced with the need to repent. Statesmen, scientists, clergymen, economists, and sociologists predict that the future outlook is gloomy for man. Amid decaying cultures, declining standards of morality, and increasing lawlessness practically all men agree that hope for the future rests on a resurgence of spiritual values. The clarion call of the hour is to repentance.

1. *National Repentance.* Nations as nations must turn to God. National sins must be confessed and forsaken. The Psalmist declares: "The wicked shall be turned into hell, and all the nations that forget God" (Psalm 9:17). No nation can escape this ultimate judgment of God unless it repents. This is the call to repentance.

2. *Personal Repentance.* A nation is made up of individuals and constitutes the sum total of all its people. National repentance begins with individual repentance. It must originate in the hearts of God's people, spread to unbelievers, and finally become a mighty, national stream of collective repentance. The individual is the key to the problem. God grant that repentance may begin today in your heart and mine!

# 29

## Faith

Everyone wants salvation. But men try to obtain it in different ways. Some think that they can be saved by their works. They try hard to keep the law and to be good; they believe that giving, doing, and striving will get them into heaven. Others hold that character is determinative and they try to develop this area of life. Their goal is to think good thoughts and to have good morals.

The Bible negates all man's effort to "earn" or "merit" salvation and announces but one way to God. Jesus Christ is the door; the key that unlocks the door is faith. Works, character and thoughts are important; but only one key fits the door— the key of faith.

Martin Luther spoke to the hearts of men when he said that faith alone (*fide sola*) saves. Man is saved by faith plus nothing else. However, lest we overemphasize salvation by faith alone, let us remember that the Bible teaches that saving faith is never alone—it never operates in a vacuum, but is always accompanied by a transformed life. One is saved by faith alone. But true faith is always accompanied by good works.

### A. The Necessity of Saving Faith.

1. The Scriptures emphasize the truth that works will never save. "Therefore by the deeds of the law there shall no flesh

be justified in his sight" (Rom. 3:20). "Knowing that a man
is not justified by the works of the law, but by the faith of
Jesus Christ . . ." (Gal. 2:16). God "who hath saved us, and
called us with an holy calling, not according to our works
. . ." (2 Tim. 1:9).

2. God does not accept any other righteousness than that of
Jesus. The effort to be saved by one's own righteousness never
succeeds. Faith substitutes Christ's righteousness for ours. "But
we are all as an unclean thing, and all our righteousnesses are
as filthy rags; and we all do fade as a leaf, and our iniquities, like
the wind, have taken us away" (Isa. 64:6). "Not by works of
righteousness which we have done, but according to his mercy
he saved us, by the washing of regeneration, and renewing of
the Holy Ghost" (Titus 3:5).

3. The Bible repeatedly stresses the fact that faith and faith
alone will save. "For by grace are ye saved through faith; and
that not of yourselves: it is the gift of God: not of works, lest
any man should boast" (Eph. 2:8,9). The Philippian jailer said,
"Sirs, what must I do to be saved? And they said, Believe on
the Lord Jesus Christ, and thou shalt be saved, and thy house"
(Acts 16:30,31). "But without faith it is impossible to please
him: for he that cometh to God must believe that he is, and
that he is a rewarder of them that diligently seek him." (Heb.
11:6; see also Rom. 3:21; 5:1; Gal. 2:16.)

## B. The Nature of Saving Faith.

An exact description of faith will help one to understand
what God requires for salvation. Some believe that faith is a
leap into the dark; that it is anti-intellectual, contrary to good
reason; and that only the untutored and the credulous possess
it. Faith is far from irrational, and believers are not necessarily
stupid or deceived. What are the three elements of true faith?

1. *Knowledge.* No man can be saved without knowing
something. Faith is not ignorance; it is not closing one's eyes to
the facts. Faith is never afraid to look the truth squarely in the

face. Man is not saved by knowledge but he cannot be saved without it. "So then faith cometh by hearing, and hearing by the word of God," for the Word of God brings knowledge. The converse of this proposition in Romans 10:17 is true. If faith must be preceded by a man's hearing the gospel, then if one does not hear the gospel he cannot have faith. The Word of God must be preached before saving faith can be assured. To be saved men must know that Christ died for them. But the bare knowledge of the historical fact that Christ died for sinners does not save a soul apart from the two steps that follow.

2. *Intellectual acceptance of the fact.* This must follow knowledge. A man must give rational assent to the facts of the gospel. This is an essential element in the pattern of faith. This truth may be illustrated as follows:

a. The devils believe that Jesus is God. They know that He can save men from their sins, but still they are not saved. When Jesus cast out the demons at Gadara, Matthew tells us, "And, behold, they cried out, saying, What have we to do with thee, Jesus, thou Son of God? Art thou come hither to torment us before the time?" (Matt. 8:29). Demons know that Jesus is the Son of God; they know that the judgment is coming; yet they are not saved. In Capernaum an unclean spirit cried out "Saying, Let us alone; what have we to do with thee, thou Jesus of Nazareth? art thou come to destroy us? I know thee who thou art, the Holy One of God" (Mark 1:24). The demon accepted the fact that Jesus was the Holy One of God. He believed but he did not have saving faith.

b. Many men in our Lord's day had knowledge adequate for salvation yet were not saved. A scribe came to our Lord and inquired about the great commandment. Jesus told him that men should love the Lord their God. To this the inquirer gave mental assent. Yet Christ informed him, "Thou art not far from the kingdom of God" (Mark 12:34). He had the facts in his possession and he gave mental assent to the facts but he was still lost; he was outside the kingdom—so near and yet so far. He needed the third element in saving faith.

3. *Personal appropriation.* Mental assent is not enough. The will must be exercised and a decision must be made. This implies action,—spiritual movement toward an object. The person who believes that Christ died for his sins is not saved . . . until he accepts or appropriates Jesus and what He has done. He must lay hold of the Saviour in childlike trust. This is the third element in saving faith. John emphasizes this truth: "But as many as received him, to them gave he power to become the sons of God, even to them that believe on his name" (John 1:12).

## C. THE OBJECT OF SAVING FAITH.

The Scriptures affirm that Jesus Christ is the object of saving faith. We are not only to believe that He is God and that He died for our sins, but we are also to put our confidence in Him. "Jesus answered and said unto them, This is the work of God, that ye believe on him whom he hath sent" (John 6:29). Paul cried out "Testifying both to the Jews, and also to the Greeks, repentance toward God, and faith toward our Lord Jesus Christ" (Acts 20:21).

What we believe about Jesus matters. In the final analysis, however, whether we believe in Him and put our trust in Him determines our everlasting destiny. At the tomb of Lazarus Jesus proclaimed the doctrine of the resurrection. Martha "saith unto him, I know that he shall rise again in the resurrection at the last day" (John 11:24). She told Jesus that she believed in the doctrine of the resurrection. But our Lord refused to stop at this point. He showed her that belief in a doctrine is insufficient. One must go beyond the doctrine and place his trust in a Person. "I am the resurrection, and the life: he that believeth in me, though he were dead, yet shall he live: And whosoever liveth and believeth in me shall never die" (John 11:25,26).

### D. The Need of Faith in the Christian's Life.

No area of the Christian life is divorced from faith. Faith is the source of all other graces, the secret of success in Christian living. The Bible teaches us that it is significant for several reasons:

1. We live by faith. ". . . the life which I now live in the flesh I live by the faith of the Son of God . . ." (Gal. 2:20).

2. We are kept and we stand firm by faith. "Who are kept by the power of God through faith . . ." (1 Peter 1:5). "Well; because of unbelief they were broken off, and thou standest by faith" (Rom. 11:20; see also 2 Cor. 1:24).

3. We resist the devil and overcome him by faith. ". . . because your adversary the devil, as a roaring lion, walketh about, seeking whom he may devour: whom resist stedfast in the faith . . ." (1 Pet. 5:8,9). "Above all, taking the shield of faith, wherewith ye shall be able to quench all the fiery darts of the wicked" (Eph. 6:16).

4. We walk by faith. "And the father of circumcision to them who are not of the circumcision only, but who also walk in the steps of that faith of our father Abraham, which he had being yet uncircumcised" (Rom. 4:12). "For we walk by faith, not by sight" (2 Cor. 5:7).

# 30

# Regeneration

Two major problems confront man. These are:

(1) *The problem of death.* By nature all mankind is dead in trespasses and sins. (See Eph. 2:1; 1 Cor. 15:22.) This problem is solved by the impartation, or implantation of divine life, known as regeneration, the spiritual birth from above.

(2) *The problem of guilt.* By nature and in conduct all mankind is sinful; man has broken the law of God and stands condemned before his Creator (cf. Rom. 3:10). Justification by faith apart from the deeds of the law is the solution to this problem.

This chapter and the next will deal with these two cardinal themes. Understand them and rejoice in God's complete provision for your spiritual needs.

The average person believes that man obtains eternal life (if such life seems desirable or available) through his character and deeds. Utilizing the wood of character and the nails of conduct, he seeks to construct a ladder to reach to the gates of glory. His effort originates below, in his own will and purposes, and it cannot succeed.

Life eternal originates above in the loving heart of God. It comes through regeneration, not reformation. It is given, not earned. Without it every man, no matter how kind, attractive or personable he may be, is dead, utterly devoid of the life of God. He exists, but he has no spiritual life. When regenerated, however, he begins to live. Now he knows that he is a child of God, that he will live forever in the presence of God, and that even while he remains on earth abundant life is his priceless possession.

## A. The Necessity of Regeneration.

1. All mankind since the Fall is by nature "born into the wrong family." Hence man must be "born again," "born from above" to enter the family of God. Our Lord denounced His enemies: "Ye are of your father the devil, and the lusts of your father ye will do" (John 8:44). This is no mere Oriental figure of speech. It is a sobering truth. No one who rejects the Saviour can rightly claim God as Father.

2. A widespread teaching today is that everyone is a child of God. This is not true. God is the Creator of all men, and to that extent He may conceivably be called their "Father." (See Acts 17:28.) Only through regeneration does one become an heir of God.

Beware of the attractive but dangerous theory known as the "universal fatherhood of God and brotherhood of man." If God is already the Father of all men, why bother to proclaim the gospel to them? Actually mankind is divided into two groups: those who have been born into the family of God, and those still out of God's family. The longing of all believers should be to win those outside of Christ to the benefits of God's family and home.

## B. The Nature of Regeneration.

Regeneration is the impartation of divine life to the believer's soul. A supernatural intervention, it marks the commencement of one's eternal life. A baby must be born before it can walk and talk. So a man must have the life of God in his heart before he can walk worthily and testify effectively for his Lord. Perhaps this is the reason Jesus compares the new birth with a natural birth. The bases of the comparison are patent:

1. In natural birth the parents, not the baby, are the responsible agents. In regeneration God, not the sinner, takes the initiative and becomes one's Father in heaven. "Of his own will begat he us" (James 1:18).

2. At birth a child enters a new sphere of existence. He must accommodate himself to new conditions. In like manner the one who is "reborn" enters a new realm of life. What he previously loved he now hates; the sins he relished he now finds distasteful. He has a new set of values, a fresh hope and confidence, and an altered horizon. (See 2 Cor. 5:17.) He has a new name. Henceforth he bears the name of his Saviour: he is a Christian.

## C. THE BASIS OF REGENERATION.

The new birth is not a solitary, unrelated act on God's part. If one is to be born from above, he must give assent to a message. This message describes the perfect work of Christ on the sinner's behalf.

1. The relationship between man's regeneration and the saving ministry of the Lord Jesus is often suggested in the Scriptures. For example: 1 Peter 1:17-23. On the basis of "the precious blood of Christ" (v. 19) one is "born again" (v. 23). The doctrines of atonement and regeneration must never be divorced. The blood of the Lamb of God, shed for the remission of sins, is the basis of the birth from above. No wonder Paul was determined to know nothing among the Corinthians "save Jesus Christ, and him crucified" (1 Cor. 2:2): he wanted his hearers to be born again. (See also Titus 3:5.)

2. Personal faith in Christ as Redeemer is the condition of regeneration. "But as many as received him, to them gave he power to become the sons of God, even to them that believe

on his name: Which were born . . ." (John 1:12,13). Receive Christ, believe in Him, and be born from above.

## D. THE PROCESS OF REGENERATION.

How does the impartation of life actually take place in the soul? Our Lord taught Nicodemus that two agencies are involved in regeneration, water and the Spirit. (See John 3:5.)

1. The Spirit is the third Person of the Trinity, who works in regenerating power upon the human heart, imparts life in place of spiritual death, and turns men from sin to God. Notice the juxtaposition of the phrases "washing of regeneration, and renewing of the Holy Ghost" (Titus 3:5).

2. The "water" does not refer to baptism. It may relate to the total cleansing, regenerative process. Some passages of Scripture seem to indicate that it may be the Word of God. James writes, for example, that God begat us "with the word of truth" (James 1:18). Peter insists that believers are born again "by the word of God, which liveth and abideth for ever" (1 Pet. 1:23). The use of water as an illustration of the Word of God is suggested in such a passage as John 15:3, but more particularly in Eph. 5:26, where Paul writes of the cleansing of the church "with the washing of water by the word."

The impartation of life takes place thus: The Holy Spirit of God, utilizing the holy Word of God, exalts the holy Son of God as Saviour. Then the Spirit woos, convicts and converts the sinner, regenerating him and causing him, through saving faith in Christ, to enter the family of God.

## E. THE RESULTS OF REGENERATION.

1. The new birth makes one a child of God. All the resources of his heavenly Father are now and forever available to him. (See John 1:12; Gal. 3:26; Rom. 8:16,17.)

2. The new birth makes one a new creation (see 2 Cor.

5:17; Gal. 6:15; Eph. 2:10), and gives one a new heart. (See Ezek. 36:26.)

3. The new birth causes believers to become "partakers of the divine nature" (2 Pet. 1:4). They are "new men" in Christ. (See Eph. 4:24; Col. 3:10.)

4. The new birth paves the way for victory over the world. (Study 1 John 3:9; 5:4,18.)

Some Christians know the precise hour of their birth from above. Others, who were brought up in the nurture of the Lord, do not know the exact time of their regeneration. In whichever of these groups one may be, if he trusts Christ as Saviour, he may rejoice in the witness of the Spirit (see Rom. 8:16), and know that he is a child of God.

# 31

# Justification

Regeneration and justification are closely related doctrines. Regeneration has to do with the change which takes place in the believer's heart; justification concerns the change in his standing before God. Regeneration refers to the impartation of life; justification to his acceptance as righteous in the eyes of God. Regeneration is the divine answer to the problem of spiritual death; justification is the divine answer to the problem of spiritual guilt.

If one understands these doctrines he will appreciate the Reformation emphasis upon the gospel of the grace of God. No man is saved by "works of righteousness," by pilgrimages, fasts, penance, or other religious rites; justification by faith, apart from works, makes possible the believer's entrance into glory.

The terms used in describing regeneration have to do with the issues of life and death; those used in describing justification, with legal, judicial issues.

A. THE INDISPENSABILITY OF JUSTIFICATION BY FAITH.

1. *The human predicament.* God is holy; man is sinful. A holy God will have no fellowship with one whose soul is

stained with sin. Between the righteous Creator and the guilty sinner a great gulf is fixed. (See Isa. 59:2.)

2. *The human effort to bridge the gulf.*

a. Man seeks to construct a bridge of character; surely, he reasons, if his character is fine and strong, he will be admitted to the presence of God. But such a bridge is far too short to reach the gates of heaven.

b. Or man tries to span the void created by sin with the bridge of conduct. He hopes that he may be saved by his deeds of goodness or mercy or love. But the bridge of conduct is a bridge of sighs: it cannot bear the sinner's weight to Heaven. (Study Rom. 3:28; Gal. 2:16; Eph. 2:9; Tit. 3:5.)

3. *The divine bridge.* Where every human bridge failed God stepped in and provided the bridge of justification by faith alone. All man-made devices to reach God are futile, inadequate, impotent. Justification by faith is the one indispensable way of restoring the guilty sinner to the heart and home of God.

## B. The Nature of Justification by Faith.

Justification is a legal act, originating in the loving will of God, on the basis of which the believer is pardoned and declared righteous in God's sight. The act relates to the sending of Christ Jesus, the Son of God, into the world to bear the sinner's guilt and death and to bring him back to God.

Three illustrations explain the doctrine:

1. *A bridge.* Justification by faith, it has already been intimated, resembles a bridge. (Study Rom. 3:21-31.)

a. *The architect.* God, not man, created the bridge. The construction was entirely of His own will and by His grace. "Being justified freely by his grace . . ." (Rom. 3:24a). Because this is true the eternal stability and the perpetual validity of the bridge are guaranteed. The structure will not collapse when the storms of adversity sweep across it. It is solid, sure, enduring. The Almighty brought it into being. (See Rom. 8:33.)

b. *The foundation.* The rock upon which the bridge stands is Calvary. God justifies the sinner, accepts him as "just," or righteous, only on the ground of Christ's atoning work upon the cross. The salvation which our Saviour wrought makes it possible for God to "be just, and the justifier of him which believeth in Jesus" (Rom. 3:26). We are declared righteous, pronounced righteous, accepted as righteous "through the redemption that is in Christ Jesus" (Rom. 3:24b).

c. *The approach.* How is one admitted to the bridge of justification? By faith alone. "Therefore we conclude that a man is justified by faith without (i.e. apart from) the deeds of the law." (Rom. 3:28; see Gal. 2:16.) This faith is not vague, mere "spiritual sensitivity." It relates to a Person. God is "the justifier of him which believeth in Jesus" (Rom. 3:26); not in Jesus as a mere teacher, or example, or leader, but as Saviour from sin. Note the emphasis upon His shed blood. (See Rom. 3:25.)

d. *The guarantee.* Christ was "raised again for our justification" (Rom. 4:25). The resurrection of our Lord is the Father's seal of approval upon His atoning death, the guarantee that the justifying transaction at Calvary is acceptable to the Father. The bridge is secure.

2. *Clothing.*

a. Man at best is by nature clothed with spiritual rags. (See Isa. 64:6.) The garments of his righteousness are moth-eaten, corrupt, decaying. This is a fearful indictment, a stern rebuke to human pride.

b. Christ has provided spotless robes of righteousness for those who, by faith, receive them. He exhorts men to procure from Him "white raiment, that thou mayest be clothed, and that the shame of thy nakedness do not appear" (Rev. 3:18).

c. His robes were woven on Calvary. Their warp was His active obedience to the law of God: He obeyed His Father's will in life and in death. Their woof was His passive obedience: He suffered according to the will of God, dying the just for the unjust to bring a lost creation back to God.

d. His robes replace the filthy rags of those who trust Him. God sees believers clad in the robes of the Saviour's righteousness and justifies them on that account.

3. *A law-court.*

a. *Man's guilt.* "All have sinned, and come short of the glory of God" (Rom. 3:23). On trial before the judgment-seat of God, all men are found guilty (cf. Rom. 3:19).

b. *The penalty of guilt.* The inexorable law of the Judge is that sin merits and must receive death (see Rom. 6:23), eternal separation from God. The character of God as just and of His law as righteous are at stake here. "The soul that sinneth, it shall die" (Ezek. 18:4).

c. *The divine Substitute.* For the sin of man someone must die. In the mercy of God Another takes the sinner's place and receives the death stroke which is the sinner's due. This Substitute is Christ. Every man must either accept the penalty his own sin merits, i.e. death; or accept the death of Christ on his behalf and be justified, i.e. declared righteous by a holy Judge.

Notice that the phrase "put to one's account" is used in connection with the doctrine of justification. This is "imputation" (cf. Rom. 4:22-24). The sin of the believer was imputed to Christ on Calvary, for he "bare our sins in his own body on the tree" (1 Pet. 2:24); the righteousness of Christ is imputed to the believer, and he is thus "accepted in the beloved" (Eph. 1:6).

## C. JUSTIFICATION AND WORKS.

1. Justification by faith alone apart from the deeds of the law is the heart of the gospel. But at this point someone may say: "Yes, but in the epistle of James the opposite teaching seems to be set forth. What is one to believe after all?"

The questioner has in mind such verses as these: "Was not

Abraham our father justified by works, when he had offered
Isaac his son upon the altar?" "Ye see then how that by works
a man is justified, and not by faith only" (James 2:21,24).

At first glance this seems to be a denial of the teaching of
justification by faith alone. A careful reading of the entire
passage, however, indicates that James is not in disagreement
with Paul. The "faith" which James has in mind and which he
insists cannot save a man is that described in verse 19: "the
devils also believe, and tremble." "Faith" here is intellectual
apprehension of truth. The devils have faith that there is one
God. The mere recognition of the reality of truth does not
save devils; nor will it save a man.

The faith that saves goes beyond the head to the heart and
will. It produces results which glorify God. Works are the
certain guarantee that faith is genuine; they are the inevitable
fruit of true faith. When James writes that "by works a man
is justified" he means that unless there are works the "faith"
is dead. It is not the genuine article after all. James does not
substitute works for faith; he insists that works must be present as a demonstration of the reality of faith.

In one's life there is either a corpse, a work-less "faith" that
is dead; or Siamese twins, faith and works. It is faith alone that
justifies. But one must be sure that works are present as a con-
comitant, a test, a proof that the faith is what it purports to
be, a total commitment of mind, heart and will to the Saviour.

2. The apostle Paul illustrates vividly the relationship between justification and works. He writes: "Abraham believed
God, and it was counted unto him for righteousness." "Faith
was reckoned to Abraham for righteousness. How was it then
reckoned? when he was in circumcision, or in uncircumcision?
Not in circumcision, but in uncircumcision. And he received
the sign of circumcision, a seal of the righteousness of the
faith which he had yet being uncircumcised" (Rom. 4:3,9-11).

The argument here is conclusive. Observe the sequence of
events. Abraham was a man of faith; his faith was reckoned,

imputed, put to his account for righteousness; he was accepted by God. After this he was circumcised. Circumcision was an outward sign or seal of his inward faith. It is absurd to intimate that circumcision made Abraham acceptable with God. Circumcision followed, it did not precede, Abraham's faith.

The application: works of righteousness, ritual, ceremonial —these follow as a logical consequence, but never precede as a necessary condition of one's acceptance with God.

## D. The Results of Justification by Faith.

1. *Assurance of salvation.* The effect of righteousness is "quietness and assurance for ever" (Isa. 32:17).

2. *Peace with God.* "Therefore being justified by faith, we have peace with God through our Lord Jesus Christ" (Rom. 5:1). All enmity between creature and Creator is gone.

3. *Freedom from condemnation.* "Who shall lay anything to the charge of God's elect? It is God that justifieth. Who is he that condemneth?" (Rom. 8:33,34).

4. *Sonship.* "That being justified by his grace, we should be made heirs according to the hope of eternal life" (Tit. 3:7).

5. *Blessings untold.* Romans 5:1-11 is a gold mine of truth. It reveals some of the marvelous blessings which result from justification. Never cease to thank God for His wonderful mercies to the children of His love.

6. *Assurance of glorification.* "And whom he justified, them he also glorified" (Rom. 8:30). Our hope of glory, but more, our certainty of Heaven, depends upon our justification by faith alone.

# 32

## *Assurance*

Christians may be certain of their salvation. The Word of God supplies men with evidence of their redemption. In spite of this fact, not all Christians possess the certainty which should be theirs and which is a logical consequence of the new birth. God has not only redeemed His people; He has also provided for them a profound assurance which they may entertain. "These things have I written unto you that believe on the name of the Son of God; that ye may know that ye have eternal life . . ." (1 John 5:13).

### A. The Meaning of Assurance.

Assurance is the intellectual and spiritual certainty that one belongs to God; that he possesses salvation. The believer KNOWS he is saved so that doubt is excluded and he is able to walk with confidence. The agony which accompanies doubt and the fears which uncertainty breeds vanish before assurance. The triumphant testimony of Paul bespeaks his personal certainty: "for I know whom I have believed, and am persuaded that he is able to keep that which I have committed unto him against that day" (2 Tim. 1:12).

## B. THE SOURCE OF ASSURANCE.

Assurance is an effect of faith, but not every believer who has saving faith has assurance. Those who would make assurance of personal salvation a test of faith are wrong. The Bible does not do this, and the experiences of too many of God's people point up the error of the procedure. Scripture and experience tell us that there is such a thing as weak faith, —faith which is genuine but which has not brought the believer out of the valley of misgivings to the plateau of assurance. The Word of God enjoins: "Let us draw near with a true heart in full assurance of faith . . ." (Heb. 10:22). While assurance is not the present possession of every heart it is attainable, and to experience it is a privilege and a duty which we ought to enjoy.

Assurance springs from a lively faith, a strong faith which the believer should possess. The Scriptures reveal further that righteousness is related to assurance: "And the work of righteousness shall be peace; and the effect of righteousness quietness and assurance for ever" (Isa. 32:17).

## C. THE GROUNDS OF ASSURANCE.

The grounds on which assurance rests are not so much internal as external; not so much subjective as objective. In an age when men are prone to depend upon feeling, emotions, intuition and intangibles, God speaks in objective fashion and points out to men the anchor of assurance to which their souls may be fastened,—an anchor which will hold amid the storms and uncertainties of life. Among the grounds for assurance are:

1. *The unconditional and universal promise of Almighty God.* Jesus declares: "All that the Father giveth me shall come to me; and him that cometh to me I will in no wise cast out" (John 6:37). The invitation goes forth: "And the Spirit and the bride say, Come. And let him that heareth say, Come. And

let him that is athirst come. And whosoever will, let him take the water of life freely" (Rev. 22:17). God is faithful. He will satisfy, as He says, those who come to Him in simple faith.

2. *The love of God.* Because God loves those whom He has purchased by blood and because this love is stronger than death and more powerful than the hosts of darkness, the believer can rest assured that when he believes in Christ he is saved. Paul suggests this in Romans when he asks: "If God be for us, who can be against us?" and continues: "Who shall separate us from the love of Christ? . . . For I am persuaded, that neither death, nor life, nor angels, nor principalities, nor powers, nor things present, nor things to come, nor height, nor depth, nor any other creature, shall be able to separate us from the love of God, which is in Christ Jesus our Lord" (see Rom. 8:31-39).

3. *The perfect finished work of Jesus and His continuous intercession for the believer.* "It is Christ that died, yea rather, that is risen again, who is even at the right hand of God, who also maketh intercession for us" (Rom. 8:34).

4. *The promise of our Lord that none of those who trust in Him shall be lost.* "My sheep hear my voice, and I know them, and they follow me: And I give unto them eternal life; and they shall never perish, neither shall any man pluck them out of my hand" (John 10:27,28).

5. *The witness of the Holy Spirit in the believer's heart.* "And hope maketh not ashamed; because the love of God is shed abroad in our hearts by the Holy Ghost which is given unto us" (Rom. 5:5). "The Spirit itself beareth witness with our spirit, that we are the children of God" (Rom. 8:16).

D. THE AREAS OF ASSURANCE.

1. *Salvation itself.* "Behold, God is my salvation; I will trust, and not be afraid: for the Lord JEHOVAH is my strength and my song; he also is become my salvation" (Isa. 12:2).

Assured that God is truly his salvation, the believer may rest in quietness of spirit and great confidence.

2. *Eternal life.* "These things have I written unto you that believe on the name of the Son of God; that ye may know that ye have eternal life . . ." (1 John 5:13).

3. *Adoption.* When saved we become God's children. The assurance of sonship, or that we have become members of the family of God, is the legitimate heritage of all who believe. "Beloved, now are we the sons of God . . ." (1 John 3:2).

4. *The election of God.* "Knowing, brethren beloved, your election of God" (1 Thess. 1:4). This is a great mystery; but it can be a source of inexpressible comfort to the elect of God.

5. *Vital union with the Lord Jesus and Almighty God.* Every believer becomes a member of the body of Christ and is linked in a vital union with Him. This union should bring assurance to every believer and fill his heart with joy unspeakable. Paul says: "Know ye not your own selves, how that Jesus Christ is in you, except ye be reprobates" (2 Cor. 13:5)? "For we are members of his body, of his flesh, and of his bones" (Eph. 5:30).

E. The Effects of Assurance.

1. The believer should never cease to praise God that the issues of eternity have been lovingly and forever settled.

2. He should walk in love towards his neighbor. Love of one's brother is demonstrable proof that his assurance is well grounded. "We know that we have passed from death unto life, because we love the brethren" (1 John 3:14; see also 1 John 5:1).

3. His testimony to the lost should be with convincing boldness based upon complete assurance. Paul was an excellent example of this sort of witnessing. His faith was unwavering. Therefore he could write to the Thessalonians that his gospel came to them not "in word only, but also in power, and in the Holy Ghost, and in much assurance" (1 Thess. 1:5). To the

very end of his ministry the apostle preached and taught "with all confidence, no man forbidding him" (Acts 28:31).

4. The believer must "hold fast the confidence and the rejoicing of the hope firm unto the end" (Heb. 3:6). He must hold the beginning of his confidence "stedfast unto the end" (Heb. 3:14). He is told: "Cast not away therefore your confidence, which hath great recompence of reward" (Heb. 10: 35).

PART SIX

# The Believer's Life with God

---

The doctrines of salvation introduce man to a new life. They are the door to a changed existence. He who passes through this portal enters the realm of righteousness and everlasting life. "Therefore if any man be in Christ, he is a new creature: old things are passed away; behold, all things are become new" (2 Cor. 5:17).

The new life in Christ is the life "not after the flesh, but after the Spirit" (Rom. 8:4). The heart of the preceding section was Calvary and the resurrection. So the core of this section is the Person and work of the Holy Spirit in one's heart, subsequent to regeneration. Without the Spirit there could be no fellowship with the Father, no consistent God-honoring walk, no growth in grace, no effectual prayer, no knowledge of the will of God, no resistance to the devil, no life on the highest plane.

This section is the watershed of the Handbook. We have opened the pages of the Bible and found in it the inerrant revelation of God; we have portrayed the nature of the unseen powers battling for the destinies of men; we have described the human predicament to which Christ alone is the answer; we have studied the Person and work of Jesus; we have found that in Him alone is life eternal; we have reached the Great Divide. Henceforth our concern must be with the outward evidences of the new inward life. "By their fruits ye shall know them" (Matt. 7:20).

Christianity works. Practical, down to earth, applicable to every human situation and need,—it transforms life in its temporal as well as its eternal context. This section and those which follow outline the relationships, duties and privileges of the Christian on his way to the Celestial City of God.

# 33

## The Believer and His God

---

Once converted, the Christian takes his place as a unit in a complicated social pattern. He sustains relationships to the world of nature and of men. The Bible has much to say about these relationships, for the Holy Spirit has not left His people to stumble in the darkness of ignorance. He has given them precise information as to their conduct in given situations.

But underlying all other relationships, indeed conditioning them, is the believer's relationship to his God. A diver's effectiveness as he labors on the ocean floor is contingent upon the air-hose which connects him with the outer air. The Christian's contacts with men and things exert an influence for truth, purity and goodness only as he maintains contact with God.

This contact is described in the Scriptures as "fellowship." In the first chapter of First John this fellowship is described. At the risk of over-simplification, but for the purpose of clarity, let us designate that fellowship as one of the Lord's "ships" and characterize it as such.

### A. A DESCRIPTION OF THE GOOD SHIP "FELLOWSHIP."

John states explicitly "and truly our fellowship is with the Father, and with his Son Jesus Christ" (1 John 1:3). To have blessed, sweet, enduring communion with God is the precious portion of the saints.

1. *The basis of fellowship.* Fellowship with one's Creator is not a vague, amorphous thing. Not a sentimental reaction of the emotions to mystic stimuli, it is a definite contact with God based upon two facts of history.

a. *The incarnation of Christ.* The first verse of First John makes this clear. John has heard, seen, and handled the Word of life. He bears witness concerning the manifested, audible, visible, tangible, incarnate life of God in Christ.

b. *Atonement through the shedding of Christ's precious blood.* This is suggested in 1 John 1:7: "we have fellowship one with another" as we walk in the light, "and the blood of Jesus Christ his Son cleanseth us from all sin."

2. *The beauty of fellowship.* Fellowship with the Father is a holy, happy realization of the nearness and love of God. It is communion with the Almighty; the enjoyment of His person and presence, a vital entering into one-ness with Him; a sharing of the divine life, an intimacy of discourse with God; a refuge from the storms of life, a release from strain, a relaxation from tension, a rest from the spiritual heat and burden of the day, a repose from the weariness and frustration of existence; an entrance into the privacy of one's closet with the knowledge that God is there.

3. *The threat to fellowship.* One divine ship cannot be wrecked—the Christian's "sonship." When born again into God's family one cannot be "unborn." Not so with fellowship. This may be broken. Therefore every believer should understand the teaching of God's Word on this theme.

## B. Dangers Which Threaten "Fellowship."

Knowledge is power. But it is protection also. Because of the hazards along a ship's way light-houses are erected, life-buoys send forth their warning signals, sea-lanes are carefully charted and pilots painstakingly instructed. If one knows the dangers he may well avoid them. The dangers which threaten our "fellowship" are:

1. *The World.* A ship is endangered by the violence of the wind. Storms, hurricanes, tempests, typhoons—these are a constant threat to the vessel. So the world imperils the believer's fellowship with God. Its tinseled delights would drive him from the path of prayer, meditation, and the study of the Word. Its enticing allurements would sweep him away from the blessedness of communion with the Lord. The wind of worldliness howls fiercely at the sails of "fellowship." It beats and rages with diabolical delight. It would fain cause the vessel to founder.

2. *The Flesh.* A ship is endangered too by the lashing of waves. Whipped into fury by the force of the wind, roaring and staggering like a drunken man, the waters leap upon the vessel, eager to engulf and destroy it. So "fellowship" with the Father is in mortal peril at the hands of the flesh. The old Adamic nature insists that its cravings be satisfied illegally and abnormally. "The flesh lusteth against the Spirit, and the Spirit against the flesh" (Gal. 5:17). In the weary process communion with the Lord is interrupted whenever the flesh is allowed to have the upper hand. But thanks be to God that the Holy Spirit, our Paraclete, will always emerge triumphant if only the believer yields to Him full control.

3. *The Devil.* A ship is endangered by submerged rocks and reefs, hidden and unseen enemies of life and limb. "Fellowship" with the Father must keep its watchman in the crow's nest day and night against the wily attacks of the devil, an invisible and exceedingly crafty foe whose delight is to wean believers from the way of communion with God. On guard, child of God, against this shrewd, implacable enemy! As you value the sweetness of your fellowship with the Lord, be on the alert.

## C. The Disaster Which Overtakes "Fellowship."

There is no sadder sight than a wreck at sea. A stately, comely vessel, built for beauty and efficiency, proudly ploughing through the waves, is suddenly struck and overwhelmed. A mighty hole caves in her noble side; she idles listlessly on the hostile flood; she is at the mercy of the current, a helpless mass of wood and steel, a painted image of despair.

O child of God, it is thus with your fellowship with God when you are betrayed by the world's sordid appeal, or by the seeming delights of carnality, or by the fiendish deceptions of the devil. The lovely vessel "Fellowship" is wrecked. It becomes a limp and useless mass. Its glory is gone, its beauty tarnished. It is a shapeless, miserable hulk.

Make no mistake. To yield to sin is to mar one's fellowship with God. Once the heavens seemed open to one's prayers; now they are closed and impenetrable. Once it was a joy to seek the communion of saints in worship; now the sound of the church bell jars one's sensitivities. Once the Bible was an open book, a precious treasure; now it is a dust-stained memento of better days. Once a happy testimony for Christ graced one's lips; now there is a numb but eloquent silence. Once a melody was in the soul; now the song of joy has changed to the discord of regret. "Fellowship" is foundering.

A word of caution here. If one has this hapless experience but finds a sort of nameless, unrepentant joy in it and no restless discontent with his condition, that is proof positive that he has never embarked in the first place upon the ship. His problem is not how to maintain fellowship with God, but how to establish it. His disaster is not a discontinuance of fellowship with God, but a failure to come by faith to the Father through Jesus Christ the Son.

"Out of fellowship with God." What a tragic state! If church members desert the sanctuary and invent excuses for their works of omission, their need is not a series of repeated invitations to "come to church" or to "support the budget." They need to be brought back, if they are truly saved, to a rich, rewarding fellowship with God. A ship at the mercy of the waves will not bring a cargo to port. It must itself first be salvaged.

Remember that sin is the only disaster that can overtake fellowship.

## D. THE DRY-DOCK FOR "FELLOWSHIP."

An astounding thing about God's dealings with his frail and faltering people is that His grace is everlasting. His mercy endureth forever. He is longsuffering and willing to pardon. But His people must do their part.

When "fellowship" with God meets disaster, a heavenly "dry-dock" is at hand,—a place of repair which saints and martyrs through the ages have gratefully frequented. This is still available to all who have been washed in the blood of the Lamb.

1. The dry-dock is the place of *repentance*. The broken portions of the vessel will not be mended until the sinning saint experiences a broken heart before the Lord he has grieved. Godly sorrow and true contrition are conditions which must be met before the vessel "Fellowship" can continue on its way. This means a frank and fearless recognition of fault, a willingness to admit error, a desire to have the matter dealt with squarely and without equivocation. It means a heart melted by the fires of divine love; eyes opened to see the heinousness of the offense; a will wrought upon by the power of the Spirit and humbled beneath the hand of the Father. It means a change of mind, a review of the values of life, a re-thinking of one's conduct, a return to a desire to glorify God alone.

2. The dry-dock is the place of *confession to God*. Repentance produces confession, which is both its logical consequence and the proof of its genuineness. God has made a solemn affir-

mation in His Word concerning this important theme: "If we confess our sins, he is faithful and just to forgive us our sins, and to cleanse us from all unrighteousness" (1 John 1:9). This does not imply that the erring saint is to make a broad, general, mechanical "confession" of sin. It must be a warm, personal, but especially a *definite* confession. The Holy Spirit has convicted him in some specific area. His sorrow outpoured in words must relate to that area, that pet, darling sphere in which his unworthy thoughts or deeds have had their fruition.

3. The dry-dock is the place of *forgiveness*. That is the glory of the text just quoted: "he is faithful and just to forgive." Our faithlessness does not alter God's faithfulness. The arms of His forgiving love are ever extended to those who sense their need and return to Him in repentant confession. "He will have mercy . . . and abundantly pardon" (Isa. 55:7). No wonder Isaiah was exultant!

4. The dry-dock is the place of *restoration*. Part of the beauty of the Psalm of the Shepherd (Psalm 23) is the phrase, "He restoreth my soul." When King David had sinned grievously against God, he cried out in agony, "Restore unto me the joy of thy salvation" (Psalm 51:12). The glory of God's forgiveness is two-fold: He blots out "the handwriting of ordinances that was against us" (Col. 2:14) and removes "our transgressions from us" (Psalm 103:12); but He also restores us to our pristine position of favor and fellowship. The vessel of our communion with Him is not only repaired. It sails once more in the service of the one who is Monarch of the waters.

## E. The Destination of "Fellowship."

Every ship on the high seas has a harbor toward which it heads, a goal upon the attainment of which it will come to rest. Christians who still sojourn on earth in fellowship with the Father know full well that some day the journey will be over. Some day faith will yield to sight, hope to fruition, expectation to realization.

The vessel "Fellowship" will glide in stately fashion into the haven of eternal rest.

This will not mean a dismantling of the ship, however. By no means! Fellowship with the Lord is sweet and inspiring out on the open sea. But when we meet our Saviour it will be inexpressibly sweeter and richer, for we shall see Him face to face. Then there will indeed be nothing between our souls and our Saviour.

# 34

# The Believer's Walk

One's profession of faith in Christ is vain unless it is accompanied by a new walk,—a walk with a new point of departure, a new direction and a new destination.

## A. The Biblical Usage of the Term "Walk."

The word "walk" is mundane. The writers of the Bible commonly use it in two senses: in its customary meaning the word denotes a transition from one place to another; but it is also employed to signify conduct, behavior, or manner of living. In this latter sense the word occurs repeatedly in the Scriptures.

Examples of the second Biblical usage of the word "walk" abound in the Old Testament. The Israelites were warned not to "forget the Lord thy God, and walk after other gods . . ." (Deut. 8:19). Samuel's sons "walked not in his ways, but turned aside after lucre, and took bribes, and perverted judgment" (1 Sam. 8:3). King Amon "walked in all the way that his father walked in, and served the idols that his father served, and worshipped them: And he forsook the Lord God of his fathers, and walked not in the way of the Lord" (2 Kings 21:21,22). A blessing is pronounced upon the man "that walketh not in the counsel of the ungodly" (Psalm 1:1). A man's heart may "walk" after his eyes (Job 31:7). The tongue of the wicked "walketh through the earth" (Psalm 73:9). The heathen "walk in darkness" (Isa. 9:2).

The New Testament writers also employ this usage of the word "walk," as the rest of this chapter will demonstrate.

## B. THE APPROPRIATENESS OF THE TERM "WALK."

The Bible with eminent fitness compares human conduct with a walk and instructs believers as to their personal walk. The appropriateness of this comparison may be seen readily.

1. *Walking is a down-to-earth procedure.* Neither exciting nor dramatic, it calls for slow and steady progress. Instead of soaring to seraphic heights, one remains on *terra firma.* So with the Christian life, which rarely has to do with mountain-top experiences, but generally with the daily, humdrum, commonplaces of life.

2. *Walking involves a starting point.* One must "arise and walk." The Christian walk originates in Christian faith. Without this faith one is totally unable even to commence to walk.

3. *Walking demands the expenditure of effort.* It is one of the most difficult feats a child must perform. It calls for a complicated interplay of muscular reactions. Similarly, the Christian life demands unceasing effort. To live on the highest plane is a feat difficult of accomplishment, demanding complicated spiritual and psychological adjustments.

4. *Walking implies progress.* A believer must not remain static. His is no armchair existence. In the nature of the case he must move forward spiritually or slip backward.

5. *Walking implies a destination.* To walk is not to meander, but to move steadily toward a goal. The Christian's spiritual destination is the City of God.

## C. THE WALK THAT GLORIFIES GOD.

1. The walk of the natural man does not glorify God. "In time past," Paul writes, "ye walked according to the course

of this world" (Eph. 2:2). The unbeliever has motivations, desires, aspirations quite distinct from those of the child of God. His walk is "according to the prince of the power of the air, the spirit that now worketh in the children of disobedience" (Eph. 2:2).

2. The walk of the saved man will glorify God if it is a "worthy" walk, for one is to walk "worthy" of his vocation. (See Eph. 4:1; also Col. 1:10 and 1 Thess. 2:12.) One has been called of God to be His child, a partaker of the divine nature. His walk should reflect the glory and dignity of his call. The Scriptures describe a "worthy" walk in detail.

3. The worthy walk is generically different from the walk of unbelievers. "This I say therefore, and testify in the Lord, that ye henceforth walk not as other Gentiles walk . . ." (Eph. 4:17). The apostle is specific: the behavior of the enemies of Christ is characterized by vanity of mind, darkness of understanding, alienation from God, blindness of heart, callous lasciviousness, and greedy uncleanness. Not so with God's people. Their mode of life should be the opposite of all this. The child of God need not be afraid to be one of God's "peculiar people." His Father in heaven has called him to humility and holiness of heart and life. When he accepted Christ as his Saviour he abandoned his old walk. Buried with Christ by baptism into death, raised from the dead with Him to a new resurrection level, he is now to "walk in newness of life" (Rom. 6:4).

4. The worthy walk reveals certain spiritual characteristics:

a. *Purity.* The believer walks as a child of light. (See Eph. 5:8.) Jesus declared: "I am the light of the world: he that followeth me shall not walk in darkness, but shall have the light of life" (John 8:12). Fellowship with God and with one's brethren in Christ is possible only to those who "walk in the light, as he is in the light." (1 John 1:6,7; see also 1 John 2:11.)

b. *Sincerity.* Having "renounced the hidden things of dishonesty," one must not walk "in craftiness" (2 Cor. 4:2). He walks openly with integrity and frankness, thus honoring God in his conduct.

c. *Obedience*. The believer walks obediently before God. John wrote: "And this is love, that we walk after his commandments. This is the commandment, That, as ye have heard from the beginning, ye should walk in it" (2 John 6). No one is saved by trying to keep God's commandments. But once saved he should strive to walk as an obedient, God-honoring, law-abiding child.

d. *Faith*. "For we walk by faith, not by sight" (2 Cor. 5:7). This is reliance, not upon carnal help or visible aid, but upon the strong arm of the Almighty.

e. *Truth*. The apostle John was a stalwart for the truth. To his spiritual children he wrote: "For I rejoiced greatly, when the brethren came and testified of the truth that is in thee, even as thou walkest in the truth. I have no greater joy than to hear that my children walk in truth" (3 John 3,4).

5. The worthy walk reveals certain outward characteristics. The believer walks:

a. *Honestly*. "The night is far spent, the day is at hand: let us therefore cast off the works of darkness, and let us put on the armour of light. Let us walk honestly, as in the day" (Rom. 13:12,13a). "And that ye study to be quiet, and to do your own business, and to work with your own hands, as we commanded you; that ye may walk honestly toward them that are without" (1 Thess. 4:11,12a). Christian integrity advertises the gospel. Reliability is a Christian grace, part and parcel of a life which magnifies the name of the Lord.

b. *Circumspectly*. "See then that ye walk circumspectly, not as fools, but as wise, Redeeming the time, because the days are evil" (Eph. 5:15,16). The child of God is to "watch his step" because others are watching it. Knowing that the days are evil, he allows no opportunity for doing good to escape him, as a wise and trustworthy servant of God.

c. *Wisely*. "Walk in wisdom toward them that are without, redeeming the time. Let your speech be alway with grace, seasoned with salt, that ye may know how ye ought to answer every man" (Col. 4:5,6).

d. *Lovingly*. "Walk in love, as Christ also hath loved us . . ." (Eph. 5:2). Love is the mainspring of Christian conduct. If one causes his brother to stumble, he is not walking "charitably" (Rom. 14:15). Love for one's neighbor is the result and demonstration of one's love for God.

## D. The Secret of a Worthy Walk.

One may walk steadfastly to the glory of God. Enoch, for example, "walked with God . . . three hundred years" (Gen. 5:22). His walk was well-pleasing to the Lord. "Before his translation he had this testimony, that he pleased God" (Heb. 11:5.)

What is the secret of such a walk? The answer is to "walk in the Spirit," that one may "not fulfil the lust of the flesh" (Gal. 5:16). Yieldedness to the Spirit is the answer. This is complete dependence, not upon mere resolutions or determinations of the will, but upon the indwelling Holy Spirit, who inclines the heart toward the good, walks beside one on the highway and leads him gently home.

# 35

# *Sanctification*

---

When a man accepts Christ as his Saviour he is justified. As we have already indicated, justification is an act of God in which He declares that, insofar as the law is concerned, justice has been satisfied. When God justifies a sinner it means that the relationship of the sinner to Himself is changed. Formerly he was alienated or separated from God by his sins. Now he is accepted as righteous. Justification, therefore, is a legal, objective act occurring outside the individual.

Regeneration, like justification, is instantaneous and occurs only once to last forever. It differs from justification in that it is subjective, and takes place within the heart. But the Christian life does not end with regeneration. Sanctification now begins.

## A. The Nature of Sanctification.

1. *Its definition.* Sanctification is to render productive of holiness or piety. The Oxford Dictionary defines it as "the action of the Holy Ghost in sanctifying or making holy the believer, by the implanting within him of the Christian graces and the destruction of the sinful affections." Obviously, then, the only sign of sanctification is holiness. "Sanctification is the work of God's free grace, whereby we are renewed

in the whole man after the image of God, and are enabled more and more to die unto sin and live unto righteousness."

2. *Its meaning.* The word "sanctification" signifies a "setting apart," a separation. Applied to believers, it means a separation from sin unto God.

In one respect the Christian has already been sanctified. "We have been sanctified through the offering of the body of Jesus Christ once for all" (Heb. 10:10 R.V.). The cross of our Saviour has separated us once for all from the guilt and penalty of sin. But we have not yet been separated from the power of sin. The more usual meaning of sanctification is the process by which the believer becomes separated in this life from the reign of sin.

3. *Its difference from justification and regeneration.* Sanctification is not a "once for all" act but is progressive and continues throughout the life of the believer. Justification relates to what Jesus has already done for us; sanctification is the effect of what He does in us. Justification relates to our standing before God; regeneration relates to our new nature; sanctification has to do with our character and conduct.

## B. The Source of Sanctification.

1. *God the Father.* "And the very God of peace sanctify you wholly; and I pray God your whole spirit and soul and body be preserved blameless unto the coming of our Lord Jesus Christ" (1 Thess. 5:23). "Jude, the servant of Jesus Christ, and brother of James, to them that are sanctified by God the Father, and preserved in Jesus Christ, and called" (Jude 1).

2. *Jesus Christ the Son.* "For both he that sanctifieth and they who are sanctified are all of one: for which cause he is not ashamed to call them brethren" (Heb. 2:11). "Wherefore Jesus also, that he might sanctify the people with his own blood, suffered without the gate" (Heb. 13:12).

3. *The Holy Spirit.* "That I should be the minister of Jesus

Christ to the Gentiles, ministering the gospel of God, that the
offering up of the Gentiles might be acceptable, being sanctified by the Holy Ghost" (Rom. 15:16). "And such were some
of you: but ye are washed, but ye are sanctified, but ye are
justified in the name of the Lord Jesus, and by the Spirit of
our God" (1 Cor. 6:11).

## C. The Purpose of Sanctification.

Two objectives are in view: Negatively, putting off the old
man, removing the principle of evil and destroying its power
in the life; and positively, putting on the new man which is
renewed in righteousness. This makes possible the growth of
the principle of righteousness until it controls all the man,—
his thoughts, feelings and actions, and until he is conformed
to the image of our Lord Jesus Christ.

1. *Putting off the old.* The Bible often refers to the death
of the old man and commands the believer to get away from
the sins which characterized his life before he was re-created
in Christ Jesus. Paul speaks of the principle involved when he
says, "Likewise reckon ye also yourselves to be dead indeed
unto sin, but alive unto God through Jesus Christ our Lord.
Let not sin therefore reign in your mortal body, that ye
should obey it in the lusts thereof" (Rom. 6:11,12). In Colossians he states, "Mortify therefore your members which are
upon the earth; fornication, uncleanness, inordinate affection,
evil concupiscence, and covetousness which is idolatry . . .
But now ye also put off all these; anger, wrath, malice, blasphemy, filthy communication out of your mouth" (Col.
3:5,8).

The apostle weighs the life of sin against the life of righteousness. He stresses the negative aspect of sanctification with
the warning that we are to flee certain sins: "Now the works
of the flesh are manifest, which are these; Adultery, fornication, uncleanness, lasciviousness, Idolatry, witchcraft, hatred,
variance, emulations, wrath, strife, seditions, heresies, Envy-

ings, murders, drunkenness, revellings, and such like: of the which I tell you before, as I have also told you in time past, that they which do such things shall not inherit the kingdom of God" (Gal. 5:19-21). Sanctification demands the elimination of those remnants of the old man which would keep the Christian from being at his spiritual best for Christ.

2. *Putting on the new.* The putting off process is essentially negative. But Christianity has never been a negative faith. Unfortunately some people seem to think that the test of sanctification is the assertion: "I don't go to the movies, I don't dance, I don't smoke, I don't do this and that." This is only one part of the story. We must preserve the negative and warn Christians to refrain from certain activities and amusements which are either dangerous in themselves or hurtful to their testimony. But beyond the negative there is the positive. We remove some things only to replace them with others which excel them as diamonds do gems of glass.

We are to "put on therefore, as the elect of God, holy and beloved, bowels of mercies, kindness, humbleness of mind, meekness, longsuffering; forbearing one another, and forgiving one another if any man have a quarrel against any . . . And above all these things put on charity, which is the bond of perfectness . . . Let the word of Christ dwell in you richly . . . And whatsoever ye do in word or deed, do all in the name of the Lord Jesus, giving thanks to God and the Father by Him" (Col. 3:12,13,14,16,17).

## D. The Evidence of Sanctification.

The sanctified believer enjoys a quality of life which sets him apart from other Christians. That life is the result of the inworking power of the Holy Spirit and manifests itself outwardly in the fruit of the Spirit, which is "love, joy, peace, longsuffering, gentleness, goodness, faith, Meekness, temperance: against such there is no law. And they that are Christ's have crucified the flesh with the affections and lusts" (Gal.

5:22-24). We should note with care that God does not speak of happiness as a fruit of the Spirit. Nowhere are we informed that we shall be free from temptation or exempt from trials, tribulations, difficulties and hardships. Indeed, the fruit of the Spirit suggests these very things. Not one of the graces mentioned becomes a part of our spiritual equipment until it has been perfected by testing. Longsuffering becomes longsuffering only when one has been sufficiently provoked to develop the quality. Faith increases and becomes triumphant when it has engaged in warfare against unbelief and has been strengthened in the conflict.

The fruit of the Spirit comprehends man in all his relationships. Love, joy and peace relate to the inner man. They deal with the Ego or Self. They cannot be manifested externally in life and action unless they first exist internally. Longsuffering, kindness and goodness relate to one's fellow men. Kindness reflects one's attitude of life; goodness his will and heart; and longsuffering his conduct in contact with men. Sanctification thus sets one right with self and others. Faith, meekness and temperance relate to one's God. Meekness suggests the attitude, faith the will and heart, and temperance the course of action. The balanced, sanctified life produces universally right relationships—to self, to others and to God.

## E. AIDS TO SANCTIFICATION.

God has not left His people to their own devices in their struggle for spiritual maturity. He has provided heavenly means to assist us. Our task is to avail ourselves of these means, intelligently and persistently.

1. *The Holy Spirit.* He works in the heart, overcomes the flesh and its corrupting influences, separates the child of God from sin and clothes him with virtue.

2. *The Word of God.* Jesus prayed to the Father: "Sanctify them through thy truth: thy word is truth" (John 17:17). Just as the body needs food for physical growth, so the soul

needs food for spiritual growth in purity and grace. This food the Word affords. Further, as the body must be often cleansed with water, so the spirit needs the cleansing of the Word. Hence our Saviour's statement: "Now ye are clean through the word which I have spoken unto you" (John 15:3).

3. *The means of grace*. Prayer, worship, the edifying ministry of the church, the communion of saints,—each has its part in furthering the believer's sanctification.

4. *Chastisement*. "For they (our fathers) verily for a few days chastened us after their own pleasure; but he for our profit, that we might be partakers of his holiness" (Heb. 12: 10). Christian character, refined in the fires of adversity, often comes forth wondrous gold.

5. *The believer's will*. "Wherefore come out from among them, and be ye separate, saith the Lord . . ." (2 Cor. 6:17). By the voluntary exercise of the will, in submission to the Holy Spirit, the child of God must separate himself from the evil that is in the world. If he would separate himself from sin he must lead a separated life.

## F. The Goal of Sanctification.

1. *The immediate goal*. The objective in one's sanctification in this life is holiness, which is conformity to Jesus Christ. Paul writes that "all things work together for good to them that love God, to them who are the called according to his purpose." But notice what follows: God's purpose for "the called" is that they "be conformed to the image of his Son." (See Rom. 8:28,29.) Holiness is being like Jesus. This is the divine standard for believers. And "this is the will of God, even your sanctification . . ." (1 Thess. 4:3).

2. *The ultimate goal*. No one attains to sinless perfection in this life. But some day the ideal which now we only approximate will be actually attained. "When he shall appear, we shall be like him . . ." (1 John 3:2). At the second com-

ing of Christ the believer's sanctification will be complete. The power of sin will be forever broken. Indeed the very presence of sin will be no more. We shall see the King in all His beauty. At the sight our conformity to Him will become a permanent reality and we shall enter into the glory prepared for the sanctified saints of God.

# 36

# *Prayer*

---

The Biblical teaching concerning prayer unfolds gradually. We must approach the subject from the standpoint of the entire Bible. Otherwise we run the risk of confusion.

Prayer is communion with God. The believer's fellowship with the Father is two-fold:

1. God speaks to us in His Holy Word: the Bible is the Father's message to His dear children.

2. We have the privilege of addressing Him in prayer. The fellowship circuit is thus complete. Prayer ought to be the Christian's native breath, his constant delight, his refuge in the moment of distress, his recourse in time of struggle, his solace in the hour of need.

## A. The Principle of Prayer.

Some teach that anyone may pray to God at any time and expect his prayers to be answered. This is untrue. Our Father in Heaven is merciful and gracious and He does answer prayer as and when He pleases. But He does not promise to answer prayers indiscriminately. Only those who fulfil God's requirement are on praying ground and may pray effectually.

This requirement is stated in 1 John 3:22: "And whatsoever we ask, we receive of him, because we keep his commandments, and do those things that are pleasing in his sight." This passage may appear to put one on legalistic ground, but the verse which follows (verse 23) clarifies the situation: "And this is his commandment, That we should believe on the name of his Son Jesus Christ, and love one another, as he gave us commandment."

Only those who are believers in the Lord Jesus Christ and who demonstrate their faith by love are in a position to pray with the expectation that their prayers will be answered.

## B. The Precepts of Prayer.

Trusting in Christ as his Saviour, the believer has established prayer-contact with the Father. If he is to be effective, however, in his prayer life, he must know and practice certain rules of prayer.

1. *Pray unto God the Father.* He is the Person addressed. (See for example, Acts 12:5.) One actually enters the presence of God when he prays, believing that God "is, and that he is a rewarder of them that diligently seek him" (Heb. 11:6). Prayer is more than the assumption of a subjective attitude. It is contact between the spirit of man and God who is a Spirit.

2. *Pray in the name of Jesus.* Christ said that no one could come unto the Father except by Him. (See John 14:6.) While this is true in the realm of salvation, it is equally true in the realm of prayer. The bases of prayer are Christ's atoning work and mediatorial intercession, not one's character, merit, or deeds.

Jesus declared: "And whatsoever ye shall ask in my name, that will I do, that the Father may be glorified in the Son. If ye shall ask anything in my name, I will do it" (John 14:13, 14). The natural man has no personal claims on God. So far as the riches of Heaven are concerned he is bankrupt. But Jesus established a divine "claim" on behalf of believers, a claim which avails in the Father's sight. Prayer in His name is the basis of one's confidence.

3. *Pray in the Spirit.* "Praying always with all prayer and supplication in the Spirit." (Eph. 6:18; compare Jude 20.) The secret of effective living is living in the Holy Spirit; the secret of effective service is serving in the Holy Spirit; the secret of effective Bible study is studying in the Holy Spirit; the secret of effective testimony is witnessing in the Holy Spirit; the secret of effective prayer is praying in the Holy Spirit.

The indwelling presence of the Holy Spirit is a reality. He provides prayer guidance for the one who is yielded to Him: "We know not what we should pray for as we ought: but the Spirit itself maketh intercession for us with groanings which cannot be uttered" (Rom. 8:26).

4. *Pray according to the will of God.* "And this is the confidence that we have in him, that, if we ask anything according to his will, he heareth us: And if we know that he hear us, whatsoever we ask, we know that we have the petitions that we desired of him" (1 John 5:14,15).

This involves an understanding and an attitude:

a. One must know the will of God. The Word of God is his textbook and the Holy Spirit, his teacher. The Bible often states God's will explicitly: some commands and directives of Scripture are clear (e.g. "For this is the will of God, even your sanctification" 1 Thess. 4:3). Situations sometimes arise, however, in which the will of God is not readily discernible. Even in such cases the lofty tenor of the Scriptures, their holy atmosphere and pervasive purity, together with the guidance of the Holy Spirit, will eventually enable the believer to know the will of God.

b. In addition to knowing the will of God, one must be prepared to submit to it. Beneath the shadow of the cross, although Christ's flesh cringed at the prospect of death, He prayed: "O my Father, if this cup may not pass away from me, except I drink it, thy will be done" (Matt. 26:42). "His sweat was as it were great drops of blood falling down to the ground" (Luke 22:44); yet His Father's will remained His supreme desire. So with the children of God. In all their praying the accomplishment of God's perfect will, no matter what it involves, must be their delight. True submission is possible only through the melting work of the Spirit of God.

5. *Pray in faith, believing.* "But let him ask in faith, nothing wavering" (James 1:6). God "is able to do exceeding abundantly above all that we ask or think" (Eph. 3:20). Faith is not an irrational leap into the dark. It is the confident outreach of the soul of one who trusts Christ and who approaches the Father in accordance with the Scriptural precepts of prayer. True Biblical faith alone can expect the removal of mountains.

6. *Pray earnestly.* Prayer is an exercise of the soul. The Lord Jesus sometimes agonized in intercession. On occasion He spent the entire night in communion with the Father. (See Luke 6:12.) Think of it! The Son of God Himself engaged in protracted prayer. How much more do we need to spend time and energy in prayer!

7. *Pray without display.* Jesus taught: "And when thou prayest, thou shalt not be as the hypocrites are: for they love to pray standing in the synagogues and in the corners of the streets, that they may be seen of men. Verily, I say unto you, They have their reward" (Matt. 6:5). True prayer is not outward show. It is God-seeking, not self-seeking; God-honoring, not self-honoring.

## C. THE PRACTICE OF PRAYER.

1. *Adoration.* As one approaches the throne of grace he should be overwhelmed with awe at the contemplation of the dignity and holiness, the ineffable majesty and glory, of the Almighty. He should ascribe to God the sovereign, transcendent, beneficent virtues which belong to Him. He should render to Him the homage of his soul.

2. *Confession.* The contemplation of the divine glory brings to the believer the realization of his sin. When Isaiah caught a beatific vision of God, he cried out: "Woe is me! for I am

undone" (Isa. 6:5). Job had the same experience. The revelation of God caused him to abhor himself, and to "repent in dust and ashes" (Job 42:6). So the one who prays today must repent and confess his transgressions to the Lord.

3. *Gratitude.* The assurance that the blood of Christ avails for the forgiveness of sins; the knowledge that God is merciful and kind and has "blessed us with all spiritual blessings in heavenly places in Christ" (Eph. 1:3); all this should inspire one with thanksgiving which finds ready expression in prayer.

4. *Petition.* God is concerned about all the believer's requests for self and for others, for causes, conditions, and circumstances. Nothing is too great or small to elicit His interest. All may be laid upon the altar of prayer. This suggests a prayer list: our Father in Heaven loves to have His children pray for definite needs.

## D. The Problems of Prayer.

1. *Iniquity is an obstacle to answered prayer.* "Behold, the Lord's hand is not shortened, that it cannot save; neither his ear heavy, that it cannot hear: But your iniquities have separated between you and your God, and your sins have hid his face from you, that he will not hear" (Isa. 59:1,2).

2. *Wrong motives hinder our prayers.* James writes: "Ye ask, and receive not, because ye ask amiss, that ye may consume it upon your lusts" (James 4:3). One's purpose in prayer should not be his own gratification or satisfaction, but the glory of God. Any other motive is base and unworthy and closes the avenue to answered prayer.

3. *The presence of idols in the heart blocks the channel of prayer.* In the days of the prophet Ezekiel, it is recorded, certain of the elders of Israel came and sat before the man of God. Apparently they expected some peculiar manifestation of the power of God. But the word of the Lord came to the prophet saying: "Son of man, these men have set up their idols in their

heart, and put the stumblingblock of their iniquity before their face: should I be enquired of at all by them?" (Ezek. 14:3). If one wants to "enquire" of the Lord effectively, he must be an iconoclast. Among the idols which he must destroy are these: an unforgiving spirit (see Mark 11:25,26); lack of love and mercy (see Prov. 21:13); continued disobedience (see Prov. 1:24-28); hypocritical formalism (see Isa. 1:2-15).

## E. The Promises of God Concerning Prayer.

1. *God answers the prayers of His children.* He is our Father. He is loving, but He is also wise. He knows what is best for His people and what will redound to His own glory. "For all the promises of God in him are yea, and in him Amen, unto the glory of God by us" (2 Cor. 1:20).

2. *God's answer may come in one of three ways.* Sometimes He replies in the affirmative: His "Yes" fills the believer's heart with joy. Sometimes the answer is negative: but His "No" is still a revelation of a heart of love. And sometimes the answer is "Wait," a challenge to continued, patient, persistent intercession.

3. *God has given examples of answered prayer.* Solomon prayed for wisdom and his prayer was answered. (See 1 Kings 3:6-9). Hezekiah prayed for deliverance from Sennacherib and his request was granted. (See 2 Kings 19:14-36.) Paul prayed that a thorn might be removed from his flesh. God answered his prayer by denying his petition. (See 2 Cor. 12:7-10.)

God has a perfect plan for the ages. However He may choose to answer, His decision is best. The attitude of true faith is this: "I thank thee, Lord, thou doest all things well."

> "Trust Him, He is ever faithful;
> Trust Him, for His will is best.
> Trust Him, for the arms of Jesus
> Are the safest place of rest."

## F. THE PERFECT PRAYER.

The Lord Jesus Christ, our supreme Teacher, has given the perfect pattern of prayer. He who would master the art of prayer should study our Lord's High Priestly prayer (see John 17) and the Lord's Prayer (see Matt. 6:9-13). Jesus introduced the latter prayer with the words: "After this manner therefore pray ye." Note in the Lord's Prayer the primary ascription of holiness, sovereignty, power and glory to God; and secondarily the supplication for the supply of the believer's material and spiritual needs.

# 37

# The Believer and the Will of God

Salvation is more than deliverance from wrath to come. Having been saved *from* something one is saved *for* something and *to* something. That something is conformity to the life of God in Christ, to His standards, commandments, and conduct. "But we all, with open face beholding as in a glass the glory of the Lord, are changed into the same image from glory to glory, even as by the Spirit of the Lord." (2 Cor. 3:18; see also 1 Thess. 4:3; 1 Peter 1:15,16.)

Jesus came to do the will of God. He taught that God had a specific and definite will for Him. Never did He affirm that He lacked a will Himself, but He consistently did the will of the Father. "Jesus saith unto them, My meat is to do the will of him that sent me, and to finish his work" (John 4:34). "I can of mine own self do nothing: as I hear, I judge: and my judgment is just; because I seek not mine own will, but the will of the Father which hath sent me" (John 5:30). Conformity to the image of Christ includes submission to the will of God. Just as Jesus knew and did God's will, so must His followers know and do God's will.

## A. Stumbling Blocks to the Performance of God's Will.

1. Some believe, unfortunately, that salvation does not include conformity to the will of God; that having been delivered from the penalty of sin they can now live as they wish. Men find it hard to understand that freedom from the penalty of sin brings the believer into a new relationship: he bears the "yoke of God." Paradoxically this yoke is one of glorious liberty; but the enemy of our souls persuades men to disbelieve this and to think of it as burdensome and galling. Salvation never means that we can do what we please unless our desires conform to the will of God.

2. Some Christians are ignorant of the truth that God has a perfect will for their lives. Their ignorance results from a failure to know the Word of God. New Christians should be instructed from the day of their regeneration concerning the will of God. If they are not so taught the fault lies in part with those who won them to Christ. Personal workers usually tell converts to read the Bible. If this is done the convert will learn something about the will of God. But the difficulty is that converts do not always read the Word of God regularly or systematically; before they reach spiritual maturity they often become defeated and disillusioned, and never discover that the will of God is pertinent to their lives.

3. Another obstacle to the performance of God's will is disobedience. The believer knows that God has a perfect will for his life, but he persistently and wilfully refuses to do that will. The refusal to accept God's will often rises from the belief that it may prove onerous or contrary to one's personal desires. Latent in one's thinking, for example, and a specific reason for his refusal to do God's will, may be the thought that God might ask him to be a preacher or a missionary. Only the obedient and submissive Christian can know the joy of being in the center of God's will.

## B. The Certainty that God Has a Perfect Will for One's Life.

The truth that God has a will for each life is taught clearly in many passages of Scripture and should be part of the believer's unchanging confidence. "For this cause we also, since the day we heard it, do not cease to pray for you, and to desire that ye might be filled with the knowledge of his will in all wisdom and spiritual understanding" (Col. 1:9). "Teach me to do thy will; for thou art my God" (Psalm 143:10). "Before I formed thee in the belly I knew thee; and before thou camest forth out of the womb I sanctified thee, and I ordained thee a prophet unto the nations." (Jer. 1:5; see also Isa. 30:19-21; Job 23:14; John 7:17.) Paul believed firmly that he was an apostle by the will of God. He was "called to be an apostle of Jesus Christ through the will of God." (1 Cor. 1:1; see 2 Cor. 1:1; Eph. 1:1.)

## C. Results of Disobeying God's Will.

Men have not always obeyed the will of God. The consequence of disobedience has been punishment, for God is displeased when we fail to do His will.

1. Abraham tried to do God's will in his own way. Promised a son of Sarah his wife, he became impatient and took Hagar, Sarah's handmaid, of whom Ishmael was born. This child of the desert was not of the line of promise. His posterity became a scourge to Christians for many centuries. Out of Ishmael have come the present day Mohammedans. (See Gen. 16.)

2. Moses struck the rock in the wilderness contrary to the expressed will of God. For this act of disobedience God punished the great law-giver by refusing him permission to lead the children of Israel into the promised land. (See Numbers 20.)

3. Saul refused to walk obediently before God and defiantly rejected the known will of God for his life. The divine verdict

was: "For rebellion is as the sin of witchcraft, and stubbornness is as iniquity and idolatry. Because thou hast rejected the word of the Lord, he hath also rejected thee from being king" (1 Sam. 15:23).

4. David tried to bring home the Ark of the Covenant, but did so in a manner contrary to the known will of God. Uzza put his hand on the Ark to steady it and died as a consequence. Disobedience was once more punished by God. (See 1 Chron. 13.)

5. Ananias and Sapphira, contrary to the revealed will of God, lied and were slain for their collusion in disobedience. (See Acts 5:1-11.)

D. The Secret of Knowing the Will of God.

In general there are three ways in which the believer may ascertain the will of God. Any one of these is subject to abuse. One must always ask God to open his heart and the eyes of his understanding that he might rightly discern the divine will.

1. *Through the Word of God.*

a. The Bible tells us *directly* in definite, unmistakable, terms what the will of God is. For example:

(1) We are commanded to lead holy lives. "For this is the will of God, even your sanctification, that ye should abstain from fornication" (1 Thess. 4:3). "But as he which hath called you is holy, so be ye holy in all manner of conversation; Because it is written, Be ye holy; for I am holy" (1 Peter 1:15, 16).

(2) We are commanded to be filled with the Holy Spirit. "And be not drunk with wine, wherein is excess; but be filled with the Spirit" (Eph. 5:18).

(3) We are commanded to take the gospel to the ends of the earth. "All power is given unto me in heaven and in earth. Go ye therefore, and teach all nations, baptizing them in the name of the Father, and of the Son, and of the Holy Ghost: Teaching them to observe all things whatsoever I have com-

manded you: and lo, I am with you alway, even unto the end of the world" (Matt. 28:18-20).

(4) We are commanded to pray. "Pray without ceasing" (1 Thess. 5:17). "Confess your faults one to another, and pray one for another . . ." (James 5:16). "I will therefore that men pray everywhere, lifting up holy hands, without wrath and doubting" (1 Tim. 2:8).

(5) We are commanded to love neither the world nor the things that are in the world; to be separated in our living; to be faithful stewards of our material possessions; and in general to live on a high and holy plane.

b. The Bible also reveals God's will *indirectly*. The Holy Spirit often takes some portion of the Word and applies it to a given situation. Saints through the ages have experienced this sort of guidance. For example:

(1) A great missionary read the 54th chapter of Isaiah. When he came to verse 6 "For the Lord hath called thee . . ." he applied the words to himself. The Holy Spirit used this verse out of its context and through it spoke to the man's heart about missionary service.

(2) Another Christian leader, believing that God wanted him on the foreign field as a missionary, was being held back because of his mother's needs. One day while waiting for a train he opened his New Testament. His eyes fell on the verse, "he that loveth father or mother more than me is not worthy of me . . ." (Matt. 10:37). The Holy Spirit spoke to him through the words, impressing him with the fact that nothing should keep him from service overseas. Of course in other cases the will of God that one remain at home might be revealed by the very fact of his responsibility for his mother.

2. *Through circumstances.* This includes the normal opening and shutting of doors which we must accept as of God. If only one door is open and the need for moving forward is obvious without any confirmation from the Holy Spirit, we may conclude that this is the door for us. If the door is defi-

nitely closed, we may regard this as the will of God. The Bible furnishes us with many examples of such guidance.

a. Gideon received a call from God but hesitated until the call was ratified by visible external circumstances. On the basis of the circumstantial evidence of the fleece he recognized God's will and led the children of Israel in victory against the Midianites.

b. David received circumstantial guidance from the Lord: "And let it be, when thou hearest the sound of a going in the tops of the mulberry trees, that then thou shalt bestir thyself: for then shall the Lord go out before thee, to smite the host of the Philistines" (2 Sam. 5:24).

c. Paul declares that God used circumstances to prevent him from acting contrary to the divine will. He writes to the church at Rome: "Now I would not have you ignorant, brethren, that oftentimes I purposed to come unto you, (but was let hitherto,) that I might have some fruit among you also, even as among other Gentiles" (Rom. 1:13). The apostle wanted to go to Rome but he was prevented from so doing by divinely arranged circumstances.

d. Adoniram Judson went to India but circumstances forced him to leave the country. Instead he went to Burma and there became a great power for God. He was instrumental in seeing thousands of Burmese find salvation in Christ. The closed door of India became the open door of Burma and thus God revealed His will.

3. *Through the inward persuasion of the Holy Spirit who speaks to our hearts when we pray and listen to His voice.* But lest we fall into the errors of intuitional guidance or the elevation of "inner light" at the expense of direct Biblical revelation, we must understand that when the Holy Spirit speaks His directions will be confirmed circumstantially. Never does the Spirit lead in a manner contrary to the Word of God. We must always be ready to distinguish our own desires from the guidance of the Holy Spirit. We must be sure that we are walking

in the Spirit and that our wills are so yielded to the will of God that we are prepared to hear His voice. Biblical examples are:

a. Jeremiah had the experience of God speaking to him. "The Word of the Lord came unto me, saying, Behold, Hanameel the son of Shallum thine uncle shall come unto thee, saying, Buy thee my field that is in Anathoth: for the right of redemption is thine to buy it" (Jer. 32:6,7). But God circumstantially confirmed the word spoken to His prophet: "So Hanameel mine uncle's son came to me in the court of the prison according to the word of the Lord, and said unto me, Buy my field, I pray thee. . . . Then I knew that this was the word of the Lord" (Jer. 32:8).

b. Paul and Timothy experienced this type of guidance. "Now when they had gone through Phrygia and the region of Galatia, and were forbidden of the Holy Ghost to preach the word in Asia" (Acts 16:6). When Paul and Barnabas were called to missionary work their guidance came directly from the Holy Spirit: "As they ministered to the Lord, and fasted, the Holy Ghost said, Separate me Barnabas and Saul for the work whereunto I have called them" (Acts 13:2).

c. Agabus, a prophet spiritually prepared, received guidance: "And when he was come unto us, he took Paul's girdle and bound his own hands and feet, and said, Thus saith the Holy Ghost, So shall the Jews at Jerusalem bind the man that owneth this girdle, and shall deliver him into the hands of the Gentiles" (Acts 21:11).

## E. Pre-requisites to Knowing God's Will.

God sometimes indicates to His children what He wishes them to do even though they are not ready to obey. A man may find that God wants him to become a minister or missionary in spite of his contrary desires. Many Christians know from the Scriptures what God's will is in relation to marriage, money, holiness, etc. And yet many do not do the will of God.

In order for one to experience constant guidance and ceaseless knowledge of the will of God, he must be willing to have
that will for his life. He must yield to the Lord and in an
irrevocable "Yes" tell Him that He has his will and life forever.
The Psalmist described this attitude of heart: "I delight to do
thy will, O my God" (Psalm 40:8). Jesus reflected the attitude: "I seek not mine own will, but the will of the Father
which hath sent me" (John 5:30). "For I came down from
heaven, not to do mine own will, but the will of him that sent
me" (John 6:38). The priest Eli counseled young Samuel,
"And it shall be, if he call thee, that thou shalt say, Speak,
Lord; for thy servant heareth" (1 Sam. 3:9). Samuel was ready
and willing to hear the voice of God. He demonstrated his
heart attitude by asking God to speak, for he would be listening and would hear.

Are you listening obediently, and are you willing to hear
the voice of God as He makes known His will for your life?
Say then with Samuel, out of the fulness of a devoted and
consecrated heart, "Speak, Lord, for thy servant heareth."

# 38

# Temptation

---

No Christian is ever exempt from temptation while in the flesh.
However spiritual a man may be and however high his aspirations, he will never reach the point at which temptation will
not strike. Temptation is inevitable because of our human nature. Even when a man has been born again his human nature
and susceptibility to temptation remain. The higher a man
ascends in his spiritual experience the greater is the possibility
that he will be tempted by the arch enemy of souls. The devil
delights to ensnare God's children. What richer reward can he
reap than that of triumphing over believers who have fallen
into his trap?

A. The Nature of Temptation.

1. The word "temptation," as used in the New Testament,
has two connotations: sometimes it means "testing" (see 1
Peter 1:6); at other times it means solicitation to evil. In this
chapter we have in mind the latter usage.

2. Temptation may be defined as the incitement of a normal
desire beyond the boundaries set by God for man.

3. Man's normal desires are to enjoy things, to acquire or
possess things, and to do things. These desires, which in them-

selves are not sinful, become sinful when they exceed the limitations imposed by God. They then become related to the three basic sins of which the apostle John speaks: "For all that is in the world, the lust of the flesh, and the lust of the eyes, and the pride of life, is not of the Father, but is of the world" (1 John 2:16). The desire to enjoy things can become the lust of the flesh; the desire to get things can become the lust of the eyes; and the desire to do things can become the vainglory of life. The temptation of Eve was within this threefold area. The fruit was good to eat, good to possess, and good to make one wise. The temptation had to do with the lust of the flesh, the lust of the eyes, and the pride of life.

4. The Christian has basic human desires. When a man is saved he still has the desire to enjoy things, the desire to get things, and the desire to do things. However, while the desires remain their object changes. The child of God wishes to enjoy things in a way that will glorify God; he wishes to obtain things for the sake of God and not for self; he wishes to do things for God and not for self. Sin is found, not in the possession of basic desires, but in their perversion.

## B. THE SOURCE OF TEMPTATION.

1. Temptation does not and cannot, in the nature of the case, come from God. "Let no man say when he is tempted, I am tempted of God: for God cannot be tempted with evil, neither tempteth he any man: but every man is tempted, when he is drawn away of his own lust, and enticed" (James 1:13, 14).

2. Temptation comes from the devil. "And Satan stood up against Israel, and provoked (enticed) David to number Israel" (1 Chron. 21:1). "Then was Jesus led up of the spirit into the wilderness to be tempted of the devil" (Matt. 4:1). "And supper being ended, the devil having now put into the heart of Judas Iscariot, Simon's son, to betray him" (John 13:2). "For this cause, when I could no longer forbear, I sent to know your

faith, lest by some means the tempter have tempted you, and our labour be in vain" (1 Thess. 3:5).

## C. THE REASON FOR TEMPTATION.

God permits His children to be tempted as a trial of their faith. "Wherein ye greatly rejoice, though now for a season, if need be, ye are in heaviness through manifold temptations: that the trial of your faith, being much more precious than of gold that perisheth, though it be tried with fire, might be found unto praise and honour and glory at the appearing of Jesus Christ" (1 Peter 1:6,7). "My brethren, count it all joy, when ye fall into divers temptations; knowing this, that the trying of your faith worketh patience" (James 1:2,3).

## D. PROTECTION AGAINST TEMPTATION.

While God does not allow us to be exempt from temptation, He limits its extent and intensity. The devil cannot ride rough-shod over God's children. God erects hedges around them designed for their protection. To understand the divine provision for our safety gives us courage and assurance in hours of trial. It also prevents us from pleading "not guilty" when we capitulate to temptation.

The fact that God shields His own is stated in the words: "There hath no temptation taken you but such as is common to man: but God is faithful, who will not suffer you to be tempted above that ye are able; but will with the temptation also make a way to escape, that ye may be able to bear it" (1 Cor. 10:13); "The Lord knoweth how to deliver the godly out of temptations, and to reserve the unjust unto the day of judgment to be punished" (2 Peter 2:9). From such passages of Scripture it is clear that our Father will not allow us to be tempted beyond what we can actually bear; He will make a way of escape for His saints; He will enable us to bear whatever temptations come; He knows how to deliver His people when temptation strikes.

## E. The Believer's Friend in the Hour of Temptation.

1. The Lord Jesus understands and sympathizes with His saints in times of temptation. We have One who knows all our sorrows and tribulations. His heart is touched by our infirmities. "For we have not an high priest which cannot be touched with the feeling of our infirmities; but was in all points tempted like as we are, yet without sin. Let us therefore come boldly to the throne of grace, that we may obtain mercy, and find grace to help in time of need" (Heb. 4:15,16).

2. Jesus is able to help those who are tempted. The Christian is weaker than the devil. In the struggle against the wiles of his adversary he requires resources which he does not in himself possess, but which belong to him because he is in Christ. Jesus has the power and the inclination to aid us. The Scriptures say, "For in that he himself hath suffered being tempted, he is able to succour them that are tempted" (Heb. 2:18).

3. Jesus intercedes with God for the saints. This intercessory work is one aspect of His high priestly ministry. Before the throne of grace our Lord pleads with God for the members of His body. He knows the Father's will and is effective in this ministry of forgiveness and protection. His effectiveness is suggested in His words to Peter: "Simon, Simon, behold, Satan hath desired to have you that he may sift you as wheat: But I have prayed for thee, that thy faith fail not: and when thou art converted, strengthen thy brethren" (Luke 22:31,32). In His priestly prayer He said, "I pray not that thou shouldest take them out of the world, but that thou shouldest keep them from the evil" (John 17:15). Christians may know that "He is able also to save them to the uttermost that come unto God by him, seeing he ever liveth to make intercession for them" (Heb. 7:25).

## F. The Christian's Duty in the Face of Temptation.

1. He is to resist temptation in faith. Yielding to temptation

is one's own fault. He cannot shift the blame to God; nor should he resort to the excuse that the temptation was beyond his God-given abilities to resist it. When the human will has been exercised to the full God has divine resources which will more than enable one to overcome temptation. We are commanded, "Above all, taking the shield of faith, wherewith ye shall be able to quench all the fiery darts of the wicked" (Eph. 6:16); "Be sober, be vigilant; because your adversary the devil, as a roaring lion, walketh about, seeking whom he may devour: Whom resist stedfast in the faith, knowing that the same afflictions are accomplished in your brethren that are in the world" (1 Peter 5:8,9). The challenge is still valid: "Ye have not yet resisted unto blood, striving against sin" (Heb. 12:4).

2. He is to guard against temptation. Our Lord tells His disciples to be awake and vigilant. Sleeping saints may be caught in the snares of the devil; but soldiers on the alert, while they may be overcome by power greater than their own, will not be subjected to a surprise attack by the enemy. Be careful not to frequent places, nor to engage in practices, which might cause you to stumble. Temptation lurks in unexpected quarters, but if one is on his guard he is not so likely to be caught unprepared. Jesus' admonition holds today: "Watch and pray, that ye enter not into temptation: the spirit indeed is willing, but the flesh is weak" (Matt. 26:41).

3. He is to employ the resources of prayer—to ask God definitely to keep him from temptation. No day should pass without his beseeching the Lord to keep him from this danger and to give him strength for life's encounters. The Lord's Prayer, the prayer perfect, is his model: "Lead us not into temptation" (Matt. 6:13).

4. He is to be careful not to be a source of temptation to others either in speech or conduct. A man or woman who brings temptation to others is being used of the devil to carry out his wicked designs. One must guard against permitting himself to become an instrument of evil. Paul writes, "Let us

not therefore judge one another any more: but judge this rather, that no man put a stumbling block or an occasion to fall in his brother's way" (Rom. 14:13).

5. He is to restore those who have been overcome by temptation but who have repented and changed their ways. Nothing that any other Christian has done is beyond the limits of one's own sin potential. Only the grace of God has kept us from falling into the sins that we hate in others. God commands that we forgive and restore when the wrong is made right and when the sinner has been dealt with on a Scriptural basis. "Brethren, if a man be overtaken in a fault, ye which are spiritual, restore such an one in the spirit of meekness; considering thyself, lest thou also be tempted" (Gal. 6:1).

### G. Restoration after One Has Yielded to Temptation.

Fellowship with one's Lord is broken when there is unconfessed sin in the life. To the extent that sin is not dealt with the believer is backslidden; he is not walking in the light. Uncorrected sin impairs one's relationship to Christ; a succession of sinful uncorrected acts produces a backslidden condition. One may be a Christian layman, or a minister of the gospel, or a theological seminary professor, and still be backslidden. But God has marvelously provided the erring believer with the following pathway of restoration to fellowship with Himself:

1. The means of cleansing: the blood of the Lord Jesus Christ. This must be applied to the sinner so that the stain and shame of his sin may be wiped out. "But if we walk in the light, as he is in the light, we have fellowship one with another, and the blood of Jesus Christ his Son cleanseth us from all sin" (1 John 1:7).

2. The method of cleansing: confession. Sins must be confessed. The confession must be made in accordance with the sin committed. If the sin is secret, confession should be secret. If the sin is public, open and notorious, confession should be

public. But confession is not to be of such a nature as to become a stumbling block or an offense to men. One is not to parade his unclean thoughts before others. It is bad enough that one entertained them without publicizing them. Since forgiveness is conditioned upon confession the believer must be careful to meet the divine requirements: "If we confess our sins, he is faithful and just to forgive us our sins, and to cleanse us from all unrighteousness" (1 John 1:9).

3. The consequence of cleansing: repayment. Where we have defrauded or taken from men what does not belong to us, repayment must be made. Where we have cheated in school examinations restitution must follow. The righting of wrong is essential to the spirit of repentance and demonstrates one's sincerity. Zacchaeus proved his repentance by his conduct: "And Zacchaeus stood, and said unto the Lord; Behold, Lord, the half of my goods I give to the poor; and if I have taken any thing from any man by false accusation, I restore him fourfold. And Jesus said unto him, This day is salvation come to this house, forasmuch as he also is a son of Abraham" (Luke 19:8,9).

The Christian walk will never be free from temptation. But a life of victory is possible. Temptation need not hold one in bondage. If he is overtaken in a fault as the result of the temptations of the devil, he need only apply the remedy and be lifted from his slough of despond to the level of victory. If he has yielded to temptation he has indeed weakened his spiritual fibre. But God has the power to raise the fallen and restore "the years the locusts have eaten." Let him apply the tested medicine of the Bible and be restored to spiritual health.

# 39

# The Believer's Warfare

The Christian life is a battle. The believer in Christ is called upon to "fight the good fight of faith" (1 Tim. 6:12). This requires spiritual consecration and stamina, and a clear understanding of the nature of the struggle. Victory is possible. But only those who appreciate the strength of the enemy and who lean for power upon the mighty arm of God will know the joy of triumph.

## A. THE ARMY OF GOD.

1. *The soldiers.* The children of God are His soldiers (see 2 Tim. 2:3) and are challenged to "war a good warfare" (1 Tim. 1:18). A man enlists in the ranks the day he puts his faith in Jesus Christ. He may not recline on flowery beds of ease nor walk the primrose path of sweet repose. The soldier's life is one of unremitting toil, strain, hardship, suffering and exposure to danger. The army of God is under attack.

2. *The Commander.* The Captain of the hosts is the Lord Jesus Christ. To Him all should yield allegiance. His word is their command; His will their desire; His purpose their objective. He directs and they must gladly obey.

3. *The banner.* This is the standard of the cross. "His blood red banner streams afar" and we follow in its train. The aton-

ing death of the Son of God, sealed by His resurrection, is symbolized to us in the banner of the cross. This is the rallying-point around which the people of God take their stand. No hammer and sickle of Communism, no rising sun of Japan, no Union Jack of England, no stars and stripes of the United States, but rather the Christian flag with its cross of red—the blood of the Lamb.

## B. THE ADVERSARY OF GOD.

"Your adversary the devil, as a roaring lion, walketh about, seeking whom he may devour" (1 Pet. 5:8). Our wrestling is not against flesh and blood. If the foe were visible and tangible our victory would be more probable. No, we wrestle "against the principalities, against the powers, against the world-rulers of this darkness, against the spiritual hosts of wickedness in the heavenly places" (Eph. 6:12 R.V.). "Against the wiles of the devil" (Eph. 6:11) we take our stand.

Ever since Adam's fall in the garden of Eden the devil has leveled his attack against the cause of the Lord. He will continue his nefarious onslaughts until his final overthrow, which, although it sometimes seems remote to those who experience his diabolical thrusts, is yet guaranteed in the Word of God. (See Rev. 20:10.)

The devil and his hosts are remarkably cunning. They know the weakest links in the chain of the Christian's character and conduct, and they concentrate their efforts in these areas. It behooves the people of God to study their own shortcomings, to know their own frailties, to understand their peculiar weaknesses, and to erect defenses at their most vulnerable points.

## C. THE ARMOUR OF GOD'S SOLDIER.

Fortunately the soldier of Christ is clad in supernatural armour and need not be afraid. He is covered with a divine panoply. The various items of his armour are repeatedly listed in the New Testament. "The weapons of our warfare are not carnal, but mighty through God to the pulling down of strongholds" (2 Cor. 10:4). We have "the armour of righteousness on the right hand and on the left" (2 Cor. 6:7).

The classic passage on this theme is the sixth chapter of Ephesians. If one is "to withstand in the evil day," he should study these words.

1. The Christian's loins are "girt about with truth" (Eph. 6:14). Paul begins at this point because the Roman soldier of old had much of his armour buckled on at his loins. The pivotal point of the believer's defenses is the truth of the living God. That truth is found in the Scriptures. Thus Satan assailed Eve with the question, "Hath God said . . . ?" (Gen. 3:1) and caused her to stumble. Thus he continues his undermining tactics today.

2. The Christian's breastplate is "of righteousness." This is, of course, two-fold. It is *imputed* righteousness, the righteousness of Christ granted to the believer and received by faith alone—a transaction which prepares one to be accepted as a child of God. But it is also *implanted* righteousness, a new life characterized by the graces of Christian character, a life that partakes of the goodness and love of God. Such a life makes a powerful impact for the cause of the Lord in the perennial conflict against sin and the devil.

3. His feet are covered, "shod with the preparation of the gospel of peace" (Eph. 6:15). No area of the body is unprotected. The basis of one's strength and confidence is the blessed gospel of Christ, through which one made his peace with God, and as the result of which, even when the adversary presses hard, one may be kept in the perfect peace of God. (See Isa. 26:3.)

4. His body is protected by "the shield of faith." This enables him "to quench all the fiery darts of the evil one" (Eph. 6:16 R.V.). Observe the imagery. The devil fashions his darts, ignites them and then projects them against the saints of God.

Faith makes Christ real in the presence of the enemy. The Christian has an impenetrable shield.

5. His head is secured by "the helmet of salvation." From top to toe there is security against the foe. Could this imply that the doubts and misgivings which assail the believer's mind are adequately met by the sturdy and enduring fact of salvation—a fact which changes not although the tide of battle surges around?

6. He has also a sword, the offensive weapon of his warfare. Must the Christian always be the attacked and never the attacker? Is his warfare always defensive and never offensive? Thank God for the "sword of the Spirit, which is the word of God" (Eph. 6:17). Just as the Lord Jesus met temptation with the sword of the Scriptures, so God's children today may brandish the same sword in their defense, and to the discomfiture of the adversary. One's danger is, not that his sword may be dented in action, but that it may grow rusty through disuse.

7. His panoply is the Lord Jesus Christ. "Put ye on the Lord Jesus Christ . . ." (Rom. 13:14). Jesus is Himself our armour in the battle against evil. We are to "put Him on." For He is Himself the truth, the sun of righteousness, the prince of peace, the object of our faith, the captain of our salvation, the Word of God incarnate. Does He not, therefore, meet the armour qualifications of Paul's letter to the Ephesians? Yea, He far transcends them.

D. THE ALLY OF THE SOLDIERS OF GOD.

Christians do not go out to meet the enemy alone. They are in holy alliance with God. When the servant of Elisha beheld the host of Syrians which had come to capture his master, he was dismayed. But the prophet encouraged him, "Fear not: for they that be with us are more than they that be with them" (2 Kings 6:16). "If God be for us, who can be against us" (Rom. 8:31): this is the grateful cry of the believing heart.

Specifically, the Holy Spirit is the Christian's support and stay in the hour of testing. He is the indwelling Paraclete: He has been called to the believer's side for times of trial. The warrior's task is to yield himself to the Spirit who will fight the battle and win for him the victory.

### E. The Assignment to Every Soldier.

Not every warrior has a place of prominence in the army of God. But every man is to stand in his allotted sphere, fulfilling his appointed task to the glory of God. Every soldier is commanded to lead:

1. *A disciplined life.* Paul writes to Timothy: "Thou therefore endure hardness, as a good soldier of Jesus Christ" (2 Tim. 2:3). The apostle kept his own body under subjection. (See 1 Cor. 9:27.) He was willing to "endure all things for the elect's sake" (2 Tim. 2:10). One must keep in trim for the fray. This involves spiritual training, the faithful use of the Word and prayer, the exercise of the soul in all that is good. The call is not for flabby, spineless warriors, but for men and women who will stand up resolutely for Jesus as disciplined, obedient servants of the cross.

2. *A disentangled life.* "No man that warreth entangleth himself with the affairs of this life" (2 Tim. 2:4). A spider-web may be as soft as silk and dainty in design. Its danger lies in its power to ensnare. Paul is not warning merely against the sordid charms of the flesh. He has in mind anything, no matter how good or worthy it may seem intrinsically, which preoccupies the believer's interest and keeps him from his rightful occupation with Christ. The "affairs" of this life often distract. They must be kept in their proper place.

### F. The Ambition of Every Soldier.

Paul summarizes this succinctly. The warrior's ambition is "that he may please him who hath chosen him to be a soldier"

(2 Tim. 2:4). This is a wonderful rule. It is applicable to any life situation.

The average man acts in such a way as to please himself. The generous man seeks to please others. But the wise man is the one who strives with all his might to please his Captain, the Lord Jesus. This involves knowledge, love and determination. One must know what Christ wants him to do, at what sector of the front he should serve, how he should use the weapons of his warfare and what strongholds of the foe he should attack. Further, he should love the Lord so strongly that if need be he would gladly lay his all upon the altar of sacrifice. And beyond that he should prove his love by a glad and determined obedience.

This is the military service which puts the Kingdom of God first, glorifies the Father, and pleases the Saviour under whose sovereign standard our warfare is waged.

## G. The Assurance of Victory.

The beautiful thing about the battle known as life is that its issue is certain, its victory is secure. Trials may perplex, temptations may smite in their fury, uncertainties may bewilder, pressures may be well-nigh over-powering. Yet in the thick of the struggle, when the strife is the keenest, the trusting believer may share the confidence of Paul: "Nay, in all these things"— and the apostle has just presented a formidable list of difficulties . . . "we are more than conquerors through him that loved us" (Rom. 8:37).

How dare one be so assured? His certainty has a solid foundation. It rests upon the nature and attributes of God Who, among other things, is omnipotent; it is based upon the availability of God's power to His people and upon the divine promises of success. The soldier must accept these promises, avail himself of divine power, and move forward to victory. The devil will oppose him constantly. He must resist him "stedfast in the faith" (1 Pet. 5:9). And when at long last the time comes for him to lay his laurels of victory down at his Captain's feet, he will be able to say with Paul: "I have fought a good fight, I have finished my course, I have kept the faith" (2 Tim. 4:7). What a triumphant affirmation!

# 40

## The Life of Victory

In dealing with sanctification we now approach an important question: How may one achieve true holiness? Holiness is the life of victory; it is life on the highest plane. One must learn to live the victorious life. How may this goal be achieved?

### A. THE DIVINE STANDARD OF VICTORY.

God does not say there are two types of Christian lives. There is only one kind of life which pleases God. Any deviation from this ideal is a failure to measure up to the divine requirements. When one misses God's mark he is not living another species of life; he is simply displaying a quality of life which is inferior to the divine plan. He who lives a blameless or holy life is called a spiritual Christian. He who departs from God's standard or falls below it is called a carnal Christian. Paul writes to the Corinthians: "And I, brethren, could not speak unto you as unto spiritual, but as unto carnal, even as unto babes in Christ. I have fed you with milk and not with meat: for hitherto ye were not able to bear it, neither yet now are ye able. For ye are yet carnal . . ." (1 Cor. 3:1-3).

1. *God desires us to be spiritual Christians.* This is the divine standard. The Word of God teaches that holiness is needed, required and commanded. The writer of Hebrews plainly says,

"Follow peace with all men, and holiness, without which no man shall see the Lord" (Heb. 12:14). Paul reminds us: "For God hath not called us unto uncleanness, but unto holiness" (1 Thess. 4:7). "Having therefore these promises, dearly beloved, let us cleanse ourselves from all filthiness of the flesh and spirit, perfecting holiness in the fear of God" (2 Cor. 7:1). "According as he hath chosen us in him before the foundation of the world, that we should be holy, and without blame before him in love" (Eph. 1:4).

2. *God has made the life of victory possible.* The divine standard is attainable. To measure up to it is a present duty, a present privilege and a present enjoyment. Victory is not something for which we must wait until we get to heaven. It is a here and now provision of love. Paul entreats us to present our bodies a "living sacrifice, holy, acceptable unto God, which is your reasonable service" (Rom. 12:1). He writes further: "And you that were sometime alienated and enemies in your mind by wicked works, yet now hath he reconciled In the body of his flesh through death, to present you holy and unblameable and unreproveable in his sight" (Col. 1:21,22). The apostle was terribly mistaken if holiness is not actually attainable in this life. For he specifically enjoins that "a bishop must be blameless, as the steward of God; not self-willed, not soon angry, not given to wine, no striker, nor given to filthy lucre; But a lover of hospitality, a lover of good men, sober, just, *holy*, temperate" (Titus 1:7,8). The holiness and the implied life of victory demanded of a bishop are the same holiness and victorious life which all Christians may enjoy.

## B. The Divine Means of Attaining Victory.

The life of victory is identified with the life which is filled with the Holy Spirit. The open secret of living triumphantly is the work of the Holy Spirit in our hearts. He alone can gain the victory. He alone enables us to become spiritual and to live life on the highest plane. At this point a distinction must be made:

1. Every believer, no matter what the quality of his Christian life may be, has received the gift of the Holy Spirit. Otherwise he would not be a true believer. "In whom ye also trusted, after that ye heard the word of truth, the gospel of your salvation: in whom also after that ye believed, ye were sealed with that Holy Spirit of promise, Which is the earnest of our inheritance until the redemption of the purchased possession, unto the praise of his glory." (Eph. 1:13,14; see John 7:39; Acts 2:4.) "Now he that hath wrought us for the selfsame thing is God, who also hath given unto us the earnest of the Spirit" (2 Cor. 5:5).

2. Not every believer is filled with the Spirit. If all Christians were already Spirit-filled, Paul would not have commanded: "And be not drunk with wine, wherein is excess; but be filled with the Spirit" (Eph. 5:18). In choosing deacons for the newly established church the advice was given: "Wherefore, brethren, look ye out from among you seven men of honest report, *full of the Holy Ghost* and wisdom, whom we may appoint over this business" (Acts 6:3). If all believers had already been full of the Holy Ghost these instructions would have been inappropriate and beside the point.

3. Every believer ought to be filled with the Spirit. Christ died to make this possible. The Christian must have the filling of the Spirit if he is to reproduce Christ's holy life. Indeed he is held responsible if he is not filled with the Spirit. For apart from such infilling the life of victory is impossible.

We are not here speaking of a second blessing or a second work of grace, nor of the baptism of the Spirit. Every believer received the baptism of the Spirit when he accepted Christ as his personal Saviour. (See 1 Cor. 12:13.) This happens once for all. There is no second baptism, although a Christian may experience the infilling of the Holy Spirit subsequent to salvation. In the normal course of events a child of God should experience the infilling of the Spirit at the time he is born again. Oftentimes, as the result of ignorance or lack of instruction, this does not occur. When the infilling takes place later one is tempted to regard it as a second work of grace, particularly because it usually involves a critical experience, when the believer in an irrevocable decision says "Yes" to God and yields to Him the undivided control of himself and all that he is.

## C. The Believer's Part in Attaining the Life of Victory.

1. *Cleansing.* This is the pre-requisite to the fullness of the Spirit. Before the Holy Spirit will fill our hearts He insists that they be cleansed. He will not occupy an unclean, defiled vessel. He is the Spirit of holiness, of truth, of faith, of wisdom, of love and of power. He refuses to infill hearts which are occupied by sin. The principle is simple: in order to be filled with the Spirit we must first be emptied of sin. This is accomplished as follows:

a. We must apply the blood of Christ by faith to our sins. The blood is the only means of cleansing. Nothing else will do this. "But if we walk in the light, as he is in the light, we have fellowship one with another, and the blood of Jesus Christ his Son cleanseth us from all sin" (1 John 1:7). But the blood will have cleansing efficacy only when:

b. We confess our sins. Unconfessed sin remains unforgiven. The blood cleanses only when it is applied; and it is applied only when we confess. The Bible teaches: "If we confess our sins, he is faithful and just to forgive us our sins, and to cleanse us from all unrighteousness" (1 John 1:9). Moreover, we must confess and put under the blood *all* known sin. "Having therefore these promises, dearly beloved, let us cleanse ourselves from *all* filthiness of the flesh and spirit, perfecting holiness in the fear of God" (2 Cor. 7:1). Nothing must be held back from God. No matter how small the item may appear to be it must be brought under the blood. The smallest known unconfessed sin can prevent us from securing the blessing of forgiveness and victory.

2. *Surrender*. Surrender, or yielding, means that the believer gives up the control of himself and his life to God. Until this step is taken self remains enthroned in the heart; and the Holy Spirit will not fill a self-controlled life. Christ and Christ alone must be King. "I beseech you therefore, brethren, by the mercies of God, that ye present your bodies a living sacrifice, holy, acceptable unto God, which is your reasonable service" (Rom. 12:1). "Neither yield ye your members as instruments of unrighteousness unto sin: but yield yourselves unto God, as those that are alive from the dead, and your members as instruments of righteousness unto God" (Rom. 6:13). We must do the yielding. We must open the doors of our hearts. The act must be done willingly, definitely and irrevocably.

3. *Faith*. In simple trust we must accept what God has promised. We must believe that once the divine conditions have been met God will faithfully perform what He has promised. So Abraham "staggered not at the promise of God through unbelief; but was strong in faith, giving glory to God; And being fully persuaded that, what he had promised, he was able also to perform. And therefore it was imputed unto him for righteousness" (Rom. 4:20-22). Saving faith receives from God the salvation He has promised. Faith for victory believes that God has fulfilled His promise and that, as we yield, we are now filled with His Holy Spirit.

4. *Action*. The believer must now *act* as a Spirit-filled child of God. A husband does not stop and ask himself the question every day whether or not he is married and whether he has the privilege of acting as a married man. He has taken the step; and having entered into the estate of marriage he now acts in accordance with the terms of his marriage vow. So the Christian, by faith filled with the Spirit of God, and maintaining due submission to his indwelling Guest, proceeds to live out in daily conduct the life of victory.

# PART SEVEN

# The Believer and the Church

In his quest after holiness and in all his new relationships as a child of God man does not walk alone. He is a member of a new society created and ordained of God for the spiritual health of the corporate fellowship. This society is the church of the living God.

Christ is the Head of His church. Believers are members of His mystical body which finds its outward expression in the visible churches throughout the world in all ages. As members of the body are closely related to the head and to the other members, so Christians everywhere, irrespective of race, color or denominational affiliation, are indissolubly linked with Christ the Head and with one another in the bonds of doctrine and charity.

The previous section was devoted to a consideration of the believer's personal, individual, particular and essentially vertical relationship to God. This section, while it continues to stress the importance of the individual and vertical relationships, sees man in his corporate, united, and essentially horizontal relationships. He is part of a Christian community which worships God together and expresses its common devotion through divinely instituted means designed for the spiritual enlargement and practical benefit of believers as well as for the worldwide extension of the faith.

As the church of Jesus Christ, believers gather together for the purpose of worship and fellowship; for the celebration of baptism and the Lord's Supper; for mutual encouragement in Christian stewardship through the pooling of their material resources to the glory of God; and for edification in the things of the Lord. Against this church of Jesus Christ "the gates of hell shall not prevail" (Matt. 16:18).

# 41

# The Church

Today rapidly changing religious currents have given rise to a re-evaluation of the church. Second only to the problem of the Word of God itself, questions involving the nature and function of the church stir the hearts and minds of theologians and ecumenical enthusiasts. On the foreign field the problem has created tensions and difficulties never experienced among peoples of European extraction who have become used to religious diversity and denominational differences.

Undoubtedly the basic question is whether the church is a visible or an invisible body. The Roman Catholic Church has always equated the true church with the visible organization. This has produced the dogma that there is no salvation outside the church, i.e. the hierarchical organization. Such a dogma leaves Protestants outside the kingdom and without salvation. Protestantism in its classical formulations has never inclined to this view. It is willing to grant that the Roman Church has true believers in it. The modern denominations have never claimed that adherents of other groups are without salvation. Quite the contrary, Presbyterians, Methodists, Baptists, Congregationalists and others who differ in peripheral but not in essential matters (that is who are agreed with respect to the doctrines of salvation) have generally held and freely stated that people of denominations other than their own may well be true believers and members of the body of Christ.

Any correct doctrine of the church (i.e. ecclesiology) must be Biblical. Earnest investigation of the Bible discloses that the word "church" (*ecclesia* in Greek) has two major meanings. It refers both to the invisible and the visible church. By the invisible church is meant all believers who are members of Christ's body, whether presently alive or dead. The body of Christ overlaps man-made barriers and is composed of true believers who have been born-again by the Spirit of the living God. The visible church or churches, on the other hand, constitute organizational Christianity as we see it in operation today. Divinely created and having its charter in the Word of God, the visible organization must not be overlooked, underestimated, nor decried.

Relationship to a visible organization, however, can by no means be equated with membership in the invisible church, the true body of Christ. Men can belong to churches as well as to lodges without being born again. False confessors simulate true faith. The wheat and the tares cannot always be easily separated. But it is also true that not all genuine believers are members of visible churches. This ought not to be the case, for the New Testament knows nothing of "solitary" Christianity. It knows only individual salvation which is followed by corporate fellowship in the divinely ordained churches created by God for the help of His people.

## A. The Invisible Church.

1. Christ is the chief cornerstone and upon Him and His atoning work the church is built. "For other foundation can no man lay than that is laid, which is Jesus Christ" (1 Cor. 3:11). "Now therefore ye are no more strangers and foreigners, but fellow-citizens with the saints, and of the household of God; And are built upon the foundation of the apostles and prophets,

Jesus Christ himself being the chief corner stone." (Eph. 2:19-20; see also 1 Peter 2:4-8.)

2. Christ is the Head of the church. No human being is to usurp this prerogative. "And hath put all things under his feet, and gave him to be the head over all things to the church" (Eph. 1:22). "For the husband is the head of the wife, even as Christ is the head of the church: and he is the saviour of the body" (Eph. 5:23).

3. The church is His body and belongs to Him. "Who now rejoice in my sufferings for you, and fill up that which is behind of the afflictions of Christ in my flesh for his body's sake, which is the church" (Col. 1:24). "And hath put all things under his feet, and gave him to be the head over all things to the church, Which is his body, the fulness of him that filleth all in all" (Eph. 1:22,23).

4. Christ has purchased the church with His own blood. "Take heed therefore unto yourselves, and to all the flock, over the which the Holy Ghost hath made you overseers, to feed the church of God, which he hath purchased with his own blood" (Acts 20:28). "Husbands, love your wives, even as Christ also loved the church, and gave himself for it" (Eph. 5:25). "Neither by the blood of goats and calves, but by his own blood he entered in once into the holy place, having obtained eternal redemption for us" (Heb. 9:12).

5. Every believer is made a member of the body of Christ, the invisible church, by the baptism of the Holy Spirit. "For by one Spirit are we all baptized into one body, whether we be Jews or Gentiles, whether we be bond or free; and have all been made to drink into one Spirit" (1 Cor. 12:13).

6. The true members of the body of Christ are one. Just as the physical body has unity and harmony in its diverse parts so the spiritual body has unity in the midst of its diversity. This unity transcends denominational and other external or organizational lines. "So we, being many, are one body in Christ, and every one members one of another" (Rom. 12:5).

"For we being many are one bread, and one body: for we are all partakers of that one bread" (1 Cor. 10:17). "For as the body is one, and hath many members, and all the members of that one body, being many, are one body: so also is Christ" (1 Cor. 12:12).

7. The church will be sinless, holy, sanctified in heaven. Christ assures us that He will perform this work and fulfill the ultimate destiny of the church. The church is a heavenly body, the members of which are engaged in a pilgrim journey until the consummation. "Husbands, love your wives, even as Christ also loved the church, and gave himself for it; That he might sanctify and cleanse it, with the washing of water by the word, That he might present it to himself a glorious church, not having spot, or wrinkle, or any such thing; but that it should be holy and without blemish" (Eph. 5:25-27).

## B. THE VISIBLE CHURCH.

The members of the body of Christ, dead and living, constitute the invisible church. But God has ordained a visible structure, the organizational church, for members of the invisible church body still resident on earth. This divine creation takes into account the need of men for corporate worship and fellowship. It is designed to aid men in tangible and concrete ways.

At times the so-called church has not been the true church of Christ. It has occasionally missed the objectives which God ordained it to pursue. Sometimes it has been a persecuting force, or a recalcitrant agency, or an unspiritual community, or a backslidden group of people. Men with spiritual insight have sometimes felt led to leave such organizations and have even gone so far as to suggest that the organized church is superfluous. Hierarchical control, ecclesiasticism, politics, schisms, heresies have rent the church, damaged its testimony, and vitiated its power.

In spite of all this we must emphasize the truth that the

visible organization is a divine creation and that it was made for men. No matter what reasons he adduces, no Christian can afford to overlook the truth that every believer must engage in corporate worship. Every true follower of Christ should be identified in some way with the Christian community. The church needs men, but even more than this, men need the church. Even if the church is not what it ought to be, we are not to bypass the church; we are to purify it and bring it back to the place which God intended for it.

Perhaps the words of John Calvin will help to clarify the distinction we have made. "In this Church (the visible) are included many hypocrites, who have nothing of Christ but the name and appearance; many persons ambitious, avaricious, envious, slanderous, and dissolute in their lives, who are tolerated for a time, either because they cannot be convicted by a legitimate process, or because discipline is not always maintained with sufficient vigor. As it is necessary, therefore, to believe in that Church, which is invisible to us, and known to God alone, so this Church, which is visible to men, we are commanded to honor, and to maintain communion with it."

1. *Tests of a true, Biblical church.* A true church can be judged by the following criteria:

a. In its basic doctrinal expression is it loyal to the cardinal truths of the Bible as held by Christendom for twenty centuries? Does it believe that the Bible is the Word of God?

b. Is it building up the saints in their most holy faith, conforming them to the image of God's dear Son? Paul declares that "all things work together for good to them that love God . . . for whom he did foreknow, he also did predestinate to be conformed to the image of his Son . . ." (Rom. 8:28, 29); and "we all, with open face beholding as in a glass the glory of the Lord, are changed into the same image from glory to glory, even as by the Spirit of the Lord" (2 Cor. 3:18). The most casual examination of the epistles shows that their purpose was to instruct believers in the faith and to promote piety, zeal and sanctified living. In seeking these same goals the true church plays an important part. To it the followers of Christ come for worship, edification, the ordinances or sacraments, but above all for instruction in the Word of the Lord.

c. Is it carrying the gospel of the Lord Jesus to the ends of the earth? The true church is a channel through which men can find Christ and be saved from their sins. Its divine formula is the Great Commission of Christ; the execution of the Saviour's command is its perpetual challenge and constant imperative. The failure of the church in this regard has been tragic. Blame for world conditions is, in part, due to the lethargy of Christians who have failed to carry out the divine commission. Nevertheless to be a true church, the body of believers must be worshipping, working and witnessing. The church is now militant, not triumphant and at rest. Its theme must be "Onward Christian soldiers, marching as to war."

2. *The organization of the church.* When Jesus spoke to Peter after the disciple's great confession of faith, He said, "thou art Peter, and upon this rock (Peter's testimony) I will build my church; and the gates of hell shall not prevail against it" (Matt. 16:18). Christ fulfilled His promise. He built His church and ordained a government for it. The church triumphant in heaven will need no human leadership: Christ the bridegroom will be there and will do all that needs to be done. But the church militant is waging its warfare on earth and God has given directions concerning its organizational structure.

Wide divergencies in church organization are evident today. The Roman Catholic pope is supposed to be the vicar of Christ and infallible when speaking concerning faith and practice. On the other hand there are groups which have neither pastors nor officers, but whose members all meet on an equal footing with respect to position and function. Christian charity must operate in this area, for good people have differed strongly over the question of church organization. Protestants, in the main, have three forms of church government: the episcopal, the representative and the congregational.

The New Testament speaks of two church offices: elder or bishop, and deacon.

a. These offices are subordinate to the Lord Himself, Who is the real Head of the church. No man should seek to usurp the place and prerogatives of Jesus Christ. Every office must be subject to Him. No Christian should aid or abet the schemes of any individual or group that seeks to deprive the Lord of His headship.

b. Church officials are the servants of the churches, not their rulers or masters. Ministers, for example, are told that they are not to be "lords over God's heritage, but being ensamples to the flock" (1 Peter 5:3). They are not to be greedy of filthy lucre, contentious, crafty, pleasers of men, nor entangled by cares nor given to wine (see Acts 20:33; Gal. 1:10; 1 Tim. 3:3; 2 Tim. 2:4; Titus 1:7; 1 Peter 5:2). They are enjoined, on the contrary, to preach the gospel, feed the sheep, build God's church, teach, exhort, strengthen, warn, comfort, watch over souls, endure hardness and war a good warfare.

And now an admonition is in order. Every child of God should believe that the visible church is God's own creation for the benefit of believers and for the extension of the gospel. He should identify himself with some visible church, engage in its activities and lend his influence to, and throw his support behind its work—praying always that every member of the visible church might be in very truth a member of the church invisible.

# 42

# The Believer's Worship

---

Worship is one of the spiritual functions and privileges enjoyed by Christians. It is more than a teaching of Scripture. It is a practice to be followed.

## A. THE URGE TO WORSHIP.

Within the human breast is an innate longing to have an external object of reverence and adoration. Men who know not the true God have expressed this longing in methods both crude and refined. The Bible tells of benighted souls whose land is full of idols. "They worship the work of their own hands, that which their own fingers have made" (Isaiah 2:8). Even Israel, when apostatizing from the Lord, felt the need of worship. She "worshipped Ashtoreth the goddess of the Zidonians, Chemosh the god of the Moabites, and Milcom the god of the children of Ammon" (1 Kings 11:33). Man seems to be restless until he can prostrate himself before some object of veneration.

For the child of God to worship is a necessity. But his is true worship, grounded upon a living relationship to God through Christ. There wells up within him a river of satisfaction, joy and spiritual enthusiasm which demands an expressional outlet in worship. Christians adore the Almighty because the Spirit of God has overwhelmed them with a yearning to render obeisance to God who has saved them and whom they have come to know and love.

## B. THE NATURE OF WORSHIP.

Worship is not primarily the outward observance of rites and ceremonies. It does not consist in the formal exercises of religion, although many of the visible forms of our faith are rooted in tradition and serve a worthy purpose. Instead, worship is an exercise of the soul. Man's inner being goes out toward God in praise, homage, and adoration. His spirit expresses gratitude, love and appreciation. He pours out his soul in devotion to his Lord.

## C. THE POSTURE IN WORSHIP.

The physical posture of the worshipper is intended to be an indication of his spiritual attitude. The Psalmist summons believers thus: "O come, let us worship and bow down: let us kneel before the Lord our maker" (Psalm 95:6). In ancient times Job "fell down upon the ground, and worshipped" (Job 1:20). When David instructed all the congregation to bless the Lord, they "bowed down their heads, and worshipped the Lord" (1 Chron. 29:20). In the days of Ezra the people "bowed their heads, and worshipped the Lord with their faces to the ground" (Neh. 8:6). Even devotees of false religions have recognized the relationship between posture and worship. Isaiah, for example, writes concerning the maker of images: ". . . he maketh a god, even his graven image: he falleth down unto it, and worshippeth it, and prayeth unto it, and saith, Deliver me; for thou art my god" (Isaiah 44:17).

## D. THE OBJECT OF TRUE WORSHIP.

The devil desires to be worshipped. To this end he tempted Jesus in the wilderness. He promised Him in exchange for His worship "all the kingdoms of the world, and the glory of them" (Matt. 4:8). Our Lord met the temptation squarely. Using "the sword of the Spirit" He parried His adversary's thrust. "Get thee hence, Satan," He cried, "for it is written, Thou shalt worship the Lord thy God, and him only shalt thou serve" (Matt. 4:10). The worship of Satan is sin.

God alone is the object of true worship. Men are not to adore graven images or likenesses: "Thou shalt not bow down thyself to them, nor serve them" (Ex. 20:5). God is jealous. He will brook no rivalry. He will be the sole object of man's worship. He will have all our homage or none. This is true for two reasons.

1. As man's Creator, Redeemer, and Sustainer, God alone is worthy of human worship. Man belongs to Him by creation and redemption, and worship is the holy bond uniting creature and Creator.

2. Any "worship" which is not directed toward God is superstition, not true worship. When King Ahaziah "served Baal, and worshipped him," he "provoked to anger the Lord God of Israel" (1 Kings 22:53). When Israel "left all the commandments of the Lord their God, and made them molten images, even two calves, and made a grove, and worshipped all the host of heaven, and served Baal" (2 Kings 17:16), God "was very angry with Israel, and removed them out of his sight" (2 Kings 17:18). When some twenty-five men were discovered by the prophet Ezekiel "with their backs toward the temple of the Lord, and their faces toward the east; and they worshipped the sun toward the east," the Lord said: "Therefore will I also deal in fury: mine eye shall not spare, neither will I have pity: and though they cry in mine ears with a loud voice, yet will I not hear them" (Ezek. 8:16,18).

Why this stern harshness? Because God rejects false worship as a repudiation of His own title to man's adoration. False worship, being nothing more than superstition directed toward unreal objects of adoration, is an insult to the Being of God, who alone is, and is "a rewarder of them that diligently seek him" (Heb. 11:6).

## E. THE BASIS OF TRUE WORSHIP.

The sacrifice of Jesus Christ, God's eternal Lamb, is the basis of true worship. An instructive passage dealing with this subject is found in the description of the tabernacle, its furniture, priesthood, and ceremonies. (See Ex. 25 ff.) The Epistle to the Hebrews is a divine commentary on this passage in Exodus. The priest could enter into the presence of God in the holy of holies only after the blood-sacrifice had been made. The logical sequence had to be observed.

Following this "pattern" (see Heb. 8:5), one does not come to God today in helter-skelter fashion. Just as the priest, before entering the tabernacle, sacrificed an animal and poured out its blood as a covering for sin, so today he who would truly worship approaches God on the ground of a perfect sacrifice for sin. The sacrifice is Christ, the Lamb of God, who has consecrated for us "a new and living way" (Heb. 10:20). On no other basis is our worship acceptable to the Father.

## F. THE PARTICIPANTS IN TRUE WORSHIP.

All believers are priests, and all may participate in worship. Many believe that worship is ineffective without some human mediator or the intervention of some saint. But the Scriptures teach differently.

Every believer in Christ has the right to exercise priestly functions. This is a priceless truth which the Protestant Reformation emphasized. By virtue of the redeeming work of Christ believers are set apart as priests and have the privilege of access to God in worship. The Lord Jesus is the "one mediator between God and men" (1 Tim. 2:5). Through Him we are "a chosen generation, a royal priesthood" (1 Pet. 2:9). Christ "loved us, and washed us from our sins in his own blood,

And hath made us kings and priests unto God and his Father"
(Rev. 1:5,6). As priests, Christians have the right to worship
the Lord and to offer up the spiritual sacrifice of praise to their
Father in heaven. There are no class distinctions when it comes
to worship. The doors to the presence of God are open to all
who are priests through faith in Christ.

The universal priesthood of believers is a glorious fact. It
involves privileges but it also imposes responsibilities which
issue in the solemn duty of worship. We must thank God that
He is accessible to the humblest saint in the hour of worship.
But we must regard as sin the failure to take advantage of the
sacred privilege of rendering homage to the Lord.

## G. The Manner of Worship.

The Psalmist declared: "O worship the Lord in the beauty
of holiness" (Psalm 96:9). The Lord Jesus gave to the woman
of Samaria a formula: "God is a Spirit: and they that worship
him must worship him in spirit and in truth" (John 4:24).
From such passages we can deduce the following:

1. True worship, whether private or public, is the worship
of the Lord "in the beauty of holiness." One must realize that
the Lord God is holy, and must approach His courts with
clean hands and a pure heart; this is the person who "shall
ascend into the hill of the Lord" (Psalm 24:3,4). One must
not harbor unconfessed sin in his life when he lifts up his soul
in worship.

2. True worship is "in spirit," not in the flesh—it is internal,
not external. To provide an atmosphere conducive to the worship of God is helpful. When, however, the audible, visible,
or tangible surroundings,—the soft music, low lights, chanted
intonations—become ends in themselves or unduly exalt the
flesh, they are an abomination to God.

3. True worship is "in truth," not in error. It must be seen
against the background of the gospel, as the privilege of the
redeemed and as directed toward the living and true God.

True worship is no mere psychological stimulus to the spirit; it is an outpouring of devotion rising from the thankful souls of God's people in accordance with the provisions of the holy Scriptures.

## H. The Importance of Public Worship.

This is not a matter for debate. It is a call to action. Let every believer "enter into his gates with thanksgiving, and into his courts with praise; be thankful unto him, and bless his name. For the Lord is good; his mercy is everlasting; and his truth endureth to all generations" (Psalm 100:4,5). Christian worship is an obligation. Note that:

1. Christ and the early church set us an example. The elements of public worship were already in evidence before the first century came to a close. Jesus did not frown upon such worship. He encouraged it. His attendance upon the services of the synagogue shows us that He endorsed public worship: "And he came to Nazareth, where he had been brought up: and, as his custom was, he went into the synagogue on the sabbath day, and stood up for to read" (Luke 4:16).

2. Paul, like his Master, left us the same example. His "manner" was to engage in public worship regularly. (Study Acts 17:1-3.)

3. The Word of God enjoins public worship. Just as God in the old dispensation demanded the presence of the children of Israel in public worship, so in the new dispensation He makes the same demand: "And let us consider one another to provoke unto love and to good works: Not forsaking the assembling of ourselves together, as the manner of some is" (Heb. 10:24,25).

# 43

# The Ordinances or Sacraments

Among Protestants two ordinances or sacraments are cele-
brated, baptism and the Lord's Supper. The Roman Catholic
Church observes seven sacraments, i.e. baptism, confirmation,
the Eucharist, penance, extreme unction, holy orders, and
matrimony. The reason for this numerical disparity is clear.
The Bible speaks of only two ordinances, baptism and the
Lord's Supper. The other five represent man-made additions
foreign to the Scriptures and introduced after the apostles had
died and the canon had been closed. Some ordinances have a
longer history than others; but none of them, apart from baptism and the Lord's Supper, has any warrant in the Word of
God. Tradition may insist that they have been observed for
many centuries. But if they do not find their source in the
Bible, no matter how long they have been taught and used,
we do not believe that they have a Scriptural right to exist.

## A. BAPTISM.

Among Protestants differences exist pertaining to baptism.
Occasionally these differences are the only barriers separating
one denomination or group from another. Most Protestant
groups believe in water baptism. The differences have to do
with the following questions:

1. *Mode of baptism.* Baptists and some other groups believe that the Biblical method of baptism is immersion. They do not believe that a person has been truly baptized if he has only been sprinkled or has simply had water poured over his head. In this view a person must be completely covered by water to be baptized properly. Others believe that the mode is unimportant. They willingly accept sprinkling, affusion, or immersion. Presbyterians, for example, while they customarily sprinkle, prescribe no single form as the only acceptable mode. A few groups believe that one must be immersed three times (trine immersion); and some believe that the one baptized must face downwards. Nearly all groups except the Baptists are lenient and will accept any mode of baptism. A person immersed in a Baptist church is acceptable in a Presbyterian church. But one who has been sprinkled in a Presbyterian church must be immersed if he is to be received into a Baptist church.

2. *Subjects of baptism.* Some groups practice believers' baptism. They baptize only those who have made a credible profession of faith in the Lord Jesus Christ as personal Saviour. These groups baptize neither infants nor children who have not reached the age of responsibility. Other bodies of believers practice infant baptism, holding that children are in a covenant relationship to God through their believing parents. Most of these groups do not teach that the baptized children will automatically grow up to be Christians, but that when they reach the age of accountability they must make a profession of faith for themselves. A few groups teach baptismal regeneration, i.e. that one is "born again" by baptism. Some Lutherans, Episcopalians, Disciples, and others hold to this view, although Protestants for the most part reject it.

3. *Necessity of baptism.* Every church group with very few exceptions teaches that baptism is essential to an obedient walk with our Lord. Almost every church requires that a person wishing to enter its fellowship be baptized. Within the

context of differing interpretations of baptism, Protestants generally insist on the rite. The warrant for their insistence is the clear teaching of the Bible: "Go ye therefore, and teach all nations, baptizing them in the name of the Father, and of the Son, and of the Holy Ghost: Teaching them to observe all things whatsoever I have commanded you: and, lo, I am with you alway, even unto the end of the world. Amen" (Matt. 28:19,20).

4. *The meaning of baptism.* To some baptism is a means of grace and to others, such as the Baptists, it is a symbolic act. To the former baptism is in varying degrees a special vehicle of grace, a sacrament which truly conveys grace to the participant. To the latter there is nothing in a baptismal service that is not equally present in an ordinary church service.

## B. THE LORD'S SUPPER.

Among Protestants differences exist in connection with the Lord's Supper. These differences are just as pronounced as those which relate to baptism, but they are less known to believers in general. Many a church member cannot explain what his denomination or group teaches about the Lord's Supper. Still fewer are able to state what other groups believe. The Lord's Supper has been less of a dividing factor among Christians than baptism has, doubtless because baptismal divergences are largely external while differences about the Lord's Supper are generally internal, relating less to form than to meaning.

1. *The different points of view.* These concern:

a. The presence of our Lord in the communion service and the elements. The Lutherans teach what is popularly called "consubstantiation." This view holds that Christ is ubiquitous and thus actually present in the communion. The bread remains bread and the wine remains wine; but in some mysterious way Jesus is there in reality and in His person. Presbyterians and others believe in the real "spiritual" presence of Christ in the elements, that He is there in a spiritual sense. Still others, such as the Baptists, believe in the symbolic presence of Christ in the ordinance: He is there just as He is at any other service of worship. The Roman Catholic Church teaches that by a miracle of consecration (called "transubstantiation") the bread and wine become the body and blood of our Lord, and that He is actually sacrificed afresh on Roman altars every day. No Protestant group of any kind holds to this Roman viewpoint. All Protestants serve the elements—the bread and the wine—to all participants; whereas the Roman Church serves only the bread to the laity and reserves the wine for the priesthood.

b. "Open" versus "Close" communion. Some churches believe that only members of a given local church have the right to participate in the communion service. They have a restricted service limited to the members of the church, and they exclude all others. Perhaps the Baptists hold to this view more consistently than any other group. But most Protestant churches invite "all believers" to participate in the service regardless of their denominational affiliations. In many instances communion breakfasts are held outside the church and include Christians from many denominations. Those who hold that communion is a church ordinance and that a school or public auditorium is not a church, object to such practices. They consider any communion service other than one held in a local church for members of that church to be a violation of Biblical precepts.

c. The frequency in observing the Lord's Supper. Christians almost universally accept the Lord's Supper as an integral part of New Testament church order and insist upon it as Biblical and necessary. While opinions differ as to whether the communion service should be held quarterly, weekly, or monthly, all agree that it should be held and that it has value for the Christian in his relationship to his Lord.

d. The meaning of the ordinance or sacrament. Some Christians believe that the Lord's Supper conveys grace and provides spiritual food for the believer; others hold that it is purely symbolic and does not convey special grace any more than a preaching service does. All, in one sense or another, believe that it is beneficial to the one who partakes. Some insist that the Supper provides the participant with definite spiritual sustenance. Others regard it primarily as a memorial of what our Lord has done, an act of worship to be observed until He comes again. But all agree that it brings the believer face to face with the fact of our Lord's death and atoning sacrifice, and that it furnishes the Christian a sacred opportunity to examine his life before partaking of the meal.

2. *The relation of the Lord's Supper to church discipline.* No one living a scandalous life should partake of the Supper. Church discipline should be wielded and such a person refused the privilege of partaking until he has repented of his sins and has been restored to fellowship. Obviously, in the case of secret sin discipline cannot be enforced. When the sin becomes public, however, it is wrong and Biblically inconsistent to permit the evildoer to partake even though he may be a church member. Perhaps this is one of the chief reasons churches lose their spiritual power—they permit persons to communicate who have no Biblical right to do so.

\* \* \*

The New Testament teaches the necessity of both baptism and the observance of the Lord's Supper. Every Christian who walks in obedience to the divine commands should be baptized and partake at the communion table. Let us be charitable toward one another about differences deeply held; let us respect these differences; and let us never condemn any group which differs with us and which refuses to open its door to those who do not meet what it considers to be the New Testament requirements for coming to the Lord's Table. No one is right at every point. Good Christians who have no differences whatever about the deity of our Lord, His virgin birth, and His vicarious atonement, do differ when it comes to the two ordinances or sacraments. Let us hold to our convictions courageously, but let us differ in the spirit of love, humility, and teachableness.

# 44

# *Stewardship*

---

Christians sometimes seem to think that the term "steward-ship" applies only to the use of money. To render an effective stewardship in God's sight one must be faithful, not only in handling his financial means, but in other areas of life as well. However, in this material age the effectiveness of one's stewardship of life may often be judged by his use of money. When a man's income is tithed, it is far more likely that the rest of his life will be dedicated to God.

Stewardship has to do with the concrete and the specific, but also with one's attitude and frame of mind. Biblical stewardship is not just the performance of certain acts; it is a life out of which acts flow as from a well of precious, satisfying waters.

A. The Meaning of Stewardship.

1. The root of the word "stewardship" conveys the idea of house management. Among the corollary concepts are the following:

a. The steward is not the owner. He does not possess the estate he manages. It is derived property, the ownership of which is vested in another.

b. The true owner has the right to demand an accounting

from the one to whom his possessions have been entrusted. This right does not depend on the steward, who has no choice in the matter. The only items for which no accounting need be rendered by the steward are those which he owns intrinsically and not by derivation. But whatever man possesses comes directly from God. Man must therefore account to God the Giver for all that God bestows. Paul tells us: "For who maketh thee to differ from another? and what hast thou that thou didst not receive? now if thou didst receive it, why dost thou glory, as if thou hadst not received it" (1 Cor. 4:7)?

2. The word "stewardship" also conveys the thought that diminution and accretion may occur depending on the use to which the entrusted possessions are put. The important question is not "What have you?" It is "What are you doing with what you have?" God demands that men account for what they have received. Three possible choices face the Christian in the use of his treasure.

a. He can fail to use it. He can leave the resources given to him undeveloped. All the iron, or diamonds encased in a thousand veins of the earth are of no avail so long as they remain unmined. Some men have native endowments and abilities. God will not hold one accountable for failing to develop gifts he does not possess. But to refuse to utilize talents one does possess is tragic. Native capacities remain valueless if they are not cultivated for the glory of God. One is often tempted to believe that his gifts are useless unless they are of the highest quality. If he does not have a beautiful voice or outstanding administrative gifts, he is prone to let such talents as he has lie fallow. Was it not a rod in the hand of Moses that turned back the waters of the Red Sea? Did not David slay Goliath with a pebble and a sling? Even a seemingly insignificant gift may become a mighty weapon for good when put to use for God.

b. He can misuse it. The gifts implanted by our Father can be developed and used, but for wrong purposes. The voice that sings the praises of God can be used in a night club. The gift of speaking which can be used to preach the gospel may also be used to create race hatred or to propagate Communism. The hand that can bring the ministry of medical healing to the native of Africa may wield the scalpel for unlawful gain. The legal gifts that can be used to assure justice in the land may also be employed to defend vicious criminals who wish to escape justice. Christians who misuse their talents thereby dishonor their Master.

c. He can use it to the glory of God. The child of God must cultivate and develop whatever God has given him, and use the gift in such a way as to benefit the Kingdom of God.

## B. AREAS OF STEWARDSHIP.

Let us examine these areas, review our lives, and decide whether our stewardship is all that it ought to be.

1. *Treasure.* Many Christians object to the idea of the tithe. They believe that the tithe does not apply to them: it is on "legal" ground, while they are under grace. Yet the principle of the tithe is written large in the Scriptures. "Ye are cursed with a curse: for ye have robbed me, even this whole nation. Bring ye all the tithes into the storehouse, that there may be meat in mine house, and prove me now herewith, saith the Lord of hosts, if I will not open you the windows of heaven, and pour you out a blessing, that there shall not be room enough to receive it" (Mal. 3:9,10). Surely we who are under grace should have no lower standard than they had who were under law. Remember that long before the law was given the principle of the tithe was written in the lives of the faithful. Abraham tithed, as it is written: "And he (Abram) gave him tithes of all" (Gen. 14:20). "Now consider how great this man was (Melchisedec), unto whom even the patriarch Abraham gave the tenth of the spoils" (Heb. 7:4). The least the Christian can do is to tithe, thereby indicating that the other ninety per cent belongs to God. The stewardship of money

does not end with what one gives. It extends to his use of what he does not give, to all his earthly goods. God has blessed His children. In loving gratitude they should return to Him a suitable portion regularly, systematically and proportionately.

2. *Time.* All men have this commodity. Each has twenty-four hours a day. This is one gift which is always immediate and which cannot be laid up for future use. We have only today. Yesterday is gone forever; what is lost is irreparably lost and can never be regained. And tomorrow never comes. Is there a proper ratio between the time spent for God and the time spent on recreation and secular pursuits? Let us be ruthlessly honest. Do we spend enough time in:

a. *Prayer?* "Pray without ceasing" (1 Thess. 5:17). "Be careful for nothing; but in every thing by prayer and supplication with thanksgiving let your requests be made known unto God" (Phil. 4:6). "I will therefore that men pray every where, lifting up holy hands, without wrath and doubting" (1 Tim. 2:8).

b. *The study of the Bible?* "Thy word have I hid in mine heart, that I might not sin against thee" (Psalm 119:11). "All scripture is given by inspiration of God, and is profitable for doctrine, for reproof, for correction, for instruction in righteousness" (2 Tim. 3:16). Does the newspaper, radio or television usurp the time which ought to be spent in the invaluable study of God's Word? Are we faithful in this matter?

c. *Personal witnessing?* Time spent in testifying for Christ is time well employed. How much of any given day do we use for this purpose? Remember that whoso "winneth souls is wise" (Prov. 11:30).

3. *Talents.* Every Christian must ask himself honestly what his gifts are and whether he is neglecting them, misusing them or using them for the glory of God. If he has a voice, athletic gifts, writing talent, a logical mind—whatever he may have, is he utilizing it in a manner pleasing to Almighty God?

4. *The use of the tongue; the attitude of the heart; and the*

*nature of one's actions.* The injunctions of the Scripture are explicit:

a. *The tongue.* "And the tongue is a fire, a world of iniquity: so is the tongue among our members, that it defileth the whole body, and setteth on fire the course of nature; and it is set on fire of hell" (James 3:6). The stewardship of speech can be more important than the stewardship of money, important as the latter may be. For with the tongue reputations may be ruined, wounds inflicted, people irreparably damaged. Truth rarely catches up with a lie.

b. *The heart.* "Keep thy heart with all diligence; for out of it are the issues of life" (Prov. 4:23). Everything in life springs from within. What a man has in his heart or inner being determines his character. External conduct reflects the condition of the heart.

c. *Actions.* ". . . I will show thee my faith by my works" (James 2:18). "Actions speak more loudly than words." One's acts are the usual criterion for determining his thoughts. One's deeds must conform to the pattern of faith and reflect the holiness of Christ. While one should not judge another's motives, he has the right to judge another's acts. We must be careful, therefore, that our actions match our profession and that both are pleasing to our Father in heaven.

## C. Accounting for One's Stewardship.

"So then every one of us shall give account of himself to God" (Rom. 14:12). "Every man's work shall be made manifest: for the day shall declare it, because it shall be revealed by fire: . . . If any man's work abide which he hath built thereupon, he shall receive a reward" (1 Cor. 3:13,14).

1. Every man will account for himself. No one will be able to criticize another's deeds or shortcomings. Stewardship is a personal, individual matter. Every redeemed child of God will stand on his own feet and give account of his own stewardship.

2. The account will be rendered at the judgment seat of

Christ which is still in the future. All Christian stewardship will come under divine scrutiny. No believer will escape rendering an account.

3. Jesus Christ is the one to whom we shall render our account. We shall not have to explain our conduct to men or to angels; to human friends or to enemies; or even to the devil. To Jesus we shall bring the accounting. And from Jesus we shall receive a just reward.

PART EIGHT

# The Believer's Outreach

The church of Jesus Christ has a message for a sin-cursed world—the glad tidings of salvation. She is more than a reservoir of truth. She is a channel of blessing unto the uttermost part of the earth. Her task is to evangelize without ceasing, to witness faithfully and persistently to the Person and work of her regnant Lord, to proclaim with no uncertain sound the fearfulness and dread consequences of sin, the coming judgment, and the refuge that is in Christ alone.

The testimony of the church is two-fold. A living organism, she is to seek to win men to Christ through the preaching of the Word, through mass evangelism, through her educational ministry, and through her multiplied organizations and activities. Every department of the life of the church should have as its primary or subsidiary aim the reaching of the unchurched for Christ.

But evangelism does not end there. Every child of God is his brother's spiritual "keeper." Every member of the church should be a witness for Christ, not merely through the example he sets, but through the message which he himself understands and has accepted, and which he knows how to share effectively with the lost. Unfortunately the church has neglected this personal aspect of her ministry. The oft-exaggerated differentiation between clergy and laity has encouraged this unwarranted error. Even the humblest saint is to be a witness for the Lord. Revival will not endure in the church until this emphasis is recaptured.

This section is dedicated to the Scriptural principles underlying the church's corporate and individual witness. May its pages serve to stir us up afresh to our solemn but joyous task.

## 45

# The Believer and the World

___

The believer finds himself in an environment known as the "world." He sustains certain relationships to his fellow-men, and must understand the will of God for his life as it relates to his environment.

The "world" as used here is not "nature." The child of God is not prevented from enjoying nature to the full. The sun, moon and stars, the glories of the sunset, the dainty simplicity of the primrose—these are evidences of God's creative skill, eloquent reminders of His provision and power. "The heavens declare the glory of God; and the firmament showeth his handiwork. Day unto day uttereth speech, and night unto night sheweth knowledge" (Psalm 19:1,2). The "world" in a Biblical sense is human society with God left out. The term describes the race of men who know not their Creator and who spurn the divine offer of redemption in Christ.

The relationship of a believer to such a world may be summarized by five prepositions.

A. THE CHRISTIAN IS IN THE WORLD.

Limited by the dimensions of space and time, he experiences the world as his physical habitat for a season. "These are in the world," the Lord Jesus said concerning His beloved followers. "I pray not that thou shouldest take them out of the world" (John 17:15).

## B. THE CHRISTIAN IS NOT OF THE WORLD.

In His High-priestly prayer Jesus said, "They are not of the world, even as I am not of the world" (John 17:14). The church is composed of "called-out ones." Christians intermingle physically with the citizens of the world, but they are not identical in origin, life, or outlook with their unbelieving neighbors.

The believer's citizenship is in heaven. He is part of a new fellowship which is totally distinct from the world system. He is a "stranger" to many who think they know him well. He is a "pilgrim" (1 Pet. 2:11) who pitches his tent for a time here below, but who is bound for the City of God.

The comparison Jesus drew between His disciples and salt, or light, is pertinent. The value of salt lies in its distinctiveness from the object salted. When it "loses its savor," surrenders its differentiating element, it has no further useful function. "It is thenceforth good for nothing, but to be cast out, and to be trodden under foot of men" (Matt. 5:13). Similarly, the service performed by light depends upon its difference from darkness. Darkness and light are mutually exclusive. So the children of God, by virtue of their new birth, present nature, and ultimate destiny, are not of the world. They form a society within the world, but they possess an inheritance, engage in activities, and enjoy a hope which distinguishes them from the world.

## C. THE CHRISTIAN IS TO HAVE VICTORY OVER THE WORLD.

Because of his proximity to the world the child of God feels its steady pressure. This pressure manifests itself through the temptation to yield to the whispered or blatant entreaties of the world.

1. The believer must steadfastly be on his guard against three types of temptation:

a. *"The lust of the flesh":* in the garden of Eden Eve saw that the fruit of the tree was "good for food"; Jesus was tempted to change a stone into bread; His people are tempted to succumb to the allurements of appetite.

b. *"The lust of the eyes":* Eve saw that the tree was "pleasant to the eyes"; Jesus was tempted to secure immediate popular acclaim by casting Himself from a pinnacle of the temple; Christians are tempted to yield to the enticements of avarice.

c. *"The pride of life":* Eve saw that the tree was "desired to make one wise"; Jesus "saw all the kingdoms of the world, and the glory of them," and was tempted to acquire their allegiance by a spiritual detour which would have avoided the cross; believers are tempted to heed the seductive appeal of undue ambition. (Study 1 John 2:15,16; Gen. 3:6 and Matt. 4:1-11.)

2. The believer must not compromise with the world. The Bible declares emphatically: "Love not the world, neither the things that are in the world. If any man love the world, the love of the Father is not in him" (1 John 2:15); "And be not conformed to this world: but be ye transformed by the renewing of your mind . . ." (Rom. 12:2); "Know ye not that the friendship of the world is enmity with God? whosoever therefore will be a friend of the world is the enemy of God" (Jas. 4:4). The Christian must give ear to these injunctions, and seek to exhibit pure and undefiled religion, one aspect of which is to "keep himself unspotted from the world" (Jas. 1:27).

3. The believer may be victorious over the world. Victory comes through yieldedness to the indwelling Holy Spirit; utilizing the means of grace; prayer and the worship and ordi-

nances of the church; the use of the Word of God; and communion with the people of God. All this, however, is based upon the Christian's faith. "And this is the victory that over-cometh the world, even our faith" (1 John 5:4b). Faith en-ables one to comprehend the nature of the conflict, its occasion, final issue, and his own relationship to it. Faith weighs the present against the future, the visible against the invisible, the temporal against the eternal. And the choice spells the differ-ence between victory and defeat.

## D. THE CHRISTIAN IS TO EXERT AN INFLUENCE UPON THE WORLD.

1. He will influence the world because his own nature has been supernaturally changed, and the Holy Spirit, resident within him, produces fruit which others will observe. In other words, his influence will be a by-product of his own salvation.

2. He will also influence the world for good because his attitudes, as well as his nature, have been changed. A new gen-erosity, tenderness, sympathy, unselfishness now characterize him. Rather than dwell in a monastery, he prefers to express his new-found love in the market-place. He is interested in philanthropy, and social and political amelioration. Wherever the gospel is proclaimed it exerts a leavening influence. The position of woman is elevated, the status of pagan life is im-proved, hospitals are organized, legislation is changed, charity is promoted, the fallen are lifted, and education is furthered.

But the temporary influences for good exerted by the gospel are not the major purpose of its proclamation. They are not to become ends in themselves. They must not be regarded as substitutes for the preaching of the gospel. They are the fruit, not the seed.

3. He will influence the world for righteousness, truth and freedom. He understands that the gospel cause to which he is devoting his life thrives when these prevail, and is threatened when injustice, falsehood and tyranny stalk the land. Believers

should not hesitate to take a resolute, progressive stand when moral issues are at stake in the conduct of world affairs. They are to be serene but not supine, charitable but not cowardly.

## E. THE CHRISTIAN IS SENT TO THE WORLD.

Our Saviour prayed "As thou hast sent me into the world, even so have I also sent them into the world" (John 17:18). Note the sequence: The Father sent the Son, out from the bosom of His love, to a hostile world of suffering, sorrow and death; so the Son sends His people out into the world, which will hate them even as it hated Him. (See John 17:14.) Every believer has a mission for his Lord.

1. The success of this mission cannot be assured unless the Christian has victory over the world. If one would lift men up to God he must himself be on a higher plane. When Abraham's nephew Lot sat in the gates of Sodom, breathing the atmosphere of iniquity in which the Sodomites reveled, it was well-nigh impossible for him to give forth an effective witness. His towns-fellows mocked him: "This one fellow came in to sojourn, and he will needs be a judge" (Gen. 19:9). Separation from tainted contacts with the world is a pre-requisite to a worthy mission to the world.

2. The mission is two-fold:

a. The child of God announces the judgment of God upon the world. He pronounces its works to be evil, its gods to be idols, its fondest creations to be but dust and ashes, its cherished dreams to be nightmares, its life to be death.

b. Over against this counsel of despair the believer offers to a lost and dying world the word of grace: "God was in Christ, reconciling the world unto himself, not imputing their trespasses unto them" (2 Cor. 5:19). The Christian's testimony is the ministry of reconciliation.

# 46

# The Believer and the Community

One is tempted to suppose that the Christian life would be easier if it could be lived in a monastery, apart from all the tensions and complexities of society. Whatever may be one's opinion about this, the fact remains that the Christian is not, and never will be, in a social vacuum. For good or ill he is a member of the community. As such he has social relationships.

## A. THE CHRISTIAN'S PERSONAL RELATIONSHIPS.

The problem begins here. One must see himself as he is:

1. *His relationship to self.* He must be ruthlessly frank. He must search his soul daily, eager to detect, confess, and abandon sin.

2. *His relationship to the means of grace.* He must read, assimilate, and apply the Word of God to his soul's need. He must engage faithfully in prayer and worship.

3. *His relationship to God.* Knowing the Lord Jesus Christ as his Saviour, he must walk humbly with his God. (See Micah 6:8.)

## B. THE CHRISTIAN'S MARITAL RELATIONSHIPS.

Wherever the Christian faith has been propagated the status of womanhood has improved. Woman is no longer a vassal, a slave or a tool. She is a person, a being for whom Christ died.

1. As Christ is the Head of the church, so the husband is the head of the wife. (See Eph. 5:23.) This does not mean that he is a tyrant. The husband is to love his wife (see Eph. 5:25), to nourish and cherish her, and to render her the respect which is her due.

2. The wife is to be subject to her husband. (See Eph. 5:24.) This is not a cringing or fawning obedience. It is respect mingled with love.

Between husband and wife there should be a mutuality, a reciprocity of interest, sympathy and tenderness. The basis for successful marriage is that the relationship be triangular: a partnership involving a man, a woman, and God.

## C. The Christian's Familial Relationships.

The parent-child relationship will be Christian if:

1. *Children obey and honor their parents.* "Children, obey your parents in the Lord: for this is right. Honour thy father and mother . . ." (Eph. 6:1,2). The divine standard for children in the home is obedience coupled with respect. This combination is attainable "in the Lord." If both parent and child are properly related to God, the child will delight in obeying and honoring the parent. The immediate solution for disobedience in the home may well be the use of discipline. The permanent solution, however, is to bring God into the picture.

2. *The parents heed God's injunctions.* "Ye fathers, provoke not your children to wrath" (Eph. 6:4). Demand, but do not threaten. Insist, but do not irritate. This is a negative precept. A positive command follows which beautifully outlines the duty of a Christian parent: "But bring them up in the nurture and admonition of the Lord:" this implies growth furthered by encouragement, and discipline administered in love. Consecrate your children to the Lord, claim them for the Lord, and surround them with Christian influences.

## D. The Christian's Ecclesiastical Relationships.

The believer is a member of the church invisible which is a living organism having its counterpart in a visible organization.

1. His primary allegiance is to Christ. Ideally, membership in the visible organization should never conflict with his membership in the body of Christ. When "loyalty" to the visible organization conflicts with loyalty to Christ, one must obey God rather than men (see Acts 5:29).

2. Members of the body (the church) are members one of another. (Study Rom. 12:4-8; 1 Cor. 12:12-27.) They are joined in mystical union, but each member of the body has a different function. The union demands both cooperation and differentiation. Each member must live in creative harmony with the rest of the body.

3. Members of the visible church should cooperate with, and be submissive to, those who hold office. "And we beseech you, brethren, to know them which labour among you, and are over you in the Lord, and admonish you; And to esteem them very highly in love for their work's sake" (1 Thess. 5:12,13). Cooperation and submission, then, should be rendered only when the leaders of the church are in the Lord and when their decisions are in accord with the Scriptures.

4. Officers of the church must not take advantage of their high position. They are to esteem their leadership as a trust from Christ, and to exercise due humility, sympathy and love in carrying out their duties.

5. The believer has a two-fold duty toward "weaker brethren" in the Christian community.

a. He must be charitable in his judgments of those whose faith is not as strong as his own (see Rom. 14:4,10,12,13). Knowing that he must himself appear before Christ's judgment-seat, he must be gentle in his criticism of others.

b. He must be careful not to put a stumbling block in his

weaker brother's path (see Rom. 14:13-15). Certain practices may be relatively harmless to the strong Christian, but if the possibility exists that they may cause a weaker brother to stumble, they should be sedulously avoided.

6. The believer should become a member of the visible organization, a church. In this way he publicly confesses his faith in Christ. He should, however, unite with a church loyal to the whole counsel of God, a church he can serve in good conscience.

7. Members of the church should share the concern of the officers in making certain that every member on the church roll is a true believer, and thus a member of the true church, the church invisible.

## E. The Christian's Political Relationships.

The Christian is a good citizen. His relationship to civil authorities is outlined in Romans 13:1-7 and 1 Peter 2:13-17.

1. The believer is "subject unto the higher powers" (Rom. 13:1), for he realizes that they are "ordained of God." Civil powers bear not the sword in vain. (See Rom. 13:4.)

2. The believer has a high sense of civic responsibility to government. He cooperates with the authorities. He votes and pays his taxes. He works for the preservation of peace and for the protection of liberty at home and abroad.

3. But the believer is a patriot, not a slave. His loyalty to government is not cringing or subservient. Only as long as the authorities grant him religious and political liberty is he compelled to render them their "dues," "tribute" and "custom" (Rom. 13:7).

## F. The Christian's Industrial Relationships.

Here the Bible lays down three broad principles:

1. *The servant and his master.* "Be obedient to them that are your masters according to the flesh, with fear and trembling, in singleness of your heart, as unto Christ; not with eye-

service, as men-pleasers; but as the servants of Christ, doing the will of God from the heart." (Eph. 6:5,6; see 1 Pet. 2:18-20.) These words were, of course, addressed to Roman slaves, but they are valid today. Christian employees must remember that they are bondslaves of Christ. They should perform their tasks as unto the Lord. Perhaps their employers are unfair. They have the right to protest and appeal. But in all their dealings they must remember that they are responsible to Christ. His standards are high and holy. (See Titus 2:9,10.)

2. *The master and his servant.* "And, ye masters, do the same things unto them, forbearing threatening: knowing that your Master also is in heaven; neither is there respect of persons with him" (Eph. 6:9). Christian employers must never forget that Christ is their Master. They are morally accountable to Him. This ideal must be their guide in every decision, in every business venture, in every relationship with subordinates.

3. *The master, the servant and God.* Management and labor relationships, if they are to be harmonious, must be a triangular proposition: management, labor and God. If the Lord is disregarded, confusion and distress will ensue. If His will is considered, even the hardest problem has a solution. When will the children of men learn this arithmetical, spiritual formula?

## G. The Christian's Race Relationships.

1. God has a plan for the races of men. He has determined "the bounds of their habitation" (Acts 17:26). Nowhere in the Bible is the assertion made that the ethnic and social barriers which have historically divided men should be artificially broken down.

2. Each race has its unique, appointed function in the divine economy. A piano has black and white keys. When these keys are played in harmony the melody is sweet. Inter-racial strife will be lessened when this simple principle is applied.

3. All races deserve equal opportunities to enjoy the good

things of life. Equality of opportunity and privilege for all men is earnestly to be desired.

4. The abiding basis of inter-racial cooperation is the presence and power of the Spirit of God. The counterpart of Babel's confusion of tongues was the new understanding which came at Pentecost when the Holy Spirit was given.

## H. The Law of Love: The Principle Underlying All Relationships.

For the child of God the key to maintaining happy, healthy, wholesome relationships with his fellow-men is genuine, self-forgetful love. This love is "the fulfilling of the law." It issues in honesty, purity, unselfishness, and is the hallmark of those who have themselves experienced in a personal way the depths of the love of Christ. (Study carefully Romans 13:8-14 and 1 Cor. 13.)

# 47

# The Believer's Witness

---

The Christian's primary task is to glorify God. In no way can he perform this task better than by witnessing for Christ. The word "witness" is derived from the Anglo-Saxon "witan," "to know." If one knows that Christ has saved him, and that mankind has no other valid hope of salvation, his responsibility is clear: he must be a witness for the Son of God.

Both in precept and illustration the Bible emphasizes the duty of witnessing.

Perhaps the simplest method of presenting the Scriptural teaching on the subject will be to study somewhat minutely a passage on personal work given to us in the book of Acts. Philip's dealings with the Ethiopian eunuch are a remarkable example of Spirit-directed and hence effective witnessing for Christ. (Read carefully Acts 8:26-40.)

A. THE PRINCIPLES UNDERLYING SUCCESSFUL
   PERSONAL WORK.

1. Christ gave to His church the task of witnessing. The heart of the Great Commission (Matt. 28:16-20) is in the words "Go, Teach." The disciples were to be empowered by the Holy Spirit and to testify step by step "unto the uttermost part of the earth" (Acts 1:8). Philip was simply obeying the marching orders of his Lord.

2. Witnessing is the duty of every believer. Philip was not an apostle. He was a deacon of the church. Testimony is the privilege, not of a select few, but of all who truly love the Lord Jesus.

3. The Christian who fails to witness for Christ is in jeopardy. When a lake has an adequate inlet but no sufficient outlet its waters become stagnant. The believer who worships, prays and reads the Word is constantly receiving blessing. If he fails to share it by witnessing, there is every possibility that he may become spiritually stagnant.

4. The story of Philip exemplifies the need of individual, personal work as well as of mass testimony. Like his Master, Philip understood the importance of dealing with solitary souls.

5. The gospel is for men of all colors, conditions and climes. The eunuch was a "foreigner" from Philip's point of view; he had a different ethnic background. He was a man of position, prestige and power. The story of salvation is for all men, black, white, and red; rich or poor; sick or sound.

6. "Religion" is not enough. A man must be introduced to Christ if he is to be saved. The eunuch had been to Jerusalem to worship: he was a worshipper. He was reading the Old Testament Scriptures: he was a Bible reader. Had Philip not found him for God, he would have remained lost.

7. The witnessing that produces permanent results is a Spirit directed enterprise from first to last. Notice that the Holy Spirit instructed Philip to join himself to the chariot; prepared the eunuch's reading and heart for the interview; presided over the conversation; and ultimately "caught away Philip." (See Acts 8:29,39.)

## B. The Purpose of Personal Work.

Many interesting themes might well have occurred to Philip as topics of conversation. The name "Philip" means "lover of horses": he might conceivably have chatted about equestrian matters! More likely, he could have dwelt upon the experiences of an Ethiopian in the temple, or the customs and history of Ethiopia, or the financial status of the African kingdom. Or he might have explained to his new friend the recent organization of the Jerusalem church, its "raison-d'être," nature, and functioning. All this would doubtless have been edifying.

Philip, however, had a job to perform. He refused to be led astray into alluring by-paths. He presented Christ to the eunuch. The conversation was Christo-centric. That is ever the goal of the church's witness: to tell men about the Saviour from sin and to urge them to put their faith in Him. Nothing else, however worthy or appealing it may seem, must be allowed to alter this purpose.

## C. THE PROGRAM OF PERSONAL WORK.

The story of Philip suggests the ever-widening outreach of the testimony of the church. He had been witnessing in Samaria (see Acts 8:5). This was in fulfillment of Jesus' words—words which outline the program of the church through the years—"and ye shall be witnesses unto me both in Jerusalem, and in all Judaea, and in Samaria, and unto the uttermost part of the earth" (Acts 1:8).

The testimony must begin at home. Fires of devotion must burn on the home altars before they can kindle sparks abroad. A church must do more than contribute to "foreign missions"; it must be concerned about the needy at its doors. A missionary candidate must do more than plan for his testimony across the sea; he must be a witness where he lives.

By the same token the church must have a world-wide vision. Its prayer life, its study of the Word, its faithfulness at home must cause it to yearn for souls everywhere without a knowledge of Christ. Its missionary zeal must embrace the lost both at home and abroad. It must concentrate on its own

"Jerusalem," but never neglect "the uttermost part of the earth," and all possible intervening areas.

## D. The Prerequisites to Personal Work.

1. *Prayer*. Philip and the other deacons had been set apart to their appointed tasks by prayer. This is fundamental to witnessing that prevails. Effective testimony must be begun, continued, bathed in prayer. God alone draws men unto Himself. (See John 6:44.)

2. *Separation*. The deacons were separated unto their particular assignment. This suggests a second basic truth: those who witness for Christ must be a separated, consecrated people, "in" the world, but not "of" the world. (Consult John 17:11, 16.) If one is to lift another to a higher plane, he must be on the higher plane himself.

3. *Humility*. Philip was a man of unselfish humility. He had an amazing ministry in Samaria, "and the people with one accord gave heed" (Acts 8:6). Yet when the angel of the Lord summoned him to the desert he arose and went. Clearly he was more concerned to do the will of God than to draw the crowds. This brand of selflessness convinces gainsayers.

4. *Obedience*. When a man desires God's will above all else he is ready to obey. Philip did not hesitate, or vacillate or count the cost when called to the wilderness. When God spoke to him he acted. This is obedience, the first-fruit of genuine devotion to God. The personal worker today must be sensitive to the will of God and ready to obey when His leading becomes clear.

5. *Enthusiasm*. When Philip was instructed by the Spirit to join the eunuch, he "ran thither to him" (Acts 8:30). This was godly enthusiasm, an eagerness to do God's will. Incidentally, had Philip delayed, the eunuch might have long since passed the glorious fifty-third chapter of Isaiah! The one who witnesses for Christ has a blessed message to deliver. Not only

should he be "sold on his product," but he must also be enthusiastic in his testimony.

6. *Compassion.* Read between the lines of Acts 8 and behold the compassion which filled Philip's heart as he approached the Ethiopian. His was true tenderness, a sympathy for the lost which should characterize every true worker for Christ.

7. *Tact.* "Understandest thou what thou readest" (Acts 8:30)? Philip was gentle, courteous, thoughtful, in his approach. His words were neither harsh, abrupt, nor repugnant. Personal workers might well take heed here.

8. *Boldness.* As his conversation with the eunuch progressed Philip revealed a courage and a directness which soon produced results. He was fishing for a soul, and his touch was firm and sure. Undue timidity is out of place when one is bent on winning a soul for Christ.

9. *Guidance.* Philip was guided, instructed and strengthened by the Holy Spirit. Apart from this no testimony will prevail. The Spirit exalts Christ through the Word, convicts the sinner, melts stubborn hearts, woos, persuades, enables men to embrace the Son of God as Saviour.

10. *Knowledge of the Word.* Philip was taught in the Scriptures. He was perfectly at home in Isaiah, for he had obviously studied the Book. So today, the man or woman of God who is led by the Spirit and instructed in the Word will be powerful in drawing others to the Saviour.

### E. The Procedure in Personal Work.

1. Philip "opened his mouth" (a very important procedure if one is to speak for Christ), "and began at the same scripture" (Acts 8:35). Begin where men are, geographically, temperamentally, spiritually. One's approach is vital. His transitions should be gentle: he is leading, persuading men, not driving or forcing them.

2. Philip used the Word to present Christ. He preached Jesus. He presented both the Person and the redemptive work

of Christ. Always remember that this is the objective in witnessing: all else is but contributory to this goal.

3. Philip pressed, gently but firmly, for a decision. The succinctness of his words to the Ethiopian is refreshing. The fish is not to be permitted too much liberty. As the Spirit leads, the line must be drawn in.

4. The eunuch believed, but Philip did not let the matter rest there. He paved the way for his convert openly to confess his new-found faith by baptism. Man believes in his heart but confesses with his lips.

5. The sequel? The experience of conversion was attended by joy. (See Acts 8:39.) We witness to men, not to confuse or embarrass them, but to make possible for them the deep and holy joy of salvation.

## F. The Passion for Personal Work.

Perhaps you are testifying faithfully for Christ. If so, thank God for the privilege, persist in well doing and give all the glory to the Lord.

If for some reason your zeal has diminished, a stern and immediate duty confronts you. Search your soul, examine your motives, weigh your life in the balances of honesty. Has something come between you and God? Is your fellowship with Him broken? What is quenching the ardent flame of your fervor? Why has your burden for the lost become light?

These are searching questions. Every believer who is not steadily witnessing for Christ should ask them fearlessly, rectify the situation and press forward with his testimony.

> The hour is late,
> The lab'rers are few;
> The harvest awaits;
> God's counting on you.

# 48

# The Believer's Work

In the realm of daily living what the Christian *does* reflects what the Christian *is*. One is redeemed for service to God and men in this life as well as for blessedness in heaven in the life to come. He is saved by faith; but his salvation is "unto good works, which God hath before ordained that we should walk in them" (Eph. 2:10).

For the Christian every area of life is sanctified. He must give tangible evidence of his redemption through service, work, vocation and ministry. "Saved to serve" is a good slogan provided that one does not limit the "serving" to church attendance and direct avenues of Christian service such as the gospel ministry, missionary work, or Christian education. Christ is Lord of life. We serve Him in whatever vocation we follow; and in every sphere of life we should seek the benediction of His divine approval.

## A. PREREQUISITES TO CHRISTIAN WORK.

1. *The new birth.* Before a man can serve God he must know Him in a personal relationship. The New Testament subsumes all of life under two commandments, the first of which is "Thou shalt love the Lord thy God with all thy heart, and with all thy soul, and with all thy mind" (Matt.

22:37). Such love, made possible through regeneration, is a condition of acceptable service to God.

2. *Consecration.* No service reaches its maximum effectiveness unless it is linked to an intelligent perception of what it involves. Christian work must be performed with the knowledge that all of life is linked to the will of God. It must spring out of a willing heart that is yielded to God. And its purpose must be to make God relevant and dominant in every area of life—at home, in the shop, in the street, as well as in the church.

3. *Motivation.* Why I do what I do determines the validity of what I do. A good act prompted by a wrong motive is not pleasing to God. The gift of money prompted by the desire to gain a reputation for liberality or to impress others is unacceptable to God. On the other hand, the smallest, most insignficant act motivated by love for God and designed to glorify Him is far better than extensive acts of charity designed to promote self. All Christian service should be rooted in the desire to glorify God, for this is the only service which is acceptable in His sight. "Ye ask, and receive not, because ye ask amiss, that ye may consume it upon your lusts" (James 4:3).

## B. The Necessity of Good Works.

1. The Roman Catholic Church teaches that men are saved by grace plus works; that works are essential and necessary to salvation, and that without them men cannot be saved. Protestant Christians deny the necessity of good works for salvation and teach that men are saved by grace alone. But Protestants do not teach that good works are irrelevant or unnecessary in the proper framework.

2. Why good works? One is saved by faith. But good works demonstrate the reality of faith. "But wilt thou know, O vain man, that faith without works is dead?" (James 2:20). James insists that all true faith will be manifested in life, and that if a man does not manifest his faith by his deeds then his "faith"

is spurious. Paul states that we build a super-structure of works upon the foundation of Jesus Christ: "Every man's work shall be made manifest: for the day shall declare it, because it shall be revealed by fire; and the fire shall try every man's work of what sort it is. If any man's work abide which he hath built thereupon, he shall receive a reward" (1 Cor. 3:13,14).

3. Good works are essential if one is to reap a reward. In heaven the saved will enjoy rewards commensurate with their works. At the judgment of believers every redeemed soul must stand before the Lord to give an account of his deeds done in the flesh. This judgment does not relate to salvation, for only the saved will appear before the Lord. It relates to rewards. Every believer will receive his reward according to his works. That it is not wrong for the child of God to look forward eagerly to his reward is clear from the experience of Moses: "Esteeming the reproach of Christ greater riches than the treasures in Egypt: for he had respect unto the recompense of the reward." (Heb. 11:26; see also Rom. 14:10,12; 2 Cor. 5:10; Heb. 6:9,10.)

## C. Types of Christian Work.

1. *Vocational calling.* Whatever position a man or woman occupies should be one in which Christ is the Lord of life. A Christian cannot be a mere businessman; he cannot be a mere teacher; he cannot be a mere lawyer; he cannot be a mere doctor; he cannot be a mere carpenter. He must be a Christian businessman; he must be a Christian teacher; he must be a Christian lawyer; he must be a Christian doctor; he must be a Christian carpenter. Whatever his vocation may be, and whatever his sex, color, or location, he must recognize, accept and practice the Lordship of Christ in respect to his calling. He must bring Christ to bear upon his life work. "The secular" does not exist in the life of the Christian. Everything is sacred.

2. *Full time Christian work.* By this is meant the employment of time and talents in a life-work context which excludes

one from working at anything else. Thus the minister of the gospel devotes full time to his calling, the missionary, church secretary, or Christian education director to his. These callings pertain to the church and its functioning. They differ from so-called "secular" jobs in that they are related specifically and exclusively to the Christian enterprise. For such vocations the call of God to the hearts of men and women is important. It is not simply a matter of seeking an outlet for one's talents and energies. Instead it is the conviction of a divine call which speaks with such force that no other occupation will satisfy or permit peace of heart.

## D. The Gifts of the Spirit in Relation to Christian Work.

Misunderstanding is common on this subject. Every Christian should be carefully instructed in order to avoid the pitfalls of error.

1. Believers are baptized by the Spirit into one body. (See 1 Cor. 12:13.) They become members of a single body which is complete in all its parts. Each part differs from the rest.

2. Every believer is given some gift by the Holy Spirit. "But the manifestation of the Spirit is given to every man to profit withal . . . . But all these worketh that one and the selfsame Spirit, dividing to every man severally as he will . . . Now ye are the body of Christ, and members in particular" (1 Cor. 12:7,11,27).

3. Christian work is simply the use or exercise of whatever gift the Holy Spirit has given the believer. One cannot use what he does not possess. He may simulate the real by the counterfeit; but that does not make his gift genuine. Specific gifts are given by the Holy Spirit as He wills. A man called to the gospel ministry, for example, should normally possess the gift of prophecy in order that he might edify, exhort, and comfort the saints. One does not choose his gifts but uses what the Holy Spirit chooses to give. "So we, being many, are one

body in Christ, and every one members one of another. Having then gifts differing according to the grace that is given to us, whether prophecy, let us prophesy according to the proportion of faith; Or ministry, let us wait on our ministering: or he that teacheth, on teaching; Or he that exhorteth, on exhortation: he that giveth, let him do it with simplicity; he that ruleth, with diligence; he that sheweth mercy, with cheerfulness" (Rom. 12:5-8).

4. The gifts of the Spirit differ in degree and kind. All come from Him and are worthy. Let no one become proud because of a seemingly greater gift; and let no one be ashamed of a smaller gift. All gifts find their source in the Holy Spirit, all are administered under the Lordship of Jesus, and all receive their efficacy from Almighty God.

5. Certain spiritual gifts are quite rare. Uninstructed people sometimes desire spectacular gifts and pay scant attention to those which seem mediocre. How quickly the heart thrills at the thought of speaking in tongues or performing miracles of healing. But the gifts of helps, governments and prophecy are often regarded less highly. While the New Testament era did not necessarily bring to an end any of the more spectacular gifts, it is perfectly plain that these have become less important than they were when the church was being established. Speaking in tongues, performing "signs," and miraculously healing the sick,—these are possible today, but they are neither necessary nor normal in church life. They are the exception rather than the rule and should be so regarded. Christians ought not to exalt men who may have these gifts. Nor are those so endowed to become the objects of public adulation.

6. The gifts of the Spirit are to be used in love. The believer's work is to be performed with a heart of love. No gift administered without love has lasting value. Paul tells us concretely that speaking in tongues, preaching the gospel, having great faith and sacrificing all material possessions are worthless unless surrounded by the atmosphere of love. While we are

encouraged to covet the gifts of the Spirit and should pray for them, essential to their proper operation and administration is love—love which Paul defines and delineates so clearly that any man may ascertain for himself whether or not he possesses it. (Study 1 Cor. 13 in detail.)

# 49

# Missions

The message of the Bible is not addressed only to the few. The Word of God knows neither black nor white, east nor west, Jew nor Gentile. It is intended for all men, and thus it is distinctively a missionary book. From beginning to end it speaks of the divine reaching down to save mankind. God sent His only begotten Son to seek and to save that which was lost, whoever and wherever the lost might be.

Seeking and saving are two vital Scriptural concepts. Both are intimately tied into the missionary picture. Just as God sent Jesus to seek and to save, so Christians are called upon to seek out the lost and to present them with the gospel message that they may be saved. In its essence missions strive to do this: to seek the lost, to reach them, and to save them.

A. The Missionary Imperative.

"Missions" is a compelling force in the lives of believers because:

1. All men without Christ are lost forever and the only way by which they can be saved is through saving faith in Jesus Christ. Thus Paul says: "Now we know that what things soever the law saith, it saith to them who are under the law: that every mouth may be stopped, and all the world may become

guilty before God" (Rom. 3:19). "For all have sinned, and come short of the glory of God" (Rom. 3:23). And Peter declares: "Neither is there salvation in any other: for there is none other name under heaven given among men, whereby we must be saved" (Acts 4:12).

2. Christians have been given a commission to tell men about Christ. "Go ye therefore, and teach all nations, baptizing them in the name of the Father, and of the Son, and of the Holy Ghost: Teaching them to observe all things whatsoever I have commanded you: and, lo, I am with you alway, even unto the end of the world" (Matt. 28:19,20). "Then said Jesus to them again, Peace be unto you: as my Father hath sent me, even so send I you" (John 20:21). "But ye shall receive power, after that the Holy Ghost is come upon you: and ye shall be witnesses unto me both in Jerusalem, and in all Judaea, and in Samaria, and unto the uttermost part of the earth" (Acts 1:8).

3. The believer's relationship to Jesus Christ compels him to witness. Even if the Lord had given us no great commission and if the Word of God were silent on the subject, the very nature of our faith, as well as our personal relationship to Christ, would demand that we propagate the gospel. We know that Christ came to redeem all men. The Word of God expressly states: "Who will have all men to be saved, and to come unto the knowledge of the truth" (1 Tim. 2:4); "And he is the propitiation for our sins: and not for our's only, but also for the sins of the whole world" (1 John 2:2). It follows logically that anyone who is savingly related to Christ will want to spread His gospel. The motives which prompt him are:

a. *Love*. Christ loved us and gave Himself for us. Can we who claim to love Him do less than give ourselves for others?

b. *Loyalty*. If we are loyal to individuals and institutions because of our intimate connections with them, how much more ought we to be loyal to the cause of the Lord Jesus Christ and obediently to make Him known.

c. *Gratitude*. Thankful to Him for what He has done for

us, we should express our gratitude by telling others the good news of salvation. We cannot repay Him for all that He did; but we can show some measure of gratitude by sharing with others the glad tidings of His love.

## B. THE MISSIONARY RESPONSIBILITY.

Christians tend to think of the missionary calling as limited to those who make it their full time vocation. In a sense this view is correct. But nowhere in the Bible is it written that missionary endeavor must be limited to the few. Missions is the task of the church at large. We have falsified the picture by separating the home field from the foreign field. With God the field is the world. Wherever men live without Christ,— that is a mission field. Every child of God should remember that:

1. No one can find Christ unless believers tell him about the Saviour. "For whosoever shall call upon the name of the Lord shall be saved. How then shall they call on him in whom they have not believed? and how shall they believe in him of whom they have not heard? and how shall they hear without a preacher? And how shall they preach, except they be sent? as it is written, How beautiful are the feet of them that preach the gospel of peace, and bring glad tidings of good things!" (Rom. 10:13-15).

2. Every Christian is to be a witness for Jesus Christ. Jesus said, "Ye are witnesses of these things" (Luke 24:48). When the church at Jerusalem was persecuted, "they were all scattered abroad throughout the regions of Judaea and Samaria, except the apostles. . . . Therefore they that were scattered abroad went every where preaching the word" (Acts 8:1,4). The apostles were not included in this dispersion. The rank and file of believers were the ones who propagated the gospel. Every man was a missionary wherever he happened to be driven.

So today personal responsibility for seeing that the gospel gets to every man rests on every believer. No Christian can excuse himself by pointing to the failure of others; nor can the labors of another permit him to claim personal exemption. All men are equally responsible in the sight of God and all are required to witness wherever they may be. All are called to be missionaries, although not all are called to engage in missionary work exclusively.

## C. The Missionary Scope.

God tells us the extent of the task He has given to us. "Go ye into all the world, . . ." (Mark 16:15). "And that repentance and remission of sins should be preached in his name among all nations, . . ." (Luke 24:47). ". . . ye shall be witnesses . . . unto the uttermost part of the earth" (Acts 1:8).

The Bible demands that the gospel be taken to the whole world. No geographical areas are excluded; no tribe is to be left out. The job is to reach the world, all men everywhere. We are not told how extensive or intensive the missionary effort shall be. We do not know how long the task must continue, or to what bounds it must reach before the work of testimony is complete. We do not know how intensively the job must be done. When has a man been told enough, and how often must the story be repeated before we have fulfilled the commission? These questions remain unanswered. We must do all that we possibly can with the knowledge we have. The great commission is still to all nations.

## D. Missionary Methods.

1. *Evangelism.* This is the direct, oral presentation of the gospel to men. It may be by radio, from the pulpit, on street corners, or in connection with the distribution of tracts. It may occur in the home, at the office, or anywhere opportunity affords. It is the most effective method, and should be the back-

bone of any direct missionary effort. The Word of God is the Sword of the Spirit and the use of that Word is basic to all evangelism.

2. *Medical missions.* Medical skill opens the doors and hearts of men and prepares them to receive the gospel. It has proved to be one of the most useful means of reaching people with the Word of God. However, medicine is not an end in itself but simply a means to an end. Whenever it is regarded as an end in itself it ceases to be a missionary agency, no matter how much physical good it may accomplish. The goal of true medical missions is the furtherance of the gospel.

3. *Education.* Like medicine, this tool is not an end in itself. We do not go to the field simply to bring literacy or knowledge, but to introduce men to Jesus Christ. Yet education can be an open door for the gospel. It is a means to an end, and that end is the gospel. Grade schools, high schools, colleges, medical schools, and seminaries are all means through which the news of salvation may be spread. Moreover, education has an additional goal. This is the training of the children of believers—a most necessary task when a Christian community has sprung up as the consequence of the preaching of the gospel.

4. *Literary work.* This includes the translation of the Bible into the language of the people, the use of the printing press in the publication of Bibles and other Christian literature, the employment of radio facilities and other direct and indirect means through which the Word of God is conveyed to the nations.

E. THE MISSIONARY PRIMACY.

In the New Testament the missionary enterprise has a central place:

1. A missionary message accompanied the birth of Jesus: "And the angel said unto them, Fear not: for, behold, I bring you good tidings of great joy, which shall be *to all people*" (Luke 2:10).

2. The Lord's Prayer is missionary in nature. Jesus taught His disciples to pray, "Thy kingdom come. Thy will be done in earth, as it is in heaven" (Matt. 6:10). We are to pray for the coming of the kingdom of God—that it may come spiritually in the hearts of men now, and that it may come soon in literal manifestation when Christ shall return to reign.

3. Jesus' first convert immediately became a missionary. "He [Andrew] first findeth his own brother Simon, and saith unto him, We have found the Messias, which is, being interpreted, the Christ. And he brought him to Jesus" (John 1:41,42).

4. The first command of the risen Lord was missionary in nature: "Peace be unto you: as my Father hath sent me, even so send I you" (John 20:21).

5. The first apostolic sermon following Pentecost had a missionary emphasis: "For the promise is unto you, and to your children, and to all that are afar off . . ." (Acts 2:39).

## F. The Missionary Urgency.

Many Christians believe in the imminent return of Christ. But one of the prophecies which must be fulfilled prior to the second advent is that the gospel first be preached to the whole world. Our Lord affirmed: "And this gospel of the kingdom shall be preached in all the world for a witness unto all nations; and then shall the end come" (Matt. 24:14). Jesus was prophesying as well as issuing a command when He said, "Ye *shall* be witnesses . . . unto the uttermost part of the earth" (Acts 1:8).

So long as our Lord tarries we know that the great commission has not been fulfilled. When He comes we shall know that the task has been completed. The fact that He delays His coming indicates that we must continue faithfully to prosecute our witness. In a sense we may hasten the coming of our Lord by busying ourselves with the most important enterprise of the church of Jesus Christ, that of getting the gospel out to every creature.

# PART NINE

# Man's Ultimate Destiny

Faithful Christian testimony produces two reactions: some accept Christ and are saved; others reject Him and are lost. "For the preaching of the cross is to them that perish foolishness; but unto us which are saved it is the power of God" (1 Cor. 1:18). This text is incisive, but it is also divisive: the gospel of Christ is a divider of men. A man is saved or he perishes. Let him call this arrangement too cut and dried, or narrow, or "tidy," if he will. The Bible teaches that in the warfare between God and the devil there is no "no man's land."

Heaven is the destination of the redeemed. Intimations of its radiant glory and hallowed blessedness are given in the Scriptures. But not until we enter its sacred portals shall we fully comprehend its infinite beatitude. Some day—and this is the certain confidence of the children of God—we shall be united with our dear Lord and with our believing loved ones whom we have "lost awhile."

Hell is the destination of the lost. The contemplation of God's utter holiness and man's fearful sinfulness make one realize that all men deserve Hell. God is not cruel because He permits some to go to a place of unending torment. Rather, He is gracious because He rescues many from the pit whose depths they deserve to sound.

God forbid that any who read this volume should scoff at the doctrines of Heaven and Hell. The divine Word speaks often and eloquently on the themes. This section is devoted to an exposition of its cardinal teaching on the subject of man's everlasting destiny.

# 50

# *Heaven*

---

Heaven is real, not imaginary. Some believe that it is a mere idea or figment of the imagination. Others assert that it is a state of mind attainable here on earth. But the Bible makes it plain that heaven, far from being an illusion or a state of mind, is real. It is the goal of a believer's hope, the end of his earthly pilgrimage, the consummation of his desires, and the fulfillment of his dreams.

## A. The Nature of Heaven.

1. *What is "heaven"?* The word is used in the Scriptures in at least three ways:

a. The lower reaches of the sky, the realm of mists and vapors. When a cloud received the ascending Christ out of His disciples' sight, the angel visitants said to them: "Why stand ye gazing up into heaven?" (Acts 1:9-11).

b. The vast area of the sun, moon and stars: "In the beginning God created the heaven and the earth" (Gen. 1:1).

c. The sphere where God preeminently dwells: "The Lord's throne is in heaven" (Psalm 11:4; see also 1 Kings 8:30; Matt. 6:9).

2. *How is heaven characterized?*

a. A place. When the Lord Jesus talked about His approaching departure to glory He said to His beloved friends, "I go to prepare a place for you" (John 14:2). The Greek word for "place" is "topos," whence "topography" is derived. Yes, our "inheritance incorruptible, and undefiled, and that fadeth not away" is "reserved in heaven" (1 Pet. 1:4). The reservation is in a definite, specific place.

b. Various other titles: e.g. a kingdom (Matt. 18:1), with its King; a city (Heb. 11:10), with its citizens; a country (Heb. 11:16), with its laws and customs; a home (John 14:2), with its happiness; an inheritance (Col. 1:12), with its possessions.

## B. THE RESIDENTS OF HEAVEN.

1. *God is in heaven.* The Lord's Prayer commences: "Our Father which art in heaven" (Matt. 6:9). Simon Peter declared of Christ, who was Himself God: "Whom the heaven must receive until the times of restitution of all things" (Acts 3:21). Jesus, as our high-priestly "fore-runner" is "within the veil" (Heb. 6:19). He has entered "into the holy place" (Heb. 9:12); "into heaven itself, now to appear in the presence of God for us" (Heb. 9:24).

2. *The angels are there.* "In the resurrection," our Lord taught, men "neither marry, nor are given in marriage, but are as the angels of God in heaven" (Matt. 22:30). Angels whose special assignment seems to be to care for little children "do always behold the face of my Father which is in heaven" (Matt. 18:10).

3. *Believers in the Lord Jesus Christ will be there.* No other way to the Father exists (see John 14:6). No "other name under heaven" (Acts 4:12) can save. One road, and only one, leads to the gates of the celestial city: the way of repentance and faith. Those who take this road will spend eternity in heaven.

4. *The wicked are excluded from heaven.* Unbelievers are

disqualified from entrance into glory. Paul says of them: "I tell you before, as I have also told you in time past, that they which do such things shall not inherit the kingdom of God" (Gal. 5:21). Again: "For this ye know, that no whoremonger, nor unclean person, nor covetous man, who is an idolater, hath any inheritance in the kingdom of Christ and of God" (Eph. 5:5). The gates of the city of light are closed to the entrance of iniquity. (See Rev. 22:14,15.)

## C. The Character and Occupation of Heaven's Residents.

1. *Character.* Believers will be spiritually perfect in heaven. In this life they yearn for holiness, yet sin abides. They struggle, they fall, they rise. The most devout saints are deeply conscious of their shortcomings. But sin is excluded from heaven. There believers will be perfectly holy. Their love for God will be unclouded by misgivings; their obedience will be joyful and complete. They will be like Christ. (See 1 John 3:2.)

2. *Occupation.* Heaven is not a place of idleness. True, those who have been weary on earth will find their rest in heaven. But resting does not imply idleness. The people of God will serve the One whom they behold face to face. Their constant adoration of the Lamb will be an occupation which will produce for their redeemed bodies and spirits the highest conceivable happiness, peace and blessedness.

## D. Recognition in Heaven.

Will believers be able to recognize one another in heaven? While the Scriptures do not throw as much light upon this subject as upon others, it is possible to pierce the veil and to reach a satisfactory reply to the question. The Bible teaches that there will be mutual recognition in heaven. One's confidence rests upon the following considerations:

1. Paul stated that when Christ appears He "shall change our vile body, that it may be fashioned like unto his glorious body, according to the working whereby he is able even to subdue all things unto himself" (Phil. 3:21). John added: "but we know that, when he shall appear, we shall be like him; for we shall see him as he is" (1 John 3:2). Our Lord's post-resurrection body was recognizable. We shall be like Him; therefore we shall be recognizable too.

2. In the story of the rich man and Lazarus, our Lord teaches that there is spirit-recognition beyond the grave. (See Luke 16:19-31; otherwise the conversation between Abraham and the rich man would be unintelligible.) How much more will there be recognition when glorified bodies and spirits are united at the resurrection.

3. Other passages of Scripture bulwark one's assurance. Abraham died in Canaan and was buried there. Yet it is written that he "was gathered to his people" (Gen. 25:8). His relatives, with the exception of Sarah, were buried hundreds of miles away. Surely there must have been a heavenly reunion and recognition. Many centuries later on the mount of transfiguration Moses and Elijah, whose spirits had departed from the earth long before, appeared and spoke with the Lord Jesus. (See Matt. 17:3.) Did not the astonished disciples recognize the guests? Glorious and triumphant fact: we shall recognize our loved ones in heaven.

4. God is love. He formed the sacred ties of human love and blessed them. Surely he would not forever shatter the bonds which He had forged when nothing would be gained by the shattering.

5. Our rational faculties will not only continue to exist, but will become more acute in our resurrection bodies. Now our knowledge is imperfect, for the flesh impairs our spiritual insight. But in heaven our sensibilities will be sharpened: the recognition which we enjoy here on earth will be even keener in glory.

## E. REWARDS IN HEAVEN.

Just to be in heaven will be unspeakable glory. Our entrance there was earned by the finished work of the Son of God on our behalf. Every believer will receive a reward.

1. *Degrees of reward.* The repentant thief who at the eleventh hour turned to Christ for salvation could not expect to receive a crown comparable to that of one who had spent a life-time in Christian testimony.

2. *Justness of reward.* Men will be rewarded according to their works. "Every man shall receive his own reward according to his own labour" (1 Cor. 3:8). "If any man's work abide . . . he shall receive a reward" (1 Cor. 3:14). There is "a prophet's reward" and "a righteous man's reward" (Matt. 10:41). So important is the Christian's reward that Paul writes: "Let no man beguile you of your reward" (Col. 2:18). John is just as insistent: "Look to yourselves, that we lose not those things which we have wrought, but that we receive a full reward" (2 John 8).

3. *Time of reward.* The rewards will be meted out at Christ's appearing. The risen Lord declared: "And, behold, I come quickly; and my reward is with me, to give every man according as his work shall be" (Rev. 22:12). Faith determines our salvation. Obedience determines our reward. At the judgment seat of Christ, before which believers will stand, every one will "receive the things done in his body, according to that he hath done, whether it be good or bad." (2 Cor. 5:10; see Rom. 14:10.)

## F. THE RADIANCE OF HEAVEN.

For the believer physical death is the emergence to a sphere of radiant, celestial, eternal light. A blaze of glory welcomes him into the presence of Christ. He gropes and falters while tabernacling in the flesh. Clouds intervene. Shadows fall across his pathway. Obscurities, perplexities darken the road. But all is different in glory. The night of sin, doubt, and despair is gone; "for there shall be no night there" (Rev. 21:25). Darkness will be permanently banished. "The city had no need of the sun, neither of the moon, to shine in it: for the glory of God did lighten it . . ." (Rev. 21:23).

And why is heaven so radiant? One stupendous answer thunders across the ages: Christ Jesus, the Light of life, is there. As it is written: "the Lamb is the light thereof" (Rev. 21:23). "The light of heaven is the face of Jesus; the joy of heaven is the presence of Jesus; the melody of heaven is the name of Jesus; the harmony of heaven is the praise of Jesus; the theme of heaven is the work of Jesus; the employment of heaven is the service of Jesus; the fulness of heaven is Jesus Himself."

# 51

## Hell

The natural heart does not wish to believe in the reality of hell. This is to be expected, for men readily reject a belief which will condemn them. Yet the concept of hell is part and parcel of the teaching of the Bible. It is closely associated with the concept of heaven. A man who does not believe in heaven will probably refuse to believe in hell.

Opinions are important only if they agree with the facts. A man may deny the existence of God; but the denial will not alter the fact that God exists. A man may deny that there is a sun; but the denial will not change the reality of its existence. So with the fact of hell. Men may dislike the idea and deny it vehemently, but their denial will not alter the fact of hell. The Bible teaches certain things about hell. To deny these truths is to call into question the rest of the Scriptural teachings.

### A. HELL: FALSE VIEWS.

1. *Annihilationism.* Some hold that God is far too gracious to condemn the souls of men to a place of everlasting punishment. Instead, He blots them out forever. Man ceases to exist in any form, material or spiritual. He is utterly annihilated.

2. *Restorationism.* In this view the love of God is regarded as a sentimental maudlin attribute. Regardless of the depth of

man's iniquity, God is too kind to permit him to suffer forever for his sins. No matter how long it may take, God will eventually restore all creation, including man, to fellowship with Himself in heaven.

3. *Presentism.* This view is widely held. Based upon sheer phantasy, its adherents insist that men experience their heaven or hell in this present life; that reward or retribution is meted out here and now on earth.

## B. HELL: A PLACE.

1. *Hell is a prepared place.* "Then shall he say also unto them on the left hand, Depart from me, ye cursed, into everlasting fire, prepared for the devil and his angels" (Matt. 25:41).

2. *Hell is a place which endures for ever.* "And these shall go away into everlasting punishment . . ." (Matt. 25:46). "The sinners in Zion are afraid; fearfulness hath surprised the hypocrites. Who among us shall dwell with the devouring fire? who among us shall dwell with everlasting burnings?" (Isa. 33:14). "And the devil that deceived them was cast into the lake of fire and brimstone, where the beast and the false prophet are, and shall be tormented day and night for ever and ever" (Rev. 20:10).

3. *Hell is a place of suffering.* "And fear not them which kill the body, but are not able to kill the soul: but rather fear him which is able to destroy both soul and body in hell" (Matt. 10:28).

4. *Hell is a place of fire and brimstone.* "The same shall drink of the wine of the wrath of God, which is poured out without mixture into the cup of his indignation; and he shall be tormented with fire and brimstone in the presence of the holy angels, and in the presence of the Lamb" (Rev. 14:10). "And whosoever was not found written in the book of life was cast into the lake of fire" (Rev. 20:15).

## C. HELL: ITS INHABITANTS.

1. The devil will be there together with the beast and the false prophet. "The beast and the false prophet . . . both were cast alive into a lake of fire burning with brimstone" (Rev. 19:20). "And the devil that deceived them was cast into the lake of fire and brimstone, where the beast and the false prophet are . . ." (Rev. 20:10).

2. Fallen angels will be there. "If God spared not the angels that sinned, but cast them down to hell, and delivered them into chains of darkness, to be reserved unto judgment" (2 Pet. 2:4). "And the angels which kept not their first estate, but left their own habitation, he hath reserved in everlasting chains under darkness unto the judgment of the great day" (Jude 6).

3. The wicked will be there. "The wicked shall be turned into hell . . ." (Psalm 9:17).

4. Anyone whose name is not written in the Lamb's Book of Life will be there. "And whosoever was not found written in the book of life was cast into the lake of fire" (Rev. 20:15).

5. Those who refuse to do the will of God will be there. "Not every one that saith unto me, Lord, Lord, shall enter into the kingdom of heaven; but he that doeth the will of my Father which is in heaven" (Matt. 7:21).

## D. HELL: THE OPPOSITE OF HEAVEN.

All men spend eternity in one of two places—heaven or hell. These places are totally different in every respect. In heaven men know neither suffering nor sorrow; in hell they experience both constantly. Heaven has nought but happy and contented people; hell has nought but unhappy and discontented people. Heaven is the place wherein no sin exists; hell is the place where sin abounds and righteousness is not to be found.

Heaven speaks to us of holiness, righteousness, justice and peace; hell reminds us of sin, defilement, death, and the justice which gives to men what they deserve for their misdeeds. If all men were good, there would be no need of hell. But all men are not good. To assert that the idea of hell is unnecessary makes a mockery of good, of God, and of justice.

### E. Hell: The Consequences of Its Denial.

To deny the existence of hell is extremely dangerous. For such a denial:

1. Repudiates the plain teaching of Scripture, and thus calls into question its credibility and authority.

2. Rejects the teaching of our Lord Jesus as false; for He told us that hell is a fearful reality. If He told us this in ignorance then His omniscience is a fiction and He cannot be God. If He did so by way of accommodation to the thinking of the people of His day then He deliberately approved what He knew was not true. Such conduct is hardly consistent with deity.

3. Undermines the Biblical teaching about heaven, or about any other major doctrine of the Christian faith. All doctrinal concepts come to us from the same source, the Bible. To accept the ones we like and deny the ones we dislike means that the truth of God is dependent on what we want to believe rather than on what the Word of God teaches. A distorted faith can be the only result when the decisions of men are permitted to determine the nature of Christian belief.

4. Makes a travesty of the teaching that men will go to hell unless they accept Christ as Saviour. If there is no hell, the Christian Church for two thousand years has been bearing false witness and preaching what is patently untrue: believers have been false witnesses, cruel and evil defamers of the truth. But so long as the Bible teaches the doctrine we must believe it and propagate it.

### F. Hell: The Possibility of Choice.

This is the time to plead with the reader. Now is the hour of decision. Before you turn this page, ask yourself this question: "Do I want to go to heaven or to hell?" We can show you how to go to heaven!

"Neither is there salvation in any other: for there is none other name under heaven given among men, whereby we must be saved" (Acts 4:12). This is the Word of God, a challenge and an appeal. Christ died for our sins to redeem our souls from hell. By personal appropriation of His work through faith you may have an abundant entrance into glory.

# PART TEN

# The Believer's Resources

---

Like roses growing beside the roadside, the promises of God adorn the Christian's pathway, inspiring him with hope and encouraging him to press on with unremitting energy to his heavenly reward. God has promised. His faithfulness is His guarantee: His Word will be fulfilled.

The promises of the Lord reveal His Father heart. Earth's pilgrimage is not easy. The road is often rocky, or dreary, or steep, or winding. Above all, it sometimes seems so very long. Were there no beacon-lights of hope, no guide-posts along the way, no points of refreshment, even the stalwart pilgrim might falter. But God knows and cares.

Stress needs to be laid repeatedly upon the oft-misunderstood truth: some of the divine promises are unconditional; others are conditional. Some apply under certain conditions and to certain people; others are universally applicable. The Bible student must be on the alert here. If he would appropriate the benefits inherent in the promises of God, he must first meet the conditions. Further, God's promises are more than lovely adornments. They serve a present purpose. The believer may indeed bask in their glory. But his duty does not stop there. Peter reminds us that by the promises of God we are to "be partakers of the divine nature, having escaped the corruption that is in the world through lust" (2 Pet. 1:4).

The concluding section of the Handbook has the dual goal of heartening the people of God, and of challenging them to lives of purity and love which daily magnify the name of the Lord Jesus. To Him be the glory for ever and ever.

# 52

## The Promises of God

---

The Bible contains nearly five thousand different promises. These promises are "exceeding great and precious" (2 Pet. 1:4) to the believer's heart. Their scope and vastness stagger our imagination unless we bear in mind the fact that our God is omnipotent, loving and kind. He is eager to bless and help His children along life's pilgrim pathway.

### A. The Certain Fulfilment of God's Promises.

God differs from men in that His promises are sure. Man often says one thing and does another. But God always does what He says He will do. If His promises are unconditional He will unconditionally perform them. If they are conditioned on something men must do, He will perform them when the conditions are met. In order, then, for God's children to claim His promises they must KNOW what the promises are and they must avail themselves of the benefits which result from the promises.

"God is not a man, that he should lie" (Num. 23:19). "He is God, the faithful God, which keepeth covenant and mercy with them that love him and keep his commandments to a thousand generations." (Deut. 7:9; see Ps. 105:8; Heb. 10:23; 2 Tim. 2:13.) "For all the promises of God in him are yea, and in him Amen, unto the glory of God by us" (2 Cor. 1:20).

## B. Promises of God Relating to the Vicissitudes of Life.

(In this section and the ones which follow one Scripture quotation occurs in each sub-section. The location of the passage is identified by the first reference, and additional appropriate passages are cited.)

1. *Trouble.* "He shall deliver thee in six troubles: yea, in seven there shall no evil touch thee." (Job 5:19; Ps. 9:9; 34:17, 19; 46:1-3; 107:19; 138:7; John 16:33.)

2. *Sickness.* It is God "who forgiveth all thine iniquities; who healeth all thy diseases" (Ps. 103:3; Ex. 15:26; Ps. 41:3; Jer. 33:6).

3. *Old age.* "And even to your old age I am he; and even to hoar hairs will I carry you: I have made, and I will bear; even I will carry, and will deliver you" (Isa. 46:4; Ps. 71:9; Prov. 16:31).

4. *Famine and want.* "They shall not be ashamed in the evil time: and in the days of famine they shall be satisfied" (Ps. 37:19; 107:9; Isa. 41:17; Zech. 10:1).

5. *Poverty and helplessness.* "For the needy shall not alway be forgotten: the expectation of the poor shall not perish for ever" (Ps. 9:18; 69:33; 132:15; Jas. 2:5).

6. *Bereavement.* "A father of the fatherless, and a judge of the widows, is God in his holy habitation" (Ps. 68:5; Ex. 22:22-24; Prov. 15:25; Jer. 49:11).

7. *Captivity.* "God setteth the solitary in families: he bringeth out those which are bound with chains: but the rebellious dwell in a dry land" (Ps. 68:6; 107:14; Isa. 49:25).

8. *Slander, evil reports.* "Blessed are ye, when men shall revile you, and persecute you, and shall say all manner of evil against you falsely, for my sake. Rejoice, and be exceeding glad: for great is your reward in heaven: for so persecuted they the prophets which were before you" (Matt. 5:11,12; Ps. 37:6; 57:3; Isa. 61:7; 1 Pet. 4:14).

9. *Injustice and oppression.* "For the oppression of the poor, for the sighing of the needy, now will I arise, saith the Lord; I will set him in safety from him that puffeth at him" (Ps. 12:5; 72:4; 146:7; Isa. 54:14).

10. *Enmity.* "And now shall mine head be lifted up above mine enemies round about me: therefore will I offer in his tabernacle sacrifices of joy; I will sing, yea, I will sing praises unto the Lord" (Ps. 27:6; 2 Kings 17:39; Isa. 54:17; Luke 18:7,8; Acts 18:10; Heb. 13:6).

11. *War.* "In famine he shall redeem thee from death: and in war from the power of the sword" (Job 5:20; Deut. 20:4; 23:14; 2 Chron. 13:12).

## C. Promises of God Relating to Material Blessings.

1. *Benefits in general.* "For the Lord God is a sun and shield: the Lord will give grace and glory: no good thing will he withhold from them that walk uprightly" (Ps. 84:11; 5:12; 23:6; Prov. 10:6; 12:2; 21:21; Rom. 8:32).

2. *Food.* "Trust in the Lord and do good; so shalt thou dwell in the land, and verily thou shalt be fed" (Ps. 37:3; Prov. 13:25; Matt. 6:26).

3. *Clothing.* "Wherefore, if God so clothe the grass of the field, which to day is, and to morrow is cast into the oven, shall he not much more clothe you, O ye of little faith?" (Matt. 6:30).

4. *Safety.* "I will both lay me down in peace, and sleep: for thou, Lord, only makest me dwell in safety" (Ps. 4:8; 112:7).

5. *Prosperity and success.* "Commit thy way unto the Lord; trust also in him; and he shall bring it to pass" (Ps. 37:5; 1:3; Isa. 65:21-23).

6. *Material needs.* "But my God shall supply all your need according to his riches in glory by Christ Jesus" (Phil. 4:19; Deut. 28:12; Ps. 112:3; Prov. 15:6).

### D. Promises of God Relating to Spiritual Blessings.

1. *The gift of faith.* "For by grace are ye saved through faith; and that not of yourselves: it is the gift of God" (Eph. 2:8).

2. *Forgiveness.* "And their sins and iniquities will I remember no more" (Heb. 10:17; Ps. 103:12; Jer. 31:34; Micah 7:18).

3. *Our right to come to God.* We have "boldness to enter into the holiest by the blood of Jesus, By a new and living way, which he hath consecrated for us, through the veil, that is to say, his flesh" (Heb. 10:19,20; Eph. 2:18; 3:12; 1 Pet. 2:24).

4. *Answered prayer.* "And call upon me in the day of trouble: I will deliver thee, and thou shalt glorify me" (Ps. 50:15; Isa. 30:19; 58:9; Jer. 29:12; Matt. 7:7,8,11; John 14:13,14; 15:7; 1 John 3:22; 5:14-16).

5. *The Holy Spirit.* "If ye then, being evil, know how to give good gifts unto your children: how much more shall your heavenly Father give the Holy Spirit to them that ask him?" (Luke 11:13; Isa. 59:21; Ezek. 36:27; John 7:38,39; John 14:16,17).

6. *Wisdom, knowledge and understanding.* "If any of you lack wisdom, let him ask of God, that giveth to all men liberally, and upbraideth not; and it shall be given him" (Jas. 1:5; Ps. 32:8; Prov. 2:6; Luke 1:77; 21:15; 1 Cor. 12:8).

7. *Help in the struggle against temptation and sin.* "There hath no temptation taken you but such as is common to man: but God is faithful, who will not suffer you to be tempted above that ye are able; but will with the temptation also make a way to escape, that ye may be able to bear it" (1 Cor. 10:13; Luke 22:31,32; Rom. 6:6,14; 7:23,25; 8:37; 2 Cor. 12:9; Gal. 1:4; Heb. 2:18; James 4:8; 2 Pet. 2:9; 1 John 4:4).

8. *Courage and strength.* "Say to them that are of a fearful heart, Be strong, fear not: behold, your God will come with

vengeance, even God with a recompence; he will come and save you" (Isa. 35:4; Ps. 29:11; 31:24; Isa. 12:2; 40:29-31).

9. *Preservation.* "And I give unto them eternal life; and they shall never perish, neither shall any man pluck them out of my hand. My Father, which gave them me, is greater than all; and no man is able to pluck them out of my Father's hand" (John 10:28,29; Rom. 8:38,39; 1 Cor. 1:8; Phil. 1:6; Jude 24).

10. *Guidance.* "The steps of a good man are ordered by the Lord: and he delighteth in his way" (Ps. 37:23; 48:14; Prov. 16:9; Isa. 42:16).

11. *Peace.* "And the peace of God, which passeth all understanding, shall keep your hearts and minds through Christ Jesus" (Phil. 4:7; Ps. 119:165; Isa. 26:3; 32:18; John 14:27).

## E. Promises of God Relating to Virtues.

1. *The forgiving spirit.* "But I say unto you, Love your enemies, bless them that curse you, do good to them that hate you, and pray for them which despitefully use you, and persecute you; That ye may be the children of your Father which is in heaven" (Matt. 5:44,45a; Mark 11:25; Luke 6:35; 1 Pet. 3:9).

2. *Purity.* "Blessed are the pure in heart: for they shall see God" (Matt. 5:8; Ps. 18:26; 73:1).

3. *Meekness.* "The meek will he guide in judgment: and the meek will he teach his way" (Ps. 25:9; 149:4; Zeph. 2:3).

4. *Humility.* "Humble yourselves therefore under the mighty hand of God, that he may exalt you in due time" (1 Pet. 5:6; Ps. 138:6; Matt. 18:4; 23:12; James 4:6).

5. *Contrition.* "The sacrifices of God are a broken spirit: a broken and a contrite heart, O God, thou wilt not despise" (Ps. 51:17; 34:18; Isa. 57:15; 66:2; Matt. 5:3).

6. *Perseverance.* "And ye shall be hated of all men for my name's sake: but he that endureth to the end shall be saved" (Matt. 10:22; 1 Cor. 15:58; Gal. 6:9; Heb. 10:23).